I0024634

THE COMPLETE TEXT OF H.R.1
TAX CUTS AND JOBS ACT

115 CONGRESS (2017-2018)

Sponsor: Rep. Brady Kevin
Committee: House —Ways and Means

Released: November 2, 2017

This Version: November 2, 2017

Text obtained from U.S. Government sources, including the Congressional Records office.

Published by Arc Manor. Arc Manor has no affiliation with any government organization or political par

ISBN: 978-1-61242-391-3

....
(Original Signature of Member)

115TH CONGRESS
1ST SESSION

H. R. 1

To provide for reconciliation pursuant to title II of the concurrent resolution on the budget for fiscal year 2018.

IN THE HOUSE OF REPRESENTATIVES

Mr. BRADY of Texas introduced the following bill; which was referred to the Committee on _____

A BILL

To provide for reconciliation pursuant to title II of the concurrent resolution on the budget for fiscal year 2018.

1   *Be it enacted by the Senate and House of Representa-*

2 *tives of the United States of America in Congress assembled,*

3 **SECTION 1. SHORT TITLE; ETC.**

4   (a) SHORT TITLE.—This Act may be cited as the

5 "Tax Cuts and Jobs Act".

6   (b) AMENDMENT OF 1986 CODE.—Except as other-

7 wise expressly provided, whenever in this Act an amend-

8 ment or repeal is expressed in terms of an amendment

9 to, or repeal of, a section or other provision, the reference

1 shall be considered to be made to a section or other provi-

2 sion of the Internal Revenue Code of 1986.

3   (c) TABLE OF CONTENTS.—The table of contents for

4 this Act is as follows:

TITLE I—TAX REFORM FOR INDIVIDUALS

Subtitle A—Simplification and Reform of Rates, Standard Deduction, and Exemptions

SEC. 1001. REDUCTION AND SIMPLIFICATION OF INDIVIDUAL INCOME TAX RATES.

(a) IN GENERAL.—Section 1 is amended by striking subsection (i) and by striking all that precedes subsection (h) and inserting the following:

1 **"SEC. 1. TAX IMPOSED.**

2   "(a) IN GENERAL.—There is hereby imposed on the

3 income of every individual a tax equal to the sum of—

4   "(1) 12 PERCENT BRACKET.—12 percent of so

5 much of the taxable income as does not exceed the

6 25-percent bracket threshold amount,

7   "(2) 25 PERCENT BRACKET.—25 percent of so

8 much of the taxable income as exceeds the 25-per-

9 cent bracket threshold amount but does not exceed

10 the 35-percent bracket threshold amount, plus

11   "(3) 35 PERCENT BRACKET.—35 percent of so

12 much of taxable income as exceeds the 35-percent

13 bracket threshold amount but does not exceed the

14 39.6 percent bracket threshold amount.

15   "(4) 39.6 PERCENT BRACKET.—39.6 percent of

16 so much of taxable income as exceeds the 39.6-per-

17 cent bracket threshold amount.

18   "(b) BRACKET THRESHOLD AMOUNTS.—For pur-

19 poses of this section—

20   "(1) 25-PERCENT BRACKET THRESHOLD

21 AMOUNT.—The term '25-percent bracket threshold

22 amount' means—

23   "(A) in the case of a joint return or sur-

24 viving spouse, $90,000,

1   "(B) in the case of an individual who is

2   the head of a household (as defined in section

3   2(b)), $67,500,

4   "(C) in the case of any other individual

5   (other than an estate or trust), an amount

6   equal to $\frac{1}{2}$ of the amount in effect for the tax-

7   able year under subparagraph (A), and

8   "(D) in the case of an estate or trust,

9        $2,550.

10   "(2) 35-PERCENT BRACKET THRESHOLD

11   AMOUNT.—The term '35-percent bracket threshold

12   amount' means—

13   "(A) in the case of a joint return or sur-

14   viving spouse, $260,000,

15   "(B) in the case of a married individual fil-

16   ing a separate return, an amount equal to $\frac{1}{2}$

17   of the amount in effect for the taxable year

18   under subparagraph (A), and

19   "(C) in the case of any other individual

20   (other than an estate or trust), $200,000, and

21   "(D) in the case of an estate or trust,

22        $9,150.

23   "(3) 39-PERCENT BRACKET THRESHOLD

24   AMOUNT.—The term '39.6-percent bracket threshold

25   amount' means—

1   "(A) in the case of a joint return or sur-

2 viving spouse, $1,000,000,

3   "(B) in the case of any other individual

4 (other than an estate or trust), an amount

5 equal to ½ of the amount in effect for the tax-

6 able year under subparagraph (A), and

7   "(C) in the case of an estate or trust,

8 $12,500.

9 "(c) INFLATION ADJUSTMENT.—

10   "(1) IN GENERAL.—In the case of any taxable

11 year beginning after 2018, each dollar amount in

12 subsection (b) (other than any amount determined

13 by reference to such a dollar amount) shall be in-

14 creased by an amount equal to—

15   "(A) such dollar amount, multiplied by

16   "(B) the cost-of-living adjustment deter-

17 mined under this subsection for the calendar

18 year in which the taxable year begins by sub-

19 stituting '2017' for '2016' in paragraph

20 (2)(A)(ii).

21 If any increase determined under the preceding sen-

22 tence is not a multiple of $100, such increase shall

23 be rounded to the next lowest multiple of $100.

24   "(2) COST-OF-LIVING ADJUSTMENT.—For pur-

25 poses of this subsection—

1   "(A) IN GENERAL.—The cost-of-living ad-

2   justment for any calendar year is the percent-

3   age (if any) by which—

4   "(i) the C-CPI-U for the preceding

5   calendar year, exceeds

6   "(ii) the normalized CPI for calendar

7   year 2016.

8   "(B) SPECIAL RULE FOR ADJUSTMENTS

9   WITH A BASE YEAR AFTER 2016.—For purposes

10   of any provision which provides for the substi-

11   tution of a year after 2016 for '2016' in sub-

12   paragraph (A)(ii), subparagraph (A) shall be

13   applied by substituting 'C-CPI-U' for 'normal-

14   ized CPI' in clause (ii).

15   "(3) NORMALIZED CPI.—For purposes of this

16   subsection, the normalized CPI for any calendar

17   year is the product of—

18   "(A) the CPI for such calendar year, mul-

19   tiplied by

20   "(B) the C-CPI-U transition multiple.

21   "(4) C-CPI-U TRANSITION MULTIPLE.—For

22   purposes of this subsection, the term 'C-CPI-U tran-

23   sition multiple' means the amount obtained by divid-

24   ing—

1   "(A) the C-CPI-U for calendar year 2016,

2   by

3   "(B) the CPI for calendar year 2016.

4   "(5) C-CPI-U.—For purposes of this sub-

5 section—

6   "(A) IN GENERAL.—The term 'C-CPI-U'

7 means the Chained Consumer Price Index for

8 All Urban Consumers (as published by the Bu-

9 reau of Labor Statistics of the Department of

10 Labor). The values of the Chained Consumer

11 Price Index for All Urban Consumers taken

12 into account for purposes of determining the

13 cost-of-living adjustment for any calendar year

14 under this subsection shall be the latest values

15 so published as of the date on which such Bu-

16 reau publishes the initial value of the Chained

17 Consumer Price Index for All Urban Con-

18 sumers for the month of August for the pre-

19 ceding calendar year.

20   "(B) DETERMINATION FOR CALENDAR

21 YEAR.—The C-CPI-U for any calendar year is

22 the average of the C-CPI-U as of the close of

23 the 12-month period ending on August 31 of

24 such calendar year.

25   "(6) CPI.—For purposes of this subsection—

1   "(A) IN GENERAL.—The term 'Consumer

2   Price Index' means the last Consumer Price

3   Index for All Urban Consumers published by

4   the Department of Labor. For purposes of the

5   preceding sentence, the revision of the Con-

6   sumer Price Index which is most consistent

7   with the Consumer Price Index for calendar

8   year 1986 shall be used.

9   "(B) DETERMINATION FOR CALENDAR

10   YEAR.—The CPI for any calendar year is the

11   average of the Consumer Price Index as of the

12   close of the 12-month period ending on August

13   31 of such calendar year.

14   "(7) DELAY OF ADJUSTMENT BASED ON C-CPI-

15 U UNTIL 2023.—Notwithstanding any other provision

16 of this title, any cost-of-living adjustment deter-

17 mined under this subsection (or by reference to this

18 subsection) shall be determined on the basis of CPI

19 rather than C-CPI-U with respect to periods before

20 January 1, 2023. Proper adjustments shall be made

21 in the application of this subsection to carry out the

22 preceding sentence.

23   "(d) SPECIAL RULES FOR CERTAIN CHILDREN WITH

24 UNEARNED INCOME.—

13

1   "(1) IN GENERAL.—In the case of any child to

2 whom this subsection applies for any taxable year—

3   "(A) the 25-percent bracket threshold

4 amount shall not be more than the taxable in-

5 come of such child for the taxable year reduced

6 by the net unearned income of such child, and

7   "(B) the 35-percent bracket threshold

8 amount shall not be more than the sum of—

9   "(i) the taxable income of such child

10   for the taxable year reduced by the net un-

11   earned income of such child, plus

12   "(ii) the dollar amount in effect under

13   subsection (b)(2)(D) for the taxable year.

14   "(C) the 39.6-percent bracket threshold

15 amount shall not be more than the sum of—

16   "(i) the taxable income of such child

17   for the taxable year reduced by the net un-

18   earned income of such child, plus

19   "(ii) the dollar amount in effect under

20   subsection (b)(3)(C).

21   "(2) CHILD TO WHOM SUBSECTION APPLIES.—

22 This subsection shall apply to any child for any tax-

23 able year if—

24   "(A) such child—

14

1   "(i) has not attained age 18 before

2   the close of the taxable year, or

3   "(ii) has attained age 18 before the

4   close of the taxable year and is described

5   in paragraph (3),

6   "(B) either parent of such child is alive at

7   the close of the taxable year, and

8   "(C) such child does not file a joint return

9   for the taxable year.

10   "(3) CERTAIN CHILDREN WHOSE EARNED IN-

11   COME DOES NOT EXCEED ONE-HALF OF INDI-

12   VIDUAL'S SUPPORT.—A child is described in this

13   paragraph if—

14   "(A) such child—

15   "(i) has not attained age 19 before

16   the close of the taxable year, or

17   "(ii) is a student (within the meaning

18   of section 7706(f)(2)) who has not attained

19   age 24 before the close of the taxable year,

20   and

21   "(B) such child's earned income (as de-

22   fined in section 911(d)(2)) for such taxable

23   year does not exceed one-half of the amount of

24   the individual's support (within the meaning of

25   section 7706(c)(1)(D) after the application of

1   section 7706(f)(5) (without regard to subpara-

2   graph (A) thereof)) for such taxable year.

3   "(4) NET UNEARNED INCOME.—For purposes

4   of this subsection—

5   "(A) IN GENERAL.—The term 'net un-

6   earned income' means the excess of—

7   "(i) the portion of the adjusted gross

8   income for the taxable year which is not

9   attributable to earned income (as defined

10   in section 911(d)(2)), over

11   "(ii) the sum of—

12   "(I) the amount in effect for the

13   taxable year under section 63(c)(2)(A)

14   (relating to limitation on standard de-

15   duction in the case of certain depend-

16   ents), plus

17   "(II) The greater of the amount

18   described in subclause (I) or, if the

19   child itemizes his deductions for the

20   taxable year, the amount of the

21   itemized deductions allowed by this

22   chapter for the taxable year which are

23   directly connected with the production

24   of the portion of adjusted gross in-

25   come referred to in clause (i).

1   "(B) LIMITATION BASED ON TAXABLE IN-

2   COME.—The amount of the net unearned in-

3   come for any taxable year shall not exceed the

4   individual's taxable income for such taxable

5   year.

6   "(e) PHASEOUT OF 12-PERCENT RATE.—

7   "(1) IN GENERAL.—The amount of tax imposed

8   by this section (determined without regard to this

9   subsection) shall be increased by 6 percent of the ex-

10   cess (if any) of—

11   "(A) adjusted gross income, over

12   "(B) the applicable dollar amount.

13   "(2) LIMITATION.—The increase determined

14   under paragraph (1) with respect to any taxpayer

15   for any taxable year shall not exceed 27.6 percent of

16   the lesser of—

17   "(A) the taxpayer's taxable income for

18   such taxable year, or

19   "(B) the 25-percent bracket threshold

20   amount in effect with respect to the taxpayer

21   for such taxable year.

22   "(3) APPLICABLE DOLLAR AMOUNT.—For pur-

23   poses of this subsection, the term 'applicable dollar

24   amount' means—

17

1   "(A) in the case of a joint return or a sur-

2   viving spouse, \$1,200,000,

3   "(B) in the case of any other individual,

4   \$1,000,000.

5   "(4) ESTATES AND TRUSTS.—Paragraph (1)

6   shall not apply in the case of an estate or trust.".

7   (b) APPLICATION OF CURRENT INCOME TAX BRACK-

8 ETS TO CAPITAL GAINS BRACKETS.—

9   (1) IN GENERAL.—

10   (A) 0-PERCENT CAPITAL GAINS BRACK-

11   ET.—Section 1(h)(1) is amended by striking

12   "which would (without regard to this para-

13   graph) be taxed at a rate below 25 percent" in

14   subparagraph (B)(i) and inserting "below the

15   15-percent rate threshold".

16   (B) 15-PERCENT CAPITAL GAINS BRACK-

17   ET.—Section 1(h)(1)(C)(ii)(I) is amended by

18   striking "which would (without regard to this

19   paragraph) be taxed at a rate below 39.6 per-

20   cent" and inserting "below the 20-percent rate

21   threshold".

22   (2) RATE THRESHOLDS DEFINED.—Section

23   1(h) is amended by adding at the end the following

24   new paragraph:

1   "(12) RATE THRESHOLDS DEFINED.—For pur-

2 poses of this subsection—

3   "(A) 15-PERCENT RATE THRESHOLD.—

4 The 15-percent rate threshold shall be—

5   "(i) in the case of a joint return or

6 surviving spouse, $77,200 (½ such amount

7 in the case of a married individual filing a

8 separate return),

9   "(ii) in the case of an individual who

10 is the head of a household (as defined in

11 section 2(b)), $51,700,

12   "(iii) in the case of any other indi-

13 vidual (other than an estate or trust), an

14 amount equal to ½ of the amount in effect

15 for the taxable year under clause (i), and

16   "(iv) in the case of an estate or trust,

17 $2,600.

18   "(B) 20-PERCENT RATE THRESHOLD.—

19 The 20-percent rate threshold shall be—

20   "(i) in the case of a joint return or

21 surviving spouse, $479,000 (½ such

22 amount in the case of a married individual

23 filing a separate return),

1   "(ii) in the case of an individual who

2   is the head of a household (as defined in

3   section 2(b)), $452,400,

4   "(iii) in the case of any other indi-

5   vidual (other than an estate or trust),

6    $425,800, and

7   "(iv) in the case of an estate or trust,

8    $12,700.

9   "(C) INFLATION ADJUSTMENT.—In the

10   case of any taxable year beginning after 2018,

11   each of the dollar amounts in subparagraphs

12   (A) and (B) shall be increased by an amount

13   equal to—

14   "(i) such dollar amount, multiplied by

15   "(ii) the cost-of-living adjustment de-

16   termined under subsection (c)(2)(A) for

17   the calendar year in which the taxable year

18   begins, determined by substituting 'cal-

19   endar year 2017' for 'calendar year 2016'

20   in clause (ii) thereof.".

21 (c) APPLICATION OF SECTION 15.—

22   (1) IN GENERAL.—Subsection (a) of section 15

23 is amended by striking "by this chapter" and insert-

24 ing "by section 11 (or by reference to any such

25 rates)".

1   (2) CONFORMING AMENDMENTS.—

2   (A) Section 15 is amended by striking sub-

3   sections (d) and (f) and by redesignating sub-

4   section (e) as subsection (d).

5   (B) Section 15(d), as redesignated by sub-

6   paragraph (A), is amended by striking "section

7   1 or 11(b)" and inserting "section 11(b)".

8   (C) Section 6013(c) is amended by striking

9   "sections 15, 443, and 7851(a)(1)(A)" and in-

10   serting "sections 443 and 7851(a)(1)(A)".

11   (3) APPLICATION TO THIS ACT.—Section 15 of

12 the Internal Revenue Code of 1986 shall not apply

13 to any change in a rate of tax imposed by chapter

14 1 of such Code which occurs by reason of any

15 amendment made by this Act (other than the

16 amendments made by section 3001).

17 (d) EFFECTIVE DATE.—

18   (1) IN GENERAL.—The amendments made by

19 this section shall apply to taxable years beginning

20 after December 31, 2017.

21   (2) SUBSECTION (c).—The amendments made

22 by subsection (c) shall take effect on the date of the

23 enactment of this Act.

1 **SEC. 1002. ENHANCEMENT OF STANDARD DEDUCTION.**

2 (a) INCREASE IN STANDARD DEDUCTION.—Section

3 63(c) is amended to read as follows:

4 "(c) STANDARD DEDUCTION.—For purposes of this

5 subtitle—

6 "(1) IN GENERAL.—Except as otherwise pro-

7 vided in this subsection, the term 'standard deduc-

8 tion' means—

9 "(A) $24,400, in the case of a joint return

10 (or a surviving spouse (as defined in section

11 2(a)),

12 "(B) three-quarters of the amount in effect

13 under subparagraph (A) for the taxable year, in

14 the case of an unmarried individual with at

15 least one qualifying child (within the meaning

16 of section 7706), and

17 "(C) one-half of the amount in effect

18 under subparagraph (A) for the taxable year, in

19 any other case.

20 "(2) LIMITATION ON STANDARD DEDUCTION IN

21 THE CASE OF CERTAIN DEPENDENTS.—In the case

22 of an individual who is a dependent of another tax-

23 payer for a taxable year beginning in the calendar

24 year in which the individual's taxable year begins,

25 the standard deduction applicable to such individual

1   for such individual's taxable year shall not exceed

2   the greater of—

3   "(A) $500, or

4   "(B) the sum of $250 and such individ-

5   ual's earned income (within the means of sec-

6   tion 32).

7   "(3) CERTAIN INDIVIDUALS, ETC., NOT ELIGI-

8   BLE FOR STANDARD DEDUCTION.—In the case of—

9   "(A) a married individual filing a separate

10   return where either spouse itemizes deductions,

11   "(B) a nonresident alien individual,

12   "(C) an individual making a return under

13   section 443(a)(1) for a period of less than 12

14   months on account of a change in his annual

15   accounting period, or

16   "(D) an estate or trust, common trust

17   fund, or partnership,

18   the standard deduction shall be zero.

19   "(4) UNMARRIED INDIVIDUAL.—For purposes

20   of this section, the term 'unmarried individual'

21   means any individual who—

22   "(A) is not married as of the close of the

23   taxable year (as determined by applying section

24   7703),

1   "(B) is not a surviving spouse (as defined

2   in section 2(a)) for the taxable year, and

3   "(C) is not a dependent of another tax-

4   payer for a taxable year beginning in the cal-

5   endar year in which the individual's taxable

6   year begins.

7   "(5) INFLATION ADJUSTMENTS.—

8   "(A) STANDARD DEDUCTION AMOUNT.—In

9   the case of any taxable year beginning after

10   2019, the dollar amount in paragraph (1)(A)

11   shall be increased by an amount equal to—

12   "(i) such dollar amount, multiplied by

13   "(ii) the cost-of-living adjustment de-

14   termined under section 1(c)(2)(A) for the

15   calendar year in which the taxable year be-

16   gins, determined by substituting 'calendar

17   year 2018' for 'calendar year 2016' in

18   clause (ii) thereof.

19   "(B) LIMITATION AMOUNT IN CASE OF

20   CERTAIN DEPENDENTS.—In the case of any

21   taxable year beginning after 2017, each of the

22   dollar amounts in paragraph (2) shall be in-

23   creased by an amount equal to—

24   "(i) such dollar amount, multiplied by

24

1   "(ii)(I) in the case of the dollar

2   amount in paragraph (2)(A), under section

3   1(c)(2)(A) for the calendar year in which

4   the taxable year begins determined by sub-

5   stituting 'calendar year 1987' for 'calendar

6   year 2016' in clause (ii) thereof, and

7   "(II) in the case of the dollar amount

8   in paragraph (2)(B), under section

9   1(c)(2)(A) for the calendar year in which

10   the taxable year begins determined by sub-

11   stituting 'calendar year 1997' for 'calendar

12   year 2016' in clause (ii) thereof.

13 If any increase determined under this paragraph is

14 not a multiple of $100, such increase shall be round-

15 ed to the next lowest multiple of $100.".

16 (b) CONFORMING AMENDMENTS.—

17   (1) Section 63(b) is amended by striking ",

18 minus—" and all that follows and inserting "minus

19 the standard deduction".

20   (2) Section 63 is amended by striking sub-

21 sections (f) and (g).

22   (3) Section 1398(c) is amended—

23   (A) by striking "BASIC" in the heading

24   thereof,

1   (B) by striking "BASIC STANDARD" in the

2   heading of paragraph (3) and inserting

3   "STANDARD", and

4   (C) by striking "basic" in paragraph (3).

5   (4) Section 3402(m)(3) is amended by striking

6 "(including the additional standard deduction under

7 section 63(c)(3) for the aged and blind)".

8   (5) Section 6014(b)(4) is amended by striking

9 "section 63(c)(5)" and inserting "section 63(c)(2)".

10   (c) EFFECTIVE DATE.—The amendment made by

11 this section shall apply to taxable years beginning after

12 December 31, 2017.

13 **SEC. 1003. REPEAL OF DEDUCTION FOR PERSONAL EXEMP-**

14   **TIONS.**

15   (a) IN GENERAL.—Part V of subchapter B of chapter

16 1 is hereby repealed.

17   (b) DEFINITION OF DEPENDENT RETAINED.—Sec-

18 tion 152, prior to repeal by subsection (a), is hereby redes-

19 ignated as section 7706 and moved to the end of chapter

20 79.

21   (c) APPLICATION TO ESTATES AND TRUSTS.—Sub-

22 section (b) of section 642 is amended—

23   (1) by striking paragraph (2)(C),

24   (2) by striking paragraph (3), and

1   (3) by striking "DEDUCTION FOR PERSONAL

2   EXEMPTION" in the heading thereof and inserting

3   "BASIC DEDUCTION".

4   (d) APPLICATION TO NONRESIDENT ALIENS.—Sec-

5 tion 873(b) is amended by striking paragraph (3).

6   (e) MODIFICATION OF WAGE WITHHOLDING

7 RULES.—

8   (1) IN GENERAL.—Section 3402(a) is amended

9   by striking paragraph (2)

10   (2) CONFORMING AMENDMENT.—Section

11   3402(a) is amended—

12   (A) by redesignating subparagraph (A)

13   and (B) of paragraph (1) as paragraphs (1)

14   and (2) and moving such redesignated para-

15   graphs 2 ems to the left, and

16   (B) by striking all that precedes "other-

17   wise provided in this section" and inserting the

18   following:

19 "(a) REQUIREMENT OF WITHHOLDING.—Except as".

20   (3) NUMBER OF EXEMPTIONS.—Section

21   3402(f)(1) is amended—

22   (A) in subparagraph (A), by striking "an

23   individual described in section 151(d)(2)" and

24   inserting "a dependent of any other taxpayer",

25   and

1   (B) in subparagraph (C), by striking "with

2 respect to whom, on the basis of facts existing

3 at the beginning of such day, there may reason-

4 ably be expected to be allowable an exemption

5 under section 151(c)" and inserting "who, on

6 the basis of facts existing at the beginning of

7 such day, is reasonably expected to be a de-

8 pendent of the employee".

9 (f) MODIFICATION OF RETURN REQUIREMENT.—

10 (1) IN GENERAL.—Paragraph (1) of section

11 6012(a) is amended to read as follows:

12 "(1) Every individual who has gross income for

13 the taxable year, except that a return shall not be

14 required of—

15   "(A) an individual who is not married (de-

16 termined by applying section 7703) and who

17 has gross income for the taxable year which

18 does not exceed the standard deduction applica-

19 ble to such individual for such taxable year

20 under section 63, or

21   "(B) an individual entitled to make a joint

22 return if—

23   "(i) the gross income of such indi-

24   vidual, when combined with the gross in-

25   come of such individual's spouse, for the

1   taxable year does not exceed the standard

2   deduction which would be applicable to the

3   taxpayer for such taxable year under sec-

4   tion 63 if such individual and such individ-

5   ual's spouse made a joint return,

6   "(ii) such individual and such individ-

7   ual's spouse have the same household as

8   their home at the close of the taxable year,

9   "(iii) such individual's spouse does not

10   make a separate return, and

11   "(iv) neither such individual nor such

12   individual's spouse is an individual de-

13   scribed in section 63(c)(2) who has income

14   (other than earned income) in excess of the

15   amount in effect under section

16   63(c)(2)(A).".

17   (2) BANKRUPTCY ESTATES.—Paragraph (8) of

18   section 6012(a) is amended by striking "the sum of

19   the exemption amount plus the basic standard de-

20   duction under section 63(c)(2)(D)" and inserting

21   "the standard deduction in effect under section

22   63(c)(1)(B)".

23   (g) CONFORMING AMENDMENTS.—

24   (1) Section 2(a)(1)(B) is amended by striking

25   "a dependent" and all that follows through "section

1 151'' and inserting ''a dependent who (within the

2 meaning of section 7706, determined without regard

3 to subsections (b)(1), (b)(2) and (d)(1)(B) thereof)

4 is a son, stepson, daughter, or stepdaughter of the

5 taxpayer''.

6   (2) Section 36B(b)(2)(A) is amended by strik-

7 ing ''section 152'' and inserting ''section 7706''.

8   (3) Section 36B(b)(3)(B) is amended by strik-

9 ing ''unless a deduction is allowed under section 151

10 for the taxable year with respect to a dependent'' in

11 the flush matter at the end and inserting ''unless

12 the taxpayer has a dependent for the taxable year''.

13   (4) Section 36B(c)(1)(D) is amended by strik-

14 ing ''with respect to whom a deduction under section

15 151 is allowable to another taxpayer'' and inserting

16 ''who is a dependent of another taxpayer''.

17   (5) Section 36B(d)(1) is amended by striking

18 ''equal to the number of individuals for whom the

19 taxpayer is allowed a deduction under section 151

20 (relating to allowance of deduction for personal ex-

21 emptions) for the taxable year'' and inserting ''the

22 sum of 1 (2 in the case of a joint return) plus the

23 number of the taxpayer's dependents for the taxable

24 year''.

1   (6) Section 36B(e)(1) is amended by striking

2 "1 or more individuals for whom a taxpayer is al-

3 lowed a deduction under section 151 (relating to al-

4 lowance of deduction for personal exemptions) for

5 the taxable year (including the taxpayer or his

6 spouse)" and inserting "1 or more of the taxpayer,

7 the taxpayer's spouse, or any dependent of the tax-

8 payer".

9   (7) Section 42(i)(3)(D)(ii)(I) is amended—

10   (A) by striking "section 152" and insert-

11   ing "section 7706", and

12   (B) by striking the period at the end and

13   inserting a comma.

14   (8) Section 72(t)(2)(D)(i)(III) is amended by

15 striking "section 152" and inserting "section 7706".

16   (9) Section 72(t)(7)(A)(iii) is amended by strik-

17 ing "section 152(f)(1)" and inserting "section

18 7706(f)(1)".

19   (10) Section 105(b) is amended—

20   (A) by striking "as defined in section 152"

21   and inserting "as defined in section 7706",

22   (B) by striking "section 152(f)(1)" and in-

23   serting "section 7706(f)(1)" and

24   (C) by striking "section 152(e)" and in-

25   serting "section 7706(e)".

31

1   (11) Section 105(c)(1) is amended by striking

2 "section 152" and inserting "section 7706".

3   (12) Section 125(e)(1)(D) is amended by strik-

4 ing "section 152" and inserting "section 7706".

5   (13) Section 132(h)(2)(B) is amended—

6   (A) by striking "section 152(f)(1)" and in-

7 serting "section 7706(f)(1)", and

8   (B) by striking "section 152(e)" and in-

9 serting "section 7706(e)".

10   (14) Section 139D(c)(5) is amended by striking

11 "section 152" and inserting "section 7706".

12   (15) Section 162(l)(1)(D) is amended by strik-

13 ing "section 152(f)(1)" and inserting "section

14 7706(f)(1)".

15   (16) Section 170(g)(1) is amended by striking

16 "section 152" and inserting "section 7706".

17   (17) Section 170(g)(3) is amended by striking

18 "section 152(d)(2)" and inserting "section

19 7706(d)(2)".

20   (18) Section 172(d) is amended by striking

21 paragraph (3).

22   (19) Section 220(b)(6) is amended by striking

23 "with respect to whom a deduction under section

24 151 is allowable to" and inserting "who is a depend-

25 ent of".

32

1   (20) Section 220(d)(2)(A) is amended by strik-

2 ing "section 152" and inserting "section 7706".

3   (21) Section 223(b)(6) is amended by striking

4 "with respect to whom a deduction under section

5 151 is allowable to" and inserting "who is a depend-

6 ent of".

7   (22) Section 223(d)(2)(A) is amended by strik-

8 ing "section 152" and inserting "section 7706".

9   (23) Section 401(h) is amended by striking

10 "section 152(f)(1)" in the last sentence and insert-

11 ing "section 7706(f)(1)".

12   (24) Section 402(l)(4)(D) is amended by strik-

13 ing "section 152" and inserting "section 7706".

14   (25) Section 409A(a)(2)(B)(ii)(I) is amended

15 by striking "section 152(a)" and inserting "section

16 7706(a)".

17   (26) Section 501(c)(9) is amended by striking

18 "section 152(f)(1)" and inserting "section

19 7706(f)(1)".

20   (27) Section 529(e)(2)(B) is amended by strik-

21 ing "section 152(d)(2)" and inserting "section

22 7706(d)(2)".

23   (28) Section 703(a)(2) is amended by striking

24 subparagraph (A) and by redesignating subpara-

33

1   graphs (B) through (F) as subparagraphs (A)

2   through (E), respectively.

3   (29) Section 874 is amended by striking sub-

4   section (b) and by redesignating subsection (c) as

5   subsection (b).

6   (30) Section 891 is amended by striking "under

7   section 151 and".

8   (31) Section 904(b) is amended by striking

9   paragraph (1).

10   (32) Section 931(b)(1) is amended by striking

11   "(other than the deduction under section 151, relat-

12   ing to personal exemptions)".

13   (33) Section 933 is amended—

14   (A) by striking "(other than the deduction

15   under section 151, relating to personal exemp-

16   tions)" in paragraph (1), and

17   (B) by striking "(other than the deduction

18   for personal exemptions under section 151)" in

19   paragraph (2).

20   (34) Section 1212(b)(2)(B)(ii) is amended to

21   read as follows:

22   "(ii) in the case of an estate or trust,

23   the deduction allowed for such year under

24   section 642(b).".

34

1   (35) Section 1361(c)(1)(C) is amended by strik-

2 ing "section 152(f)(1)(C)" and inserting "section

3 7706(f)(1)(C)".

4   (36) Section 1402(a) is amended by striking

5 paragraph (7).

6   (37) Section 2032A(c)(7)(D) is amended by

7 striking "section 152(f)(2)" and inserting "section

8 7706(f)(2)".

9   (38) Section 3402(m)(1) is amended by striking

10 "other than the deductions referred to in section

11 151 and".

12   (39) Section 3402(r)(2) is amended by striking

13 "the sum of—" and all that follows and inserting

14 "the standard deduction in effect under section

15 63(c)(1)(B).".

16   (40) Section 5000A(b)(3)(A) is amended by

17 striking "section 152" and inserting "section 7706".

18   (41) Section 5000A(c)(4)(A) is amended by

19 striking "the number of individuals for whom the

20 taxpayer is allowed a deduction under section 151

21 (relating to allowance of deduction for personal ex-

22 emptions) for the taxable year" and inserting "the

23 sum of 1 (2 in the case of a joint return) plus the

24 number of the taxpayer's dependents for the taxable

25 year".

1   (42) Section 6013(b)(3)(A) is amended—

2   (A) by striking "had less than the exemp-

3   tion amount of gross income" in clause (ii) and

4   inserting "had no gross income",

5   (B) by striking "had gross income of the

6   exemption amount or more" in clause (iii) and

7   inserting "had any gross income", and

8   (C) by striking the flush language fol-

9   lowing clause (iii).

10   (43) Section 6014(b)(4), as amended by the

11   preceding provisions of this Act, is amended by

12   striking "where the taxpayer itemizes his deductions

13   or".

14   (44) Section 6103(l)(21)(A)(iii) is amended to

15   read as follows:

16   "(iii) the number of the taxpayer's de-

17   pendents,".

18   (45) Section 6213(g)(2) is amended by striking

19   subparagraph (H).

20   (46) Section 6334(d)(2) is amended to read as

21   follows:

22   "(2) EXEMPT AMOUNT.—

23   "(A) IN GENERAL.—For purposes of para-

24   graph (1), the term 'exempt amount' means an

25   amount equal to—

1 "(i) the standard deduction, divided

2 by

3 "(ii) 52.

4 "(B) VERIFIED STATEMENT.—Unless the

5 taxpayer submits to the Secretary a written and

6 properly verified statement specifying the facts

7 necessary to determine the proper amount

8 under subparagraph (A), subparagraph (A)

9 shall be applied as if the taxpayer were a mar-

10 ried individual filing a separate return with no

11 dependents.".

12 (47) Section 7702B(f)(2)(C)(iii) is amended by

13 striking "section 152(d)(2)" and inserting "section

14 7706(d)(2)".

15 (48) Section 7703(a) is amended by striking

16 "part V of subchapter B of chapter 1 and".

17 (49) Section 7703(b)(1) is amended by striking

18 "section 152(f)(1)" and all that follows and insert-

19 ing "section 7706(f)(1),".

20 (50) Section 7706(a), as redesignated by this

21 section, is amended by striking "this subtitle" and

22 inserting "subtitle A".

23 (51)(A) Section 7706(d)(1)(B), as redesignated

24 by this section, is amended by striking "the exemp-

1   tion amount (as defined in section 151(d))" and in-
2   serting "$4,150".

3   (B) Section 7706(d), as redesignated by this
4   section, is amended by adding at the end the fol-
5   lowing new paragraph:

6   "(6) INFLATION ADJUSTMENT.—In the case of
7   any calendar year beginning after 2018, the $4,150
8   amount in paragraph (1)(B) shall be increased by an
9   amount equal to—

10   "(A) such dollar amount, multiplied by

11   "(B) the cost-of-living adjustment deter-
12   mined under section 1(c)(2)(A) for such cal-
13   endar year, determined by substituting 'cal-
14   endar year 2017' for 'calendar year 2016' in
15   clause (ii) thereof.

16   If any increase determined under the preceding sen-
17   tence is not a multiple of $100, such increase shall
18   be rounded to the next lowest multiple of $100.".

19   (52) The table of sections for chapter 79 is
20   amended by adding at the end the following new
21   item:

"Sec. 7706. Dependent defined.".

22   (h) EFFECTIVE DATE.—The amendments made by
23   this section shall apply to taxable years beginning after
24   December 31, 2017.

1 **SEC. 1004. MAXIMUM RATE ON BUSINESS INCOME OF INDI-**

2 **VIDUALS.**

3 (a) IN GENERAL.—Part I of subchapter A of chapter

4 1 is amended by inserting after section 3 the following

5 new section:

6 **"SEC. 4. 25 PERCENT MAXIMUM RATE ON BUSINESS IN-**

7 **COME OF INDIVIDUALS.**

8 "(a) REDUCTION IN TAX TO ACHIEVE 25 PERCENT

9 MAXIMUM RATE.—The tax imposed by section 1 shall be

10 reduced by the sum of—

11 "(1) 10 percent of the lesser of—

12 "(A) qualified business income, or

13 "(B) the excess (if any) of—

14 "(i) taxable income reduced by net

15 capital gain (as defined in section

16 1(h)(11)(A)), over

17 "(ii) the maximum dollar amount for

18 the 25-percent rate bracket which applies

19 to the taxpayer under section 1 for the

20 taxable year, and

21 "(2) 4.6 percent of the excess (if any) of—

22 "(A) the lesser of—

23 "(i) qualified business income, or

24 "(ii) the excess (if any) determined

25 under paragraph (1)(B), over

26 "(B) the excess of—

1   "(i) the maximum dollar amount for

2   the 35-percent rate bracket which applies

3   to the taxpayer under section 1 for the

4   taxable year, over

5   "(ii) the maximum dollar amount for

6   the 25-percent rate bracket which applies

7   to the taxpayer under section 1 for the

8   taxable year.

9   "(b) QUALIFIED BUSINESS INCOME.—For purposes

10 of this section, the term 'qualified business income' means

11 the excess (if any) of—

12   "(1) the sum of—

13   "(A) 100 percent of any net business in-

14   come derived from any passive business activity,

15   plus

16   "(B) the capital percentage of any net

17   business income derived from any active busi-

18   ness activity, over

19   "(2) the sum of—

20   "(A) 100 percent of any net business loss

21   derived from any passive business activity,

22   "(B) except as provided in subsection

23   (e)(3)(A), 30 percent of any net business loss

24   derived from any active business activity, plus

1   "(C) any carryover business loss deter-

2   mined for the preceding taxable year.

3   "(c) DETERMINATION OF NET BUSINESS INCOME OR

4   LOSS.—For purposes of this section—

5   "(1) IN GENERAL.—Net business income or loss

6   shall be determined with respect to any business ac-

7   tivity by appropriately netting items of income, gain,

8   deduction, and loss with respect to such business ac-

9   tivity.

10   "(2) WAGES, ETC.—Any wages (as defined in

11   section 3401), payments described in subsection (a)

12   or (c) of section 707, or directors' fees received by

13   the taxpayer which are properly attributable to any

14   business activity shall be taken into account under

15   paragraph (1) as an item of income with respect to

16   such business activity.

17   "(3) EXCEPTION FOR CERTAIN INVESTMENT-

18   RELATED ITEMS.—There shall not be taken into ac-

19   count under paragraph (1)—

20   "(A) any item of short-term capital gain,

21   short-term capital loss, long-term capital gain,

22   or long-term capital loss,

23   "(B) any dividend, income equivalent to a

24   dividend, or payment in lieu of dividends de-

25   scribed in section 954(c)(1)(G),

41

1   "(C) any interest income other than inter-
2   est income which is properly allocable to a trade
3   or business,

4   "(D) any item of gain or loss described in
5   subparagraph (C) or (D) of section 954(c)(1)
6   (applied by substituting 'business activity' for
7   'controlled foreign corporation'),

8   "(E) any item of income, gain, deduction,
9   or loss taken into account under section
10   954(c)(1)(F) (determined without regard to
11   clause (ii) thereof and other than items attrib-
12   utable to notional principal contracts entered
13   into in transactions qualifying under section
14   1221(a)(7)),

15   "(F) any amount received from an annuity
16   which is not received in connection with the
17   trade or business of the business activity, and

18   "(G) any item of deduction or loss properly
19   allocable to an amount described in any of the
20   preceding subparagraphs.

21   "(4) APPLICATION OF RESTRICTIONS APPLICA-
22 BLE TO DETERMINING TAXABLE INCOME.—Net busi-
23 ness income or loss shall be appropriately adjusted
24 so as only to take into account any amount of in-
25 come, gain, deduction, or loss to the extent such

42

1   amount affects the determination of taxable income

2   for the taxable year.

3   "(5) CARRYOVER BUSINESS LOSS.—For pur-

4   poses of subsection (b)(2)(C), the carryover business

5   loss determined for any taxable year is the excess (if

6   any) of the sum described in subsection (b)(2) over

7   the sum described in subsection (b)(1) for such tax-

8   able year.

9   "(d) PASSIVE AND ACTIVE BUSINESS ACTIVITY.—

10 For purposes of this section—

11   "(1) PASSIVE BUSINESS ACTIVITY.—The term

12   'passive business activity' means any passive activity

13   as defined in section 469(c) determined without re-

14   gard to paragraphs (3) and (6)(B) thereof.

15   "(2) ACTIVE BUSINESS ACTIVITY.—The term

16   'active business activity' means any business activity

17   which is not a passive business activity.

18   "(3) BUSINESS ACTIVITY.—The term 'business

19   activity' means any activity (within the meaning of

20   section 469) which involves the conduct of any trade

21   or business.

22   "(e) CAPITAL PERCENTAGE.—For purposes of this

23 section—

1   "(1) IN GENERAL.—Except as otherwise pro-

2 vided in this section, the term 'capital percentage'

3 means 30 percent.

4   "(2) INCREASED PERCENTAGE FOR CAPITAL-IN-

5 TENSIVE BUSINESS ACTIVITIES.—In the case of a

6 taxpayer who elects the application of this paragraph

7 with respect to any active business activity (other

8 than a specified service activity), the capital percent-

9 age shall be equal to the applicable percentage (as

10 defined in subsection (f)) for each taxable year with

11 respect to which such election applies. Any election

12 made under this paragraph shall apply to the tax-

13 able year for which such election is made and each

14 of the 4 subsequent taxable years. Such election

15 shall be made not later than the due date (including

16 extensions) for the return of tax for the taxable year

17 for which such election is made, and, once made,

18 may not be revoked.

19   "(3) TREATMENT OF SPECIFIED SERVICE AC-

20 TIVITIES.—

21   "(A) IN GENERAL.—In the case of any ac-

22   tive business activity which is a specified service

23   activity—

24   "(i) the capital percentage shall be 0

25   percent, and

1   "(ii) subsection (b)(2)(B) shall be ap-

2   plied by substituting '0 percent' for '30

3   percent'.

4   "(B) EXCEPTION FOR CAPITAL-INTENSIVE

5 SPECIFIED SERVICE ACTIVITIES.—If—

6   "(i) the taxpayer elects the application

7   of this subparagraph with respect to such

8   activity for any taxable year, and

9   "(ii) the applicable percentage (as de-

10   fined in subsection (f)) with respect to

11   such activity for such taxable year is at

12   least 10 percent,

13 then subparagraph (A) shall not apply and the

14 capital percentage with respect to such activity

15 shall be equal to such applicable percentage.

16   "(C) SPECIFIED SERVICE ACTIVITY.—The

17 term 'specified service activity' means any activ-

18 ity involving the performance of services de-

19 scribed in section 1202(e)(3)(A), including in-

20 vesting, trading, or dealing in securities (as de-

21 fined in section 475(c)(2)), partnership inter-

22 ests, or commodities (as defined in section

23 475(e)(2)).

24   "(4) REDUCTION IN CAPITAL PERCENTAGE IN

25 CERTAIN CASES.—The capital percentage (deter-

1 mined after the application of paragraphs (2) and

2 (3)) with respect to any active business activity shall

3 not exceed 1 minus the quotient (not greater than

4 1) of—

5   "(A) any amounts described in subsection

6   (c)(2) which are taken into account in deter-

7   mining the net business income derived from

8   such activity, divided by

9   "(B) such net business income.

10   "(f) APPLICABLE PERCENTAGE.—For purposes of

11 this section—

12   "(1) IN GENERAL.—The term 'applicable per-

13   centage' means, with respect to any active business

14   activity for any taxable year, the quotient (not great-

15   er than 1) of—

16   "(A) the specified return on capital with

17   respect to such activity for such taxable year,

18   divided by

19   "(B) the taxpayer's net business income

20   derived from such activity for such taxable year.

21   "(2) SPECIFIED RETURN ON CAPITAL.—The

22   term 'specified return on capital' means, with re-

23   spect to any active business activity referred to in

24   paragraph (1), the excess of—

25   "(A) the product of—

1   "(i) the deemed rate of return for the

2   taxable year, multiplied by

3   "(ii) the asset balance with respect to

4   such activity for such taxable year, over

5   "(B) an amount equal to the interest

6   which is paid or accrued, and for which a de-

7   duction is allowed under this chapter, with re-

8   spect to such activity for such taxable year.

9   "(3) DEEMED RATE OF RETURN.—The term

10   'deemed rate of return' means, with respect to any

11   taxable year, the Federal short-term rate (deter-

12   mined under section 1274(d) for the month in which

13   or with which such taxable year ends) plus 7 per-

14   centage points.

15   "(4) ASSET BALANCE.—

16   "(A) IN GENERAL.—The asset balance

17   with respect to any active business activity re-

18   ferred to in paragraph (1) for any taxable year

19   equals the taxpayer's adjusted basis of the

20   property used in connection with such activity

21   as of the end of the taxable year (determined

22   without regard to sections 168(k) and 179).

23   "(B) APPLICATION TO ACTIVITIES CAR-

24   RIED ON THROUGH PARTNERSHIPS AND S COR-

25   PORATIONS.—In the case of any active business

1   activity carried on through a partnership or S

2   corporation, the taxpayer shall take into ac-

3   count such taxpayer's distributive or pro rata

4   share (as the case may be) of the asset balance

5   with respect to such activity as determined

6   under this paragraph with respect to the part-

7   nership's or S corporation's adjusted basis of

8   the property used in connection with such activ-

9   ity by the partnership or S corporation.

10   "(g) REGULATIONS.—The Secretary may issue such

11 regulations or other guidance as may be necessary or ap-

12 propriate to carry out the purposes of this section, includ-

13 ing regulations or other guidance—

14   "(1) which ensures that no amount is taken

15   into account under subsection (f)(4) with respect to

16   more than one activity, and

17   "(2) which treats all specified service activities

18   of the taxpayer as a single business activity for pur-

19   poses of this section to the extent that such activi-

20   ties would be treated as a single employer under

21   subsection (a) or (b) of section 52 or subsection (m)

22   or (o) of section 414.

23   "(h) REFERENCES.—Any reference in this title to

24 section 1 shall be treated as including a reference to this

48

1 section unless the context of such reference clearly indi-

2 cates otherwise.".

3 (b) 25 PERCENT RATE FOR CERTAIN DIVIDENDS OF

4 REAL ESTATE INVESTMENT TRUSTS AND COOPERA-

5 TIVES.—Section 1(h) is amended by adding at the end the

6 following new paragraph:

7 "(12) 25 PERCENT RATE FOR CERTAIN DIVI-

8 DENDS OF REAL ESTATE INVESTMENT TRUSTS AND

9 COOPERATIVES.—

10 "(A) IN GENERAL.—For purposes of this

11 subsection, net capital gain (as defined in para-

12 graph (11)) and unrecaptured section 1250

13 gain (as defined in paragraph (6)) shall each be

14 increased by specified dividend income.

15 "(B) SPECIFIED DIVIDEND INCOME.—For

16 purposes of this paragraph, the term 'specified

17 dividend income' means—

18 "(i) in the case of any dividend re-

19 ceived from a real estate investment trust,

20 the portion of such dividend which is nei-

21 ther—

22 "(I) a capital gain dividend (as

23 defined in section 852(b)(3)), nor

1   "(II) taken into account in deter-

2   mining qualified dividend income (as

3   defined in paragraph (11)), and

4   "(ii) any dividend which is includible

5   in gross income and which is received from

6   an organization or corporation described in

7   section 501(c)(12) or 1381(a).".

8 (b) NET EARNINGS FROM SELF-EMPLOYMENT.—

9   (1) APPLICATION TO LABOR PERCENTAGE OF

10 DISTRIBUTIVE AND PRO RATA SHARES.—Section

11 1402(a) is amended—

12   (A) by striking "the gross income derived

13   by an individual from any trade or business car-

14   ried on by such individual, less the deductions

15   allowed by this subtitle which are attributable

16   to such trade or business, plus his distributive

17   share (whether or not distributed) of income or

18   loss described in section 702(a)(8) from any

19   trade or business carried on by a partnership of

20   which he is a member" and inserting "the labor

21   percentage of the gross income derived by an

22   individual from any trade or business carried on

23   by such individual, less the labor percentage of

24   the deductions allowed by this subtitle which

25   are attributable to such trade or business, plus

1   the labor percentage of such individual's dis-

2   tributive share (whether or not distributed) of

3   income or loss described in section 702(a)(8)

4   from any trade or business carried on by a

5   partnership of which such individual is a mem-

6   ber, plus the labor percentage of such individ-

7   ual's pro rata share (whether or not distrib-

8   uted) of nonseparately computed income or loss

9   (as defined in section 1366(a)(2)) from any

10   trade or business carried on by an S corpora-

11   tion in which such individual is a shareholder'',

12   and

13   (B) by striking "and such distributive

14   share of partnership ordinary income or loss"

15   and inserting ", such distributive share of part-

16   nership ordinary income or loss, and such pro

17   rata share of S corporation nonseparately com-

18   puted income or loss".

19   (2) LABOR PERCENTAGE.—Section 1402 is

20   amended by adding at the end the following new

21   subsection:

22   "(m) LABOR PERCENTAGE.—

23   "(1) IN GENERAL.—For purposes of this sec-

24   tion, the term 'labor percentage' means, with respect

25   to any income or loss, the excess (expressed as a

1 percentage) of 1 minus the capital percentage (ex-

2 pressed as a decimal) with respect to such income or

3 loss.

4   "(2) CAPITAL PERCENTAGE.—For purposes of

5 paragraph (1), the term 'capital percentage' means

6 the percentage which applied with respect to such

7 income or loss under section 4(b)(1)(B).

8   "(3) ADJUSTMENT FOR S CORPORATION

9 WAGES.—For purposes of this subsection, proper ad-

10 justment shall be made for wages paid to the tax-

11 payer with respect to any trade or business carried

12 on by an S corporation in which the taxpayer is a

13 shareholder.".

14   (3) APPLICATION TO RENTAL INCOME.—Section

15 1402(a) is amended by striking paragraph (1).

16   (4) APPLICATION TO LIMITED PARTNERS.—Sec-

17 tion 1402(a) is amended by striking paragraph (13).

18   (c) CLERICAL AMENDMENT.—The table of sections

19 for part I of subchapter A of chapter 1 is amended by

20 inserting after the item relating to section 3 the following

21 new item:

"Sec. 4. 25 percent maximum rate on business income of individuals.".

22   (d) EFFECTIVE DATE.—The amendments made by

23 this section shall apply to taxable years beginning after

24 December 31, 2017.

52

1   (e) TRANSITION RULE.—In the case of any taxable

2 year which includes December 31, 2017, the amendment

3 made by subsection (a) shall apply with respect to such

4 taxable year adjusted—

5   (1) so as to apply with respect to the rates of

6   tax in effect under section 1 of the Internal Revenue

7   Code of 1986 with respect to such taxable year (and

8   so as to achieve a 25 percent effective rate of tax

9   on the business income (determined without regard

10   to paragraph (2)) in the same manner as such

11   amendment applies to taxable years beginning after

12   such date with respect to the rates of tax in effect

13   for such years), and

14   (2) by reducing the amount of the reduction in

15   tax (as otherwise determined under paragraph (1))

16   by the amount which bears the same proportion to

17   the amount of such reduction as the number of days

18   in the taxable year which are before January 1,

19   2018, bears to the number of days in the entire tax-

20   able year.

21 **SEC. 1005. CONFORMING AMENDMENTS RELATED TO SIM-**

22   **PLIFICATION OF INDIVIDUAL INCOME TAX**

23   **RATES.**

24   (a) AMENDMENTS RELATED TO MODIFICATION OF

25 INFLATION ADJUSTMENT.—

53

1   (1) Section 36B(b)(3)(A)(ii)(II) is amended by

2 striking "consumer price index" and inserting "C-

3 CPI-U (as defined in section 1(c))".

4   (2) Section 41(e)(5)(C) is amended to read as

5 follows:

6   "(C) Cost-of-living adjustment de-

7   fined.—

8   "(i) In general.—The cost-of-living

9   adjustment for any calendar year is the

10   cost-of-living adjustment for such calendar

11   year determined under section 1(c)(2)(A),

12   by substituting 'calendar year 1987' for

13   'calendar year 2016' in clause (ii) thereof.

14   "(ii) Special rule where base pe-

15   riod ends in a calendar year other

16   than 1983 or 1984.—If the base period of

17   any taxpayer does not end in 1983 or

18   1984, clause (i) shall be applied by sub-

19   stituting the calendar year in which such

20   base period ends for 1987.".

21   (3) Section 42(e)(3)(D)(ii) is amended by strik-

22 ing "section 1(f)(3) for such calendar year by sub-

23 stituting 'calendar year 2008' for 'calendar year

24 1992' in subparagraph (B) thereof" and inserting

25 "section 1(c)(2)(A) for such calendar year by sub-

54

1   stituting 'calendar year 2008' for 'calendar year

2   2016' in clause (ii) thereof''.

3   (4) Section 42(h)(3)(H)(i)(II) is amended by

4   striking "section 1(f)(3) for such calendar year by

5   substituting 'calendar year 2001' for 'calendar year

6   1992' in subparagraph (B) thereof'' and inserting

7   "section 1(c)(2)(A) for such calendar year by sub-

8   stituting 'calendar year 2001' for 'calendar year

9   2016' in clause (ii) thereof''.

10   (5) Section 45R(d)(3)(B)(ii) is amended by

11   striking "section 1(f)(3) for the calendar year, deter-

12   mined by substituting 'calendar year 2012' for 'cal-

13   endar year 1992' in subparagraph (B) thereof'' and

14   inserting "'section 1(c)(2)(A) for such calendar

15   year, determined by substituting "calendar year

16   2012" for "calendar year 2016" in clause (ii) there-

17   of' ''.

18   (6) Section 125(i)(2) is amended—

19   (A) by striking "section 1(f)(3) for the cal-

20   endar year in which the taxable year begins by

21   substituting 'calendar year 2012' for 'calendar

22   year 1992' in subparagraph (B) thereof'' in

23   subparagraph (B) and inserting "section

24   1(c)(2)(A) for the calendar year in which the

25   taxable year begins", and

1   (B) by striking "$50" both places it ap-

2   pears in the last sentence and inserting

3   "$100".

4   (7) Section 162(o)(3) is amended by inserting

5 "as in effect before enactment of the Tax Cuts and

6 Jobs Act" after "section 1(f)(5)".

7   (8) Section 220(g)(2) is amended by striking

8 "section 1(f)(3) for the calendar year in which the

9 taxable year begins by substituting 'calendar year

10 1997' for 'calendar year 1992' in subparagraph (B)

11 thereof" and inserting "section 1(c)(2)(A) for the

12 calendar year in which the taxable year begins, de-

13 termined by substituting 'calendar year 1997' for

14 'calendar year 2016' in clause (ii) thereof".

15   (9) Section 223(g)(1) is amended by striking all

16 that follows subparagraph (A) and inserting the fol-

17 lowing:

18   "(B) the cost-of-living adjustment deter-

19   mined under section 1(c)(2)(A) for the calendar

20   year in which the taxable year begins, deter-

21   mined—

22   "(i) by substituting for 'calendar year

23   2016' in clause (ii) thereof—

24   "(I) except as provided in clause

25   (ii), 'calendar year 1997', and

56

1   "(II) in the case of each dollar

2   amount in subsection (c)(2)(A), 'cal-

3   endar year 2003', and

4   "(ii) by substituting 'March 31' for

5   'August 31' in paragraphs (5)(B) and

6   (6)(B) of section 1(c).

7   The Secretary shall publish the dollar amounts

8 as adjusted under this subsection for taxable

9 years beginning in any calendar year no later

10 than June 1 of the preceding calendar year.".

11   (10) Section 430(c)(7)(D)(vii)(II) is amended

12 by striking "section 1(f)(3) for the calendar year,

13 determined by substituting 'calendar year 2009' for

14 'calendar year 1992' in subparagraph (B) thereof"

15 and inserting "section 1(c)(2)(A) for the calendar

16 year, determined by substituting 'calendar year

17 2009' for 'calendar year 2016' in clause (ii) there-

18 of".

19   (11) Section 512(d)(2)(B) is amended by strik-

20 ing "section 1(f)(3) for the calendar year in which

21 the taxable year begins, by substituting 'calendar

22 year 1994' for 'calendar year 1992' in subparagraph

23 (B) thereof"and inserting "section 1(c)(2)(A) for the

24 calendar year in which the taxable year begins, de-

1   termined by substituting 'calendar year 1994' for
2   'calendar year 2016' in clause (ii) thereof''.

3   (12) Section 513(h)(2)(C)(ii) is amended by
4   striking ''section 1(f)(3) for the calendar year in
5   which the taxable year begins by substituting 'cal-
6   endar year 1987' for 'calendar year 1992' in sub-
7   paragraph (B) thereof'' and inserting ''section
8   1(c)(2)(A) for the calendar year in which the taxable
9   year begins, determined by substituting 'calendar
10   year 1987' for 'calendar year 2016' in clause (ii)
11   thereof''.

12   (13) Section 831(b)(2)(D)(ii) is amended by
13   striking ''section 1(f)(3) for such calendar year by
14   substituting 'calendar year 2013' for 'calendar year
15   1992' in subparagraph (B) thereof'' and inserting
16   ''section 1(c)(2)(A) for such calendar year by sub-
17   stituting 'calendar year 2013' for 'calendar year
18   2016' in clause (ii) thereof''.

19   (14) Section 877A(a)(3)(B)(i)(II) is amended
20   by striking ''section 1(f)(3) for the calendar year in
21   which the taxable year begins, by substituting 'cal-
22   endar year 2007' for 'calendar year 1992' in sub-
23   paragraph (B) thereof'' and inserting ''section
24   1(c)(2)(A) for the calendar year in which the taxable
25   year begins, determined by substituting 'calendar

58

1   year 2007' for 'calendar year 2016' in clause (ii)
2   thereof''.

3   (15) Section 911(b)(2)(D)(ii)(II) is amended by
4   striking "section 1(f)(3) for the calendar year in
5   which the taxable year begins, determined by sub-
6   stituting '2004' for '1992' in subparagraph (B)
7   thereof'' and inserting "section 1(c)(2)(A) for the
8   calendar year in which the taxable year begins, de-
9   termined by substituting 'calendar year 2004' for
10 'calendar year 2016' in clause (ii) thereof''.

11   (16) Section 1274A(d)(2) is amended to read
12 as follows:

13   "(2) INFLATION ADJUSTMENT.—

14   "(A) IN GENERAL.—In the case of any
15   debt instrument arising out of a sale or ex-
16   change during any calendar year after 2018,
17   each adjusted dollar amount shall be increased
18   by an amount equal to—

19   "(i) such adjusted dollar amount,
20   multiplied by

21   "(ii) the cost-of-living adjustment de-
22   termined under section 1(c)(2)(A) for such
23   calendar year, determined by substituting
24   'calendar year 2017' for 'calendar year
25   2016' in clause (ii) thereof.

1   "(B) Adjusted dollar amounts.—For

2   purposes of this paragraph, the term 'adjusted

3   dollar amount' means the dollar amounts in

4   subsections (b) and (c), in each case as in effect

5   for calendar year 2018.

6   "(C) Rounding.—Any increase under sub-

7   paragraph (A) shall be rounded to the nearest

8   multiple of $100.''.

9   (17) Section 2010(c)(3)(B)(ii) is amended by

10   striking ''section 1(f)(3) for such calendar year by

11   substituting 'calendar year 2010' for 'calendar year

12   1992' in subparagraph (B) thereof'' and inserting

13   ''section 1(c)(2)(A) for such calendar year, deter-

14   mined by substituting 'calendar year 2010' for 'cal-

15   endar year 2016' in clause (ii) thereof''.

16   (18) Section 2032A(a)(3)(B) is amended by

17   striking ''section 1(f)(3) for such calendar year by

18   substituting 'calendar year 1997' for 'calendar year

19   1992' in subparagraph (B) thereof'' and inserting

20   ''section 1(c)(2)(A) for such calendar year, deter-

21   mined by substituting 'calendar year 1997' for 'cal-

22   endar year 2016' in clause (ii) thereof''.

23   (19) Section 2503(b)(2)(B) is amended by

24   striking ''section 1(f)(3) for such calendar year by

25   substituting 'calendar year 1997' for 'calendar year

1   1992' in subparagraph (B) thereof'' and inserting

2   ''section 1(c)(2)(A) for the calendar year, deter-

3   mined by substituting 'calendar year 1997' for 'cal-

4   endar year 2016' in clause (ii) thereof''.

5   (20) Section 4161(b)(2)(C)(i)(II) is amended by

6   striking ''section 1(f)(3) for such calendar year, de-

7   termined by substituting '2004' for '1992' in sub-

8   paragraph (B) thereof'' and inserting ''section

9   1(c)(2)(A) for such calendar year, determined by

10 substituting 'calendar year 2004' for 'calendar year

11 2016' in clause (ii) thereof''.

12 (21) Section 4261(e)(4)(A)(ii) is amended by

13 striking ''section 1(f)(3) for such calendar year by

14 substituting the year before the last nonindexed year

15 for 'calendar year 1992' in subparagraph (B) there-

16 of'' and inserting ''section 1(c)(2)(A) for such cal-

17 endar year, determined by substituting the year be-

18 fore the last nonindexed year for 'calendar year

19 2016' in clause (ii) thereof''.

20 (22) Section 4980I(b)(3)(C)(v)(II) is amended

21 (A) by striking ''section 1(f)(3)'' and in-

22 serting ''section 1(c)(2)(A)'',

23 (B) by striking ''subparagraph (B)'' and

24 inserting ''clause (ii)'', and

1   (C) by striking "1992" and inserting

2   "2016".

3   (23) Section 5000A(c)(3)(D)(ii) is amended—

4   (A) by striking "section 1(f)(3)" and in-

5   serting "section 1(c)(2)(A)",

6   (B) by striking "subparagraph (B)" and

7   inserting "clause (ii)", and

8   (C) by striking "1992" and inserting

9   "2016".

10   (24) Section 6039F(d) is amended by striking

11   "section 1(f)(3), except that subparagraph (B)

12   thereof" and inserting "section 1(c)(2)(A), except

13   that clause (ii) thereof".

14   (25) Section 6323(i)(4)(B) is amended by strik-

15   ing "section 1(f)(3) for the calendar year, deter-

16   mined by substituting 'calendar year 1996' for 'cal-

17   endar year 1992' in subparagraph (B) thereof" and

18   inserting "section 1(c)(2)(A) for the calendar year,

19   determined by substituting 'calendar year 1996' for

20   'calendar year 2016' in clause (ii) thereof".

21   (26) Section 6334(g)(1)(B) is amended by

22   striking "section 1(f)(3) for such calendar year, by

23   substituting 'calendar year 1998' for 'calendar year

24   1992' in subparagraph (B) thereof" and inserting

25   "section 1(c)(2)(A) for such calendar year, deter-

62

1   mined by substituting 'calendar year 1999' for 'cal-

2   endar year 2016' in clause (ii) thereof''.

3   (27) Section 6601(j)(3)(B) is amended by strik-

4   ing ''section 1(f)(3) for such calendar year by sub-

5   stituting 'calendar year 1997' for 'calendar year

6   1992' in subparagraph (B) thereof'' and inserting

7   ''section 1(c)(2)(A) for such calendar year by sub-

8   stituting 'calendar year 1997' for 'calendar year

9   2016' in clause (ii) thereof''.

10   (28) Section 6651(i)(1) is amended by striking

11   ''section 1(f)(3) determined by substituting 'calendar

12   year 2013' for 'calendar year 1992' in subparagraph

13   (B) thereof'' and inserting ''section 1(c)(2)(A) deter-

14   mined by substituting 'calendar year 2013' for 'cal-

15   endar year 2016' in clause (ii) thereof''.

16   (29) Section 6721(f)(1) is amended—

17   (A) by striking ''section 1(f)(3)'' and in-

18   serting ''section 1(c)(2)(A)'',

19   (B) by striking ''subparagraph (B)'' and

20   inserting ''clause (ii)'', and

21   (C) by striking ''1992'' and inserting

22   ''2016''.

23   (30) Section 6722(f)(1) is amended—

24   (A) by striking ''section 1(f)(3)'' and in-

25   serting ''section 1(c)(2)(A)'',

1   (B) by striking "subparagraph (B)" and
2   inserting "clause (ii)", and

3   (C) by striking "1992" and inserting
4   "2016".

5   (31) Section 6652(c)(7)(A) is amended by strik-
6   ing "section 1(f)(3) determined by substituting 'cal-
7   endar year 2013' for 'calendar year 1992' in sub-
8   paragraph (B) thereof" and inserting "section
9   1(c)(2)(A) determined by substituting 'calendar year
10   2013' for 'calendar year 2016' in clause (ii) there-
11   of".

12   (32) Section 6695(h)(1) is amended by striking
13   "section 1(f)(3) determined by substituting 'calendar
14   year 2013' for 'calendar year 1992' in subparagraph
15   (B) thereof" and inserting "section 1(c)(2)(A) deter-
16   mined by substituting 'calendar year 2013' for 'cal-
17   endar year 2016' in clause (ii) thereof".

18   (33) Section 6698(e)(1) is amended by striking
19   " section 1(f)(3) determined by substituting 'cal-
20   endar year 2013' for 'calendar year 1992' in sub-
21   paragraph (B) thereof" and inserting "section
22   1(c)(2)(A) determined by substituting 'calendar year
23   2013' for 'calendar year 2016' in clause (ii) there-
24   of".

64

1   (34) Section 6699(e)(1) is amended by striking

2   "section 1(f)(3) determined by substituting 'calendar

3   year 2013' for 'calendar year 1992' in subparagraph

4   (B) thereof" and inserting "section 1(c)(2)(A) deter-

5   mined by substituting 'calendar year 2013' for 'cal-

6   endar year 2016' in clause (ii) thereof".

7   (35) Section 7345(f)(2) is amended by striking

8   "section 1(f)(3) for the calendar year, determined by

9   substituting 'calendar year 2015' for 'calendar year

10   1992' in subparagraph (B) thereof" and inserting

11   "section 1(c)(2)(A) for the calendar year, deter-

12   mined by substituting 'calendar year 2015' for 'cal-

13   endar year 2016' in clause (ii) thereof".

14   (36) Section 7430(c)(1) is amended by striking

15   "section 1(f)(3) for such calendar year, by sub-

16   stituting 'calendar year 1995' for 'calendar year

17   1992' in subparagraph (B) thereof" in the flush text

18   at the end and inserting "section 1(c)(2)(A) for such

19   calendar year, determined by substituting 'calendar

20   year 1995' for 'calendar year 2016' in clause (ii)

21   thereof".

22   (37) Section 7872(g)(5) is amended to read as

23   follows:

24   "(5) INFLATION ADJUSTMENT.—

1   "(A) IN GENERAL.—In the case of any

2   loan made during any calendar year after 2018

3   to which paragraph (1) applies, the adjusted

4   dollar amount shall be increased by an amount

5   equal to—

6   "(i) such adjusted dollar amount,

7   multiplied by

8   "(ii) the cost-of-living adjustment de-

9   termined under section 1(c)(2)(A) for such

10   calendar year, determined by substituting

11   'calendar year 2017' for 'calendar year

12   2016' in clause (ii) thereof.

13   "(B) ADJUSTED DOLLAR AMOUNT.—For

14   purposes of this paragraph, the term 'adjusted

15   dollar amount' means the dollar amount in

16   paragraph (2) as in effect for calendar year

17   2018.

18   "(C) ROUNDING.—Any increase under sub-

19   paragraph (A) shall be rounded to the nearest

20   multiple of $100.".

21   (b) OTHER CONFORMING AMENDMENTS.—

22   (1) Section 36B(b)(3)(B)(ii)(I)(aa) is amended

23   to read as follows:

24   "(aa) who is described in

25   section 1(b)(1)(B) and who does

1   not have any dependents for the

2   taxable year,''.

3   (2) Section 486B(b)(1) is amended—

4   (A) by striking "maximum rate in effect"

5 and inserting "highest rate specified", and

6   (B) by striking "section 1(e)" and insert-

7 ing "section 1".

8   (3) Section 511(b)(1) is amended by striking

9 "section 1(e)" and inserting "section 1".

10   (4) Section 641(a) is amended by striking "sec-

11 tion 1(e) shall apply to the taxable income" and in-

12 serting "section 1 shall apply to the taxable in-

13 come".

14   (5) Section 641(c)(2)(A) is amended to read as

15 follows:

16   "(A) Except to the extent provided in sec-

17   tion 1(h), the rate of tax shall be treated as

18   being the highest rate of tax set forth in section

19   1(a).''.

20   (6) Section 646(b) is amended to read as fol-

21 lows:

22   "(b) TAXATION OF INCOME OF TRUST.—Except as

23 provided in subsection (f)(1)(B)(ii), there is hereby im-

24 posed on the taxable income of an electing Settlement

25 Trust a tax at the rate specified in section 1(a)(1). Such

1 tax shall be in lieu of the income tax otherwise imposed

2 by this chapter on such income.".

3   (7) Section 685(c) is amended by striking "Sec-

4   tion 1(e)" and inserting "Section 1".

5   (8) Section 904(b)(3)(E)(ii)(I) is amended by

6   striking "set forth in subsection (a), (b), (c), (d), or

7   (e) of section 1 (whichever applies)" and inserting

8   "the highest rate of tax specified in section 1".

9   (9) Section 1398(c)(2) is amended by striking

10   "subsection (d) of".

11   (10) Section 3402(p)(1)(B) is amended by

12   striking "any percentage applicable to any of the 3

13   lowest income brackets in the table under section

14   1(c)," and inserting "12 percent, 25 percent,".

15   (11) Section 3402(q)(1) is amended by striking

16   "the product of third lowest rate of tax applicable

17   under section 1(c) and" and inserting "25 percent

18   of".

19   (12) Section 3402(r)(3) is amended by striking

20   "the amount of tax which would be imposed by sec-

21   tion 1(c) (determined without regard to any rate of

22   tax in excess of the fourth lowest rate of tax applica-

23   ble under section 1(c)) on an amount of taxable in-

24   come equal to" and inserting "an amount equal to

25   the product of 25 percent multiplied by".

1   (13) Section 3406(a)(1) is amended by striking

2 "the product of the fourth lowest rate of tax applica-

3 ble under section 1(c) and" and inserting "25 per-

4 cent of".

5   (14) Section 6103(e)(1)(A)(iii) is amended by

6 striking "section 1(g) (as in effect on the day before

7 the enactment of theTax Cuts and Jobs Act)".

8 (c) EFFECTIVE DATE.—The amendments made by

9 this section shall apply to taxable years beginning after

10 December 31, 2017.

Subtitle B—Simplification and Reform of Family and Individual Tax Credits

SEC. 1101. ENHANCEMENT OF CHILD TAX CREDIT AND NEW FAMILY TAX CREDIT.

16 (a) INCREASE IN CREDIT AMOUNT AND ADDITION OF

17 OTHER DEPENDENTS.—

18   (1) IN GENERAL.—Section 24(a) is amended—

19   (A) by striking "qualifying child" and inserting

20 "dependent",

21   (B) by striking "for which the taxpayer is al-

22 lowed a deduction under section 151", and

23   (C) by striking "an amount equal to $1,000."

24 and inserting the following: "an amount equal to—

1   "(1) in the case of a qualifying child, $1,600,

2   and

3   "(2) for taxable years beginning before January

4   1, 2023, in the case of the taxpayer (each spouse in

5   the case of a joint return) and any dependent to

6   whom paragraph (1) does not apply, $300.".

7   (2) CONFORMING AMENDMENTS.—

8   (A) Section 24(c) is amended—

9   (i) by redesignating paragraphs (1) and

10   (2) as paragraphs (2) and (3), respectively,

11   (ii) by striking "152(c)" in paragraph (2)

12   (as so redesignated) and inserting "7706(c)",

13   (iii) by inserting before paragraph (2) (as

14   so redesignated) the following new paragraph:

15   "(1) DEPENDENT.—

16   "(A) IN GENERAL.—The term 'dependent'

17   shall have the meaning given such term by sec-

18   tion 7706.

19   "(B) CERTAIN INDIVIDUALS NOT TREATED

20   AS DEPENDENTS.—In the case of an individual

21   with respect to whom a credit under this section

22   is allowable to another taxpayer for a taxable

23   year beginning in the calendar year in which

24   the individual's taxable year begins, the amount

25   applicable to such individual under subsection

70

1   (a) for such individual's taxable year shall be
2   zero.'',

3   (iv) in paragraph (3) (as so redesig-
4   nated)—

5   (I) by striking "term 'qualifying
6   child'" and inserting "terms 'qualifying
7   child' and 'dependent'", and

8   (II) by striking "152(b)(3)" and in-
9   serting "7706(b)(3)", and

10   (v) in the heading by striking "QUALI-
11   FYING" and inserting "DEPENDENT; QUALI-
12   FYING"

13   (B) The heading for section 24 is amended by
14   inserting "**AND FAMILY**" after "**CHILD**".

15   (C) The table of sections for subpart A of part
16   IV of subchapter A of chapter 1 is amended by
17   striking the item relating to section 24 and inserting
18   the following new item:

"Sec. 24. Child and dependent tax credit.''.

19   (b) ELIMINATION OF MARRIAGE PENALTY.—Section
20 24(b)(2) is amended—

21   (1) by striking "$110,000" in subparagraph (A) and
22 inserting "$230,000",

23   (2) by inserting "and" at the end of subparagraph
24 (A),

1   (3) by striking "$75,000 in the case of an individual

2 who is not married" and all that follows through the pe-

3 riod at the end and inserting "one-half of the amount in

4 effect under subparagraph (A) for the taxable year in the

5 case of any other individual.".

6   (c) CREDIT REFUNDABLE UP TO $1,000 PER

7 CHILD.—

8   (1) IN GENERAL.—Section 24(d)(1)(A) is amended

9 by striking all that follows "under this section" and insert-

10 ing the following: "determined—

11   "(i) without regard to this subsection

12   and the limitation under section 26(a),

13   "(ii) without regard to subsection

14   (a)(2), and

15   "(iii) by substituting '$1,000' for

16   '$1,600' in subsection (a)(1), or".

17   (2) INFLATION ADJUSTMENT.—Section 24(d) is

18 amended by inserting after paragraph (2) the following

19 new paragraph:

20   "(3) INFLATION ADJUSTMENT.—In the case of

21   any taxable year beginning in a calendar year after

22   2017, the $1,000 amount in paragraph (1)(A)(iii)

23   shall be increased by an amount equal to—

24   "(A) such dollar amount, multiplied by

72

1   "(B) the cost-of-living adjustment under

2   section 1(c)(2)(A) for such calendar year.

3   Any increase determined under the preceding sen-

4 tence shall be rounded to the next highest multiple

5 of $100 and shall not exceed the amount in effect

6 under subsection (a)(2).".

7   (d) EFFECTIVE DATE.—The amendments made by

8 this section shall apply to taxable years beginning after

9 December 31, 2017.

10 **SEC. 1102. REPEAL OF NONREFUNDABLE CREDITS.**

11   (a) REPEAL OF SECTION 22.—

12   (1) IN GENERAL.—Subpart A of part IV of sub-

13   chapter A of chapter 1 is amended by striking sec-

14   tion 22 (and by striking the item relating to such

15   section in the table of sections for such subpart).

16   (2) CONFORMING AMENDMENT.—

17   (A) Section 86(f) is amended by striking

18   paragraph (1) and by redesignating paragraphs

19   (2), (3), and (4) as paragraphs (1), (2), and

20   (3), respectively.

21   (B)(i) Subsections (c)(3)(B) and (d)(4)(A)

22   of section 7706, as redesignated by this Act,

23   are each amended by striking "(as defined in

24   section 22(e)(3)".

1   (ii) Section 7706(f), as redesignated by

2   this Act, is amended by redesignating para-

3   graph (7) as paragraph (8) and by inserting

4   after paragraph (6) the following new para-

5   graph:

6   "(7) PERMANENT AND TOTAL DISABILITY DE-

7   FINED.—An individual is permanently and totally

8   disabled if he is unable to engage in any substantial

9   gainful activity by reason of any medically deter-

10   minable physical or mental impairment which can be

11   expected to result in death or which has lasted or

12   can be expected to last for a continuous period of

13   not less than 12 months. An individual shall not be

14   considered to be permanently and totally disabled

15   unless he furnishes proof of the existence thereof in

16   such form and manner, and at such times, as the

17   Secretary may require.".

18   (iii) Section 415(c)(3)(C)(i) is amended by

19   striking "22(e)(3)" and inserting "7706(f)(7)".

20   (iv) Section 422(c)(6) is amended by strik-

21   ing "22(e)(3)" and inserting "7706(f)(7)".

22   (b) REPEAL OF SECTION 23.—Subpart A of part IV

23 of subchapter A of chapter 1 is amended by striking sec-

24 tion 23 (and by striking the item relating to such section

25 in the table of sections for such subpart).

74

1   (c) TERMINATION OF SECTION 25.—Section 25, as

2 amended by section 3601, is amended by adding at the

3 end the following new subsection:

4   "(k) TERMINATION.—No credit shall be allowed

5 under this section with respect to any mortgage credit cer-

6 tificate issued after December 31, 2017.".

7   (d) REPEAL OF SECTION 30D.—

8   (1) IN GENERAL.—Subpart B of part IV of

9   subchapter A of chapter 1 is amended by striking

10   section 30D (and by striking the item relating to

11   such section in the table of sections for such sub-

12   part).

13   (2) CONFORMING AMENDMENTS.—

14   (A) Section 38(b) is amended by striking

15   paragraph (35).

16   (B) Section 1016(a) is amended by strik-

17   ing paragraph (37).

18   (C) Section 6501(m) is amended by strik-

19   ing "30D(e)(4),".

20   (e) EFFECTIVE DATE.—

21   (1) IN GENERAL.—Except as provided in para-

22   graphs (2) and (3), the amendments made by this

23   section shall apply to taxable years beginning after

24   December 31, 2017.

1   (2) SUBSECTION (c).—The amendment made

2 by subsection (c) shall apply to taxable years ending

3 after December 31, 2017.

4   (3) SUBSECTION (d).—The amendments made

5 by subsection (d) shall apply to vehicles placed in

6 service in taxable years beginning after December

7 31, 2017.

8 **SEC. 1103. REFUNDABLE CREDIT PROGRAM INTEGRITY.**

9 (a) SOCIAL SECURITY NUMBER REQUIRED TO CLAIM

10 THE REFUNDABLE PORTION OF THE CHILD TAX CRED-

11 IT.—

12   (1) IN GENERAL.—Section 24(d), as amended

13 by the preceding provisions of this Act, is amended

14 by redesignating paragraph (5) as paragraph (4)

15 and by adding at the end the following new para-

16 graph:

17   "(5) IDENTIFICATION REQUIREMENT.—

18   "(A) IN GENERAL.—Paragraph (1) shall

19   not apply to any taxpayer for any taxable year

20   unless the taxpayer includes the taxpayer's so-

21   cial security number on the return of tax for

22   such taxable year.

23   "(B) JOINT RETURNS.—In the case of a

24   joint return, the requirement of subparagraph

25   (A) shall be treated as met if the social security

1   number of either spouse is included on such re-

2   turn.

3   "(C) SOCIAL SECURITY NUMBER.—For

4   purposes of this paragraph, the term 'social se-

5   curity number' means a social security number

6   issued to an individual by the Social Security

7   Administration (but only if the social security

8   number is issued to a citizen of the United

9   States or pursuant to subclause (I) (or that

10   portion of subclause (III) that relates to sub-

11   clause (I)) of section 205(c)(2)(B)(i) of the So-

12   cial Security Act).".

13   (2) OMISSIONS TREATED AS MATHEMATICAL OR

14   CLERICAL ERROR.—

15   (A) IN GENERAL.—Section 6213(g)(2)(I)

16   is amended to read as follows:

17   "(I) an omission of a correct social secu-

18   rity number required under section 24(d)(5)

19   (relating to refundable portion of child tax cred-

20   it), or a correct TIN required under section

21   24(e) (relating to child tax credit), to be in-

22   cluded on a return,".

23   (3) CLERICAL AMENDMENT.—The heading for

24   section 24(e) is amended by striking "IDENTIFICA-

77

1   TION REQUIREMENTS" and inserting "GENERAL

2   IDENTIFICATION REQUIREMENTS".

3   (b) SOCIAL SECURITY NUMBER MUST BE PRO-

4   VIDED.—

5   (1) IN GENERAL.—Section 25A(f)(1)(A), as

6   amended by section 1201 of this Act, is amended by

7   striking "taxpayer identification number" each place

8   it appears and inserting "social security number".

9   (2) OMISSION TREATED AS MATHEMATICAL OR

10   CLERICAL ERROR.—Section 6213(g)(2)(J) is amend-

11   ed by striking "TIN" and inserting "social security

12   number and employer identification number".

13   (c) INDIVIDUALS PROHIBITED FROM ENGAGING IN

14   EMPLOYMENT IN UNITED STATES NOT ELIGIBLE FOR

15   EARNED INCOME TAX CREDIT.—Section 32(m) is amend-

16   ed—

17   (1) by striking "(other than:" and all that fol-

18   lows through "of the Social Security Act)", and

19   (2) by inserting before the period at the end the

20   following: ", but only if, in the case of subsection

21   (c)(1)(E), the social security number is issued to a

22   citizen of the United States or pursuant to subclause

23   (I) (or that portion of subclause (III) that relates to

24   subclause (I)) of section 205(c)(2)(B)(i) of the So-

25   cial Security Act".

1   (d) EFFECTIVE DATE.—The amendments made by
2 this section shall apply to taxable years beginning after
3 December 31, 2017.

Subtitle C—Simplification and Reform of Education Incentives

SEC. 1201. AMERICAN OPPORTUNITY TAX CREDIT.

7   (a) IN GENERAL.—Section 25A is amended to read
8 as follows:

"SEC. 25A. AMERICAN OPPORTUNITY TAX CREDIT.

10   "(a) IN GENERAL.—In the case of an individual,
11 there shall be allowed as a credit against the tax imposed
12 by this chapter for the taxable year an amount equal to
13 the sum of—

14   "(1) 100 percent of so much of the qualified
15   tuition and related expenses paid by the taxpayer
16   during the taxable year (for education furnished to
17   any eligible student for whom an election is in effect
18   under this section for such taxable year during any
19   academic period beginning in such taxable year) as
20   does not exceed $2,000, plus

21   "(2) 25 percent of so much of such expenses so
22   paid as exceeds the dollar amount in effect under
23   paragraph (1) but does not exceed twice such dollar
24   amount.

1   "(b) PORTION OF CREDIT REFUNDABLE.—40 per-

2 cent of the credit allowable under subsection (a)(1) (deter-

3 mined without regard to this subsection and section 26(a)

4 and after application of all other provisions of this section)

5 shall be treated as a credit allowable under subpart C (and

6 not under this part). The preceding sentence shall not

7 apply to any taxpayer for any taxable year if such tax-

8 payer is a child to whom section 1(d) applies for such tax-

9 able year.

10   "(c) LIMITATION BASED ON MODIFIED ADJUSTED

11 GROSS INCOME.—

12   "(1) IN GENERAL.—The amount allowable as a

13   credit under subsection (a) for any taxable year shall

14   be reduced (but not below zero) by an amount which

15   bears the same ratio to the amount so allowable (de-

16   termined without regard to this subsection and sub-

17   section (b) but after application of all other provi-

18   sions of this section) as—

19   "(A) the excess of—

20   "(i) the taxpayer's modified adjusted

21   gross income for such taxable year, over

22   "(ii) $80,000 (twice such amount in

23   the case of a joint return), bears to

24   "(B) $10,000 (twice such amount in the

25   case of a joint return).

1   "(2) MODIFIED ADJUSTED GROSS INCOME.—

2 For purposes of this subsection, the term 'modified

3 adjusted gross income' means the adjusted gross in-

4 come of the taxpayer for the taxable year increased

5 by any amount excluded from gross income under

6 section 911, 931, or 933.

7   "(d) OTHER LIMITATIONS.—

8   "(1) CREDIT ALLOWED ONLY FOR 5 TAXABLE

9 YEARS.—An election to have this section apply may

10 not be made for any taxable year if such an election

11 (by the taxpayer or any other individual) is in effect

12 with respect to such student for any 5 prior taxable

13 years.

14   "(2) CREDIT ALLOWED ONLY FOR FIRST 5

15 YEARS OF POSTSECONDARY EDUCATION.—

16   "(A) IN GENERAL.—No credit shall be al-

17   lowed under subsection (a) for a taxable year

18   with respect to the qualified tuition and related

19   expenses of an eligible student if the student

20   has completed (before the beginning of such

21   taxable year) the first 5 years of postsecondary

22   education at an eligible educational institution.

23   "(B) FIFTH YEAR LIMITATIONS.—In the

24   case of an eligible student with respect to whom

25   an election has been in effect for 4 preceding

1   taxable years for purposes of the fifth taxable

2   year—

3   "(i) the amount of the credit allowed

4   under this section for the taxable year

5   shall not exceed an amount equal to 50

6   percent of the credit otherwise determined

7   with respect to such student under this

8   section (without regard to this subpara-

9   graph), and

10   "(ii) the amount of the credit deter-

11   mined under subsection (b) and allowable

12   under subpart C shall not exceed an

13   amount equal to 40 percent of the amount

14   determined with respect to such student

15   under clause (i).

16   "(e) DEFINITIONS.—For purposes of this section—

17   "(1) ELIGIBLE STUDENT.— The term 'eligible

18   student' means, with respect to any academic period,

19   a student who—

20   "(A) meets the requirements of section

21   484(a)(1) of the Higher Education Act of 1965

22   (20 U.S.C. 1091(a)(1)), as in effect on August

23   5, 1997, and

1   "(B) is carrying at least ½ the normal

2   full-time work load for the course of study the

3   student is pursuing.

4   "(2) QUALIFIED TUITION AND RELATED EX-

5 PENSES.—

6   "(A) IN GENERAL.—The term 'qualified

7   tuition and related expenses' means tuition,

8   fees, and course materials, required for enroll-

9   ment or attendance of—

10   "(i) the taxpayer,

11   "(ii) the taxpayer's spouse, or

12   "(iii) any dependent of the taxpayer,

13   at an eligible educational institution for courses

14   of instruction of such individual at such institu-

15   tion.

16   "(B) EXCEPTION FOR EDUCATION INVOLV-

17   ING SPORTS, ETC.—Such term does not include

18   expenses with respect to any course or other

19   education involving sports, games, or hobbies,

20   unless such course or other education is part of

21   the individual's degree program.

22   "(C) EXCEPTION FOR NONACADEMIC

23   FEES.—Such term does not include student ac-

24   tivity fees, athletic fees, insurance expenses, or

1   other expenses unrelated to an individual's aca-

2   demic course of instruction.

3   "(3) ELIGIBLE EDUCATIONAL INSTITUTION.—

4 The term 'eligible educational institution' means an

5 institution—

6   "(A) which is described in section 481 of

7   the Higher Education Act of 1965 (20 U.S.C.

8   1088), as in effect on August 5, 1997, and

9   "(B) which is eligible to participate in a

10   program under title IV of such Act.

11   "(f) SPECIAL RULES.—

12   "(1) IDENTIFICATION REQUIREMENTS.—

13   "(A) STUDENT.—No credit shall be al-

14   lowed under subsection (a) to a taxpayer with

15   respect to the qualified tuition and related ex-

16   penses of an individual unless the taxpayer in-

17   cludes the name and taxpayer identification

18   number of such individual on the return of tax

19   for the taxable year, and such taxpayer identi-

20   fication number was issued on or before the due

21   date for filing such return.

22   "(B) TAXPAYER.—No credit shall be al-

23   lowed under this section if the identifying num-

24   ber of the taxpayer was issued after the due

25   date for filing the return for the taxable year.

1   "(C) INSTITUTION.—No credit shall be al-

2   lowed under this section unless the taxpayer in-

3   cludes the employer identification number of

4   any institution to which qualified tuition and

5   related expenses were paid with respect to the

6   individual.

7   "(2) ADJUSTMENT FOR CERTAIN SCHOLAR-

8   SHIPS, ETC.—The amount of qualified tuition and

9   related expenses otherwise taken into account under

10   subsection (a) with respect to an individual for an

11   academic period shall be reduced (before the applica-

12   tion of subsection (c)) by the sum of any amounts

13   paid for the benefit of such individual which are allo-

14   cable to such period as—

15   "(A) a qualified scholarship which is ex-

16   cludable from gross income under section 117,

17   "(B) an educational assistance allowance

18   under chapter 30, 31, 32, 34, or 35 of title 38,

19   United States Code, or under chapter 1606 of

20   title 10, United States Code, and

21   "(C) a payment (other than a gift, be-

22   quest, devise, or inheritance within the meaning

23   of section 102(a)) for such individual's edu-

24   cational expenses, or attributable to such indi-

25   vidual's enrollment at an eligible educational in-

1   stitution, which is excludable from gross income

2   under any law of the United States.

3   "(3) TREATMENT OF EXPENSES PAID BY DE-

4   PENDENT.—If an individual is a dependent of an-

5   other taxpayer for a taxable year beginning in the

6   calendar year in which such individuals taxable year

7   begins—

8   "(A) no credit shall be allowed under sub-

9   section (a) to such individual for such individ-

10   ual's taxable year, and

11   "(B) qualified tuition and related expenses

12   paid by such individual during such individual's

13   taxable year shall be treated for purposes of

14   this section as paid by such other taxpayer.

15   "(4) TREATMENT OF CERTAIN PREPAY-

16   MENTS.—If qualified tuition and related expenses

17   are paid by the taxpayer during a taxable year for

18   an academic period which begins during the first 3

19   months following such taxable year, such academic

20   period shall be treated for purposes of this section

21   as beginning during such taxable year.

22   "(5) DENIAL OF DOUBLE BENEFIT.—No credit

23   shall be allowed under this section for any amount

24   for which a deduction is allowed under any other

25   provision of this chapter.

1   "(6) NO CREDIT FOR MARRIED INDIVIDUALS

2 FILING SEPARATE RETURNS.—If the taxpayer is a

3 married individual (within the meaning of section

4 7703), this section shall apply only if the taxpayer

5 and the taxpayer's spouse file a joint return for the

6 taxable year.

7   "(7) NONRESIDENT ALIENS.—If the taxpayer is

8 a nonresident alien individual for any portion of the

9 taxable year, this section shall apply only if such in-

10 dividual is treated as a resident alien of the United

11 States for purposes of this chapter by reason of an

12 election under subsection (g) or (h) of section 6013.

13   "(8) RESTRICTIONS ON TAXPAYERS WHO IM-

14 PROPERLY CLAIMED CREDIT IN PRIOR YEAR.—

15   "(A) TAXPAYERS MAKING PRIOR FRAUDU-

16 LENT OR RECKLESS CLAIMS.—

17   "(i) IN GENERAL.—No credit shall be

18 allowed under this section for any taxable

19 year in the disallowance period.

20   "(ii) DISALLOWANCE PERIOD.—For

21 purposes of clause (i), the disallowance pe-

22 riod is—

23   "(I) the period of 10 taxable

24 years after the most recent taxable

25 year for which there was a final deter-

1 mination that the taxpayer's claim of

2 credit under this section was due to

3 fraud, and

4   "(II) the period of 2 taxable

5 years after the most recent taxable

6 year for which there was a final deter-

7 mination that the taxpayer's claim of

8 credit under this section was due to

9 reckless or intentional disregard of

10 rules and regulations (but not due to

11 fraud).

12   "(B) TAXPAYERS MAKING IMPROPER

13 PRIOR CLAIMS.—In the case of a taxpayer who

14 is denied credit under this section for any tax-

15 able year as a result of the deficiency proce-

16 dures under subchapter B of chapter 63, no

17 credit shall be allowed under this section for

18 any subsequent taxable year unless the taxpayer

19 provides such information as the Secretary may

20 require to demonstrate eligibility for such cred-

21 it.

22 "(g) INFLATION ADJUSTMENT.—

23   "(1) IN GENERAL.—In the case of a taxable

24 year beginning after 2018, the $80,000 amount in

G:\M\15\BRADTX\BRADTX_045.XML

1 subsection (c)(1)(A)(ii) shall each be increased by an
2 amount equal to—

3   "(A) such dollar amount, multiplied by

4   "(B) the cost-of-living adjustment deter-
5   mined under section 1(c)(2)(A) for the calendar
6   year in which the taxable year begins, deter-
7   mined by substituting 'calendar year 2017' for
8   'calendar year 2016' in clause (ii) thereof.

9   "(2) ROUNDING.—If any amount as adjusted
10   under paragraph (1) is not a multiple of $1,000,
11   such amount shall be rounded to the next lowest
12   multiple of $1,000.

13   "(h) REGULATIONS.—The Secretary may prescribe
14 such regulations or other guidance as may be necessary
15 or appropriate to carry out this section, including regula-
16 tions providing for a recapture of the credit allowed under
17 this section in cases where there is a refund in a subse-
18 quent taxable year of any amount which was taken into
19 account in determining the amount of such credit.".

20   (b) CONFORMING AMENDMENTS.—

21   (1) Section 72(t)(7)(B) is amended by striking
22   "section 25A(g)(2)" and inserting "section
23   25A(f)(2)".

g:\VHLC\110217\110217.061.xml   (679209|10)
November 2, 2017 (10:46 a.m.)

89

1   (2) Section 529(c)(3)(B)(v)(I) is amended by

2   striking "section 25A(g)(2)" and inserting "section

3   25A(f)(2)".

4   (3) Section 529(e)(3)(B)(i) is amended by strik-

5   ing "section 25A(b)(3)" and inserting "section

6   25A(d)".

7   (4) Section 530(d)(2)(C) is amended—

8   (A) by striking "section 25A(g)(2)" in

9   clause (i)(I) and inserting "section 25A(f)(2)",

10   and

11   (B) by striking "HOPE AND LIFETIME

12   LEARNING CREDITS" in the heading and insert-

13   ing "AMERICAN OPPORTUNITY TAX CREDIT".

14   (5) Section 530(d)(4)(B)(iii) is amended by

15   striking "section 25A(g)(2)" and inserting "section

16   25A(d)(4)(B)".

17   (6) Section 6050S(e) is amended by striking

18   "subsection (g)(2)" and inserting "subsection

19   (f)(2)".

20   (7) Section 6211(b)(4)(A) is amended by strik-

21   ing "subsection (i)(6)" and inserting "subsection

22   (b)".

23   (8) Section 6213(g)(2)(J) is amended by strik-

24   ing "TIN required under section 25A(g)(1)" and in-

1   serting "TIN, and employer identification number,

2   required under section 25A(f)(1)".

3   (9) Section 6213(g)(2)(Q) is amended to read

4   as follows:

5   "(Q) an omission of information required

6   by section 25A(f)(8)(B) or an entry on the re-

7   turn claiming the credit determined under sec-

8   tion 25A(a) for a taxable year for which the

9   credit is disallowed under section

10   25A(f)(8)(A).".

11   (10) Section 1004(c) of division B of the Amer-

12   ican Recovery and Reinvestment Tax Act of 2009 is

13   amended—

14   (A) in paragraph (1)—

15   (i) by striking "section 25A(i)(6)"

16   each place it appears and inserting "sec-

17   tion 25A(b)", and

18   (ii) by striking "with respect to tax-

19   able years beginning after 2008 and before

20   2018" each place it appears and inserting

21   "with respect to each taxable year",

22   (B) in paragraph (2), by striking "Section

23   25A(i)(6)" and inserting "Section 25A(b)", and

24   (C) in paragraph (3)(C), by striking "sub-

25   section (i)(6)" and inserting "subsection (b)".

1 (11) The table of sections for subpart A of part

2 IV of subchapter A of chapter 1 is amended by

3 striking the item relating to section 25A and insert-

4 ing the following new item:

"Sec. 25A. American opportunity tax credit.".

5 (c) EFFECTIVE DATE.—The amendments made by

6 this section shall apply to taxable years beginning after

7 December 31, 2017.

8 **SEC. 1202. CONSOLIDATION OF EDUCATION SAVINGS**

9   **RULES.**

10 (a) NO NEW CONTRIBUTIONS TO COVERDELL EDU-

11 CATION SAVINGS ACCOUNT.—Section 530(b)(1)(A) is

12 amended to read as follows:

13 "(A) Except in the case of rollover con-

14 tributions, no contribution will be accepted after

15 December 31, 2017.".

16 (b) LIMITED DISTRIBUTION ALLOWED FOR ELEMEN-

17 TARY AND SECONDARY TUITION.—

18 (1) IN GENERAL.—Section 529(c) is amended

19 by adding at the end the following new paragraph:

20 "(7) TREATMENT OF ELEMENTARY AND SEC-

21 ONDARY TUITION.—Any reference in this subsection

22 to the term 'qualified higher education expense' shall

23 include a reference to expenses for tuition in connec-

24 tion with enrollment at an elementary or secondary

25 school.".

1   (2) LIMITATION.—Section 529(e)(3)(A) is
2   amended by adding at the end the following: "The
3   amount of cash distributions from all qualified tui-
4   tion programs described in subsection (b)(1)(A)(ii)
5   with respect to a beneficiary during any taxable
6   year, shall, in the aggregate, include not more than
7    $10,000 in expenses for tuition incurred during the
8   taxable year in connection with the enrollment or at-
9   tendance of the beneficiary as an elementary or sec-
10   ondary school student at a public, private, or reli-
11   gious school.".

12   (c) ROLLOVERS TO QUALIFIED TUITION PROGRAMS
13   PERMITTED.—Section 530(d)(5) is amended by inserting
14   ", or into (by purchase or contribution) a qualified tuition
15   program (as defined in section 529)," after "into another
16   Coverdell education savings account".

17   (d) DISTRIBUTIONS FROM QUALIFIED TUITION PRO-
18   GRAMS FOR CERTAIN EXPENSES ASSOCIATED WITH REG-
19   ISTERED APPRENTICESHIP PROGRAMS.—Section
20   529(e)(3) is amended by adding at the end the following
21   new subparagraph:

22   "(C) CERTAIN EXPENSES ASSOCIATED
23   WITH REGISTERED APPRENTICESHIP PRO-
24   GRAMS.—The term 'qualified higher education
25   expenses' shall include books, supplies, and

1   equipment required for the enrollment or at-

2   tendance of a designated beneficiary in an ap-

3   prenticeship program registered and certified

4   with the Secretary of Labor under section 1 of

5   the National Apprenticeship Act (29 U.S.C.

6   50).''.

7   (e) UNBORN CHILDREN ALLOWED AS ACCOUNT

8 BENEFICIARIES.—Section 529(e) is amended by adding at

9 the end the following new paragraph:

10   ''(6) TREATMENT OF UNBORN CHILDREN.—

11   ''(A) IN GENERAL.—Nothing shall prevent

12   an unborn child from being treated as a des-

13   ignated beneficiary or an individual under this

14   section.

15   ''(B) UNBORN CHILD.—For purposes of

16   this paragraph—

17   ''(i) IN GENERAL.—The term 'unborn

18   child' means a child in utero.

19   ''(ii) CHILD IN UTERO.—The term

20   'child in utero' means a member of the

21   species homo sapiens, at any stage of de-

22   velopment, who is carried in the womb.''.

23   (f) EFFECTIVE DATES.—

24   (1) IN GENERAL.—Except as otherwise pro-

25   vided in this subsection, the amendments made by

1   this section shall apply to contributions made after

2   December 31, 2017.

3   (2) ROLLOVERS TO QUALIFIED TUITION PRO-

4   GRAMS.—The amendments made by subsection (b)

5   shall apply to distributions after December 31,

6   2017.

7 **SEC. 1203. REFORMS TO DISCHARGE OF CERTAIN STUDENT**

8   **LOAN INDEBTEDNESS.**

9   (a) TREATMENT OF STUDENT LOANS DISCHARGED

10 ON ACCOUNT OF DEATH OR DISABILITY.—Section 108(f)

11 is amended by adding at the end the following new para-

12 graph:

13   "(5) DISCHARGES ON ACCOUNT OF DEATH OR

14   DISABILITY.—

15   "(A) IN GENERAL.—In the case of an indi-

16   vidual, gross income does not include any

17   amount which (but for this subsection) would

18   be includible in gross income by reasons of the

19   discharge (in whole or in part) of any loan de-

20   scribed in subparagraph (B) if such discharge

21   was—

22   "(i) pursuant to subsection (a) or (d)

23   of section 437 of the Higher Education

24   Act of 1965 or the parallel benefit under

1   part D of title IV of such Act (relating to

2   the repayment of loan liability),

3   "(ii) pursuant to section 464(c)(1)(F)

4   of such Act, or

5   "(iii) otherwise discharged on account

6   of the death or total and permanent dis-

7   ability of the student.

8   "(B) LOANS DESCRIBED.—A loan is de-

9   scribed in this subparagraph if such loan is—

10   "(i) a student loan (as defined in

11   paragraph (2)), or

12   "(ii) a private education loan (as de-

13   fined in section 140(7) of the Consumer

14   Credit   Protection   Act   (15   U.S.C.

15   1650(7))).".

16   (b) EXCLUSION FROM GROSS INCOME FOR PAY-

17 MENTS MADE UNDER INDIAN HEALTH SERVICE LOAN

18 REPAYMENT PROGRAM.—

19   (1) IN GENERAL.—Section 108(f)(4) is amend-

20   ed by inserting "under section 108 of the Indian

21   Health Care Improvement Act," after "338I of such

22   Act,".

23   (2) CLERICAL AMENDMENT.—The heading for

24   section 108(f)(4) is amended by striking "AND CER-

96

1 TAIN" and inserting ", INDIAN HEALTH SERVICE

2 LOAN REPAYMENT PROGRAM, AND CERTAIN".

3 (c) EFFECTIVE DATES.—

4   (1) SUBSECTION (a).—The amendment made

5 by subsection (a)(1) shall apply to discharges of in-

6 debtedness after December 31, 2017.

7   (2) SUBSECTION (b).—The amendments made

8 by subsection (b) shall apply to amounts received in

9 taxable years beginning after December 31, 2017.

10 **SEC. 1204. REPEAL OF OTHER PROVISIONS RELATING TO**

11   **EDUCATION.**

12 (a) IN GENERAL.—Subchapter B of chapter 1 is

13 amended—

14   (1) in part VII by striking sections 221 and

15 222 (and by striking the items relating to such sec-

16 tions in the table of sections for such part),

17   (2) in part VII by striking sections 135 and

18 127 (and by striking the items relating to such sec-

19 tions in the table of sections for such part), and

20   (3) by striking subsection (d) of section 117.

21 (b) CONFORMING AMENDMENT RELATING TO SEC-

22 TION 221.—

23   (1) Section 62(a) is amended by striking para-

24 graph (17).

1 (2) Section 163(h)(2) is amended by striking

2 subparagraph (F).

3 (3) Section 6050S(a) is amended—

4 (A) by inserting "or" at the end of para-

5 graph (1),

6 (B) by striking "or" at the end of para-

7 graph (2), and

8 (C) by striking paragraph (3).

9 (4) Section 6050S(e) is amended by striking all

10 that follows "thereof)" and inserting a period.

11 (c) CONFORMING AMENDMENT RELATING TO SEC-

12 TION 222.—Section 62(a) is amended by striking para-

13 graph (18).

14 (d) CONFORMING AMENDMENTS RELATING TO SEC-

15 TION 127.—

16 (1) Section 125(f)(1) is amended by striking

17 "127,".

18 (2) Section 132(j)(8) is amended by striking

19 "which are not excludable from gross income under

20 section 127".

21 (3) Section 414(n)(3)(C) is amended by strik-

22 ing "127,".

23 (4) Section 414(t)(2) is amended by striking

24 "127,".

1   (5) Section 3121(a)(18) is amended by striking

2   "127,".

3   (6) Section 3231(e) is amended by striking

4   paragraph (6).

5   (7) Section 3306(b)(13) is amended by "127,".

6   (8) Section 3401(a)(18) is amended by striking

7   "127,".

8   (9) Section 6039D(d)(1) is amended by striking

9   ", 127".

10   (e) CONFORMING AMENDMENTS RELATING TO SEC-

11   TION 117(d).—

12   (1) Section 117(c)(1) is amended—

13   (A) by striking "subsections (a) and (d)"

14   and inserting "subsection (a)", and

15   (B) by striking "or qualified tuition reduc-

16   tion".

17   (2) Section 414(n)(3)(C) is amended by strik-

18   ing "117(d),".

19   (3) Section 414(t)(2) is amended by striking

20   "117(d),".

21   (f) EFFECTIVE DATES.—

22   (1) IN GENERAL.—Except as otherwise pro-

23   vided in this subsection, the amendments made by

24   this section shall apply to taxable years beginning

25   after December 31, 2017.

1 (2) AMENDMENTS RELATING TO SECTION

2 117(d).—The amendments made by subsections

3 (a)(3) and (e) shall apply to amounts paid or in-

4 curred after December 31, 2017.

Subtitle D—Simplification and Reform of Deductions

SEC. 1301. REPEAL OF OVERALL LIMITATION ON ITEMIZED DEDUCTIONS.

9 (a) IN GENERAL.—Part 1 of subchapter B of chapter

10 1 is amended by striking section 68 (and the item relating

11 to such section in the table of sections for such part).

12 (b) EFFECTIVE DATE.—The amendments made by

13 this section shall apply to taxable years beginning after

14 December 31, 2017.

SEC. 1302. MORTGAGE INTEREST.

16 (a) MODIFICATION OF LIMITATIONS.—

17 (1) IN GENERAL.—Section 163(h)(3) is amend-

18 ed to read as follows:

19   "(3) QUALIFIED RESIDENCE INTEREST.—For

20 purposes of this subsection—

21   "(A) IN GENERAL.—The term 'qualified

22   residence interest' means any interest which is

23   paid or accrued during the taxable year on in-

24   debtedness which—

1   "(i) is incurred in acquiring, con-

2   structing, or substantially improving any

3   qualified residence (determined as of the

4   time the interest is accrued) of the tax-

5   payer, and

6   "(ii) is secured by such residence.

7   Such term also includes interest on any indebt-

8   edness secured by such residence resulting from

9   the refinancing of indebtedness meeting the re-

10   quirements of the preceding sentence (or this

11   sentence); but only to the extent the amount of

12   the indebtedness resulting from such refi-

13   nancing does not exceed the amount of the refi-

14   nanced indebtedness.

15   "(B) LIMITATION.—

16   "(i) IN GENERAL.—The aggregate

17   amount of indebtedness taken into account

18   under subparagraph (A) for any period

19   shall not exceed $500,000 (half of such

20   amount in the case of a married individual

21   filing a separate return).

22   "(C) TREATMENT OF INDEBTEDNESS IN-

23   CURRED ON OR BEFORE NOVEMBER 2, 2017.—

24   "(i) IN GENERAL.—In the case of any

25   pre-November 2, 2017, indebtedness, this

1   paragraph shall apply as in effect imme-

2   diately before the enactment of the Tax

3   Cuts and Jobs Act.

4   "(ii) PRE-NOVEMBER 2, 2017, INDEBT-

5   EDNESS.—For purposes of this subpara-

6   graph, the term 'pre-November 2, 2017,

7   indebtedness' means—

8   "(I) any principal residence ac-

9   quisition indebtedness which was in-

10   curred on or before November 2,

11   2017, or

12   "(II) any principal residence ac-

13   quisition indebtedness which is in-

14   curred after November 2, 2017, to re-

15   finance indebtedness described in

16   clause (i) (or refinanced indebtedness

17   meeting the requirements of this

18   clause) to the extent (immediately

19   after the refinancing) the principal

20   amount of the indebtedness resulting

21   from the refinancing does not exceed

22   the principal amount of the refinanced

23   indebtedness (immediately before the

24   refinancing).

1   "(iii) LIMITATION ON PERIOD OF RE-

2   FINANCING.—clause (ii)(II) shall not apply

3   to any indebtedness after—

4   "(I) the expiration of the term of

5   the original indebtedness, or

6   "(II) if the principal of such

7   original indebtedness is not amortized

8   over its term, the expiration of the

9   term of the 1st refinancing of such in-

10   debtedness (or if earlier, the date

11   which is 30 years after the date of

12   such 1st refinancing).

13   "(iv) BINDING CONTRACT EXCEP-

14   TION.—In the case of a taxpayer who en-

15   ters into a written binding contract before

16   November 2, 2017, to close on the pur-

17   chase of a principal residence before Janu-

18   ary 1, 2018, and who purchases such resi-

19   dence before April 1, 2018, subparagraphs

20   (A) and (B) shall be applied by sub-

21   stituting 'April 1, 2018' for 'November 2,

22   2017'.".

23   (2) CONFORMING AMENDMENTS.—

24   (A) Section 108(h)(2) is by striking "for

25   '$1,000,000 ($500,000' in clause (ii) thereof"

1   and inserting "for '$500,000 ($250,000' in

2   paragraph (2)(A), and '$1,000,000' for

3   '$500,000' in paragraph (2)(B), thereof"

4   (B) Section 163(h) is amended—

5   (i) by striking subparagraphs (E) and

6   (F) in paragraph (4), and

7   (ii) by striking paragraph (5).

8 (b) TAXPAYERS LIMITED TO 1 QUALIFIED RESI-

9 DENCE.—Section 163(h)(4)(A)(i) is amended to read as

10 follows:

11   "(i) IN GENERAL.—The term 'quali-

12   fied residence' means the principal resi-

13   dence (within the meaning of section 121)

14   of the taxpayer. Rules similar to the rules

15   of paragraph (3)(C) shall apply for pur-

16   poses of the preceding sentence.".

17 (c) EFFECTIVE DATES.—

18   (1) IN GENERAL.—The amendments made by

19 this section shall apply to interest paid or accrued

20 in taxable years beginning after December 31, 2017,

21 with respect to indebtedness incurred before, on, or

22 after such date.

23   (2) TREATMENT OF GRANDFATHERED INDEBT-

24 EDNESS.—For application of the amendments made

25 by this section to grandfathered indebtedness, see

1   paragraph (3)(C), and the second sentence of para-

2   graph (4)(A)(i), of section 163(h) of the Internal

3   Revenue Code of 1986, as amended by this section.

4   **SEC. 1303. REPEAL OF DEDUCTION FOR CERTAIN TAXES**

5   **NOT PAID OR ACCRUED IN A TRADE OR BUSI-**

6   **NESS.**

7   (a) IN GENERAL.—Section 164(b)(5) is amended to

8   read as follows:

9   "(5) LIMITATION IN CASE OF INDIVIDUALS.—In

10   the case of a taxpayer other than a corporation—

11   "(A) foreign real property taxes (other

12   than taxes which are paid or accrued in car-

13   rying on a trade or business or an activity de-

14   scribed in section 212) shall not be taken into

15   account under subsection (a)(1),

16   "(B) the aggregate amount of taxes (other

17   than taxes which are paid or accrued in car-

18   rying on a trade or business or an activity de-

19   scribed in section 212) taken into account

20   under subsection (a)(1) and for any taxable

21   year shall not exceed $10,000 ($5,000 in the

22   case of a married individual filing a separate re-

23   turn),

24   "(C) subsection (a)(2) shall only apply to

25   taxes which are paid or accrued in carrying on

1   a trade or business or an activity described in

2   section 212, and

3   "(D) subsection (a)(3) shall not apply to

4   State and local taxes.".

5   (b) EFFECTIVE DATE.—The amendments made by

6 this section shall apply to taxable years beginning after

7 December 31, 2017.

8 **SEC. 1304. REPEAL OF DEDUCTION FOR PERSONAL CAS-**

9   **UALTY LOSSES.**

10   (a) IN GENERAL.—Section 165(c) is amended by in-

11 serting "and" at the end of paragraph (1), by striking

12 "; and" at the end of paragraph (2) and inserting a pe-

13 riod, and by striking paragraph (3).

14   (b) CONFORMING AMENDMENTS.—

15   (1) Section 165(h) is amended to read as fol-

16   lows:

17   "(h) SPECIAL RULE WHERE PERSONAL CASUALTY

18 GAINS EXCEED PERSONAL CASUALTY LOSSES.—

19   "(1) IN GENERAL.—If the personal casualty

20   gains for any taxable year exceed the personal cas-

21   ualty losses for such taxable year—

22   "(A) all such gains shall be treated as

23   gains from sales or exchanges of capital assets,

24   and

106

1   "(B) all such losses shall be treated as

2   losses from sales or exchanges of capital assets.

3   "(2) DEFINITIONS OF PERSONAL CASUALTY

4   GAIN AND PERSONAL CASUALTY LOSS.—For pur-

5   poses of this subsection—

6   "(A) PERSONAL CASUALTY LOSS.—The

7   term 'personal casualty loss' means any loss of

8   property not connected with a trade or business

9   or a transaction entered into for profit, if such

10   loss arises from fire, storm, shipwreck, or other

11   casualty, or from theft.

12   "(B) PERSONAL CASUALTY GAIN.—The

13   term 'personal casualty gain' means the recog-

14   nized gain from any involuntary conversion of

15   property which is described in subparagraph

16   (A) arising from fire, storm, shipwreck, or other

17   casualty, or from theft.".

18   (2) Subsection (i) of section 165 is amended—

19   (A) in paragraph (1)—

20   (i) by striking "(as defined by clause

21   ii) of subsection (h)(3)(C))", and

22   (ii) by striking "(as defined by clause

23   (i) of such subsection)",

24   (B) by striking "(as defined by subsection

25   (h)(3)(C)(i)" in paragraph (4), and

1   (C) by adding at the end the following new

2 paragraph:

3   "(5) FEDERALLY DECLARED DISASTER.—For

4 purposes of this subsection—

5   "(A) FEDERALLY DECLARED DISASTER.—

6   The term 'federally declared disaster' means

7   any disaster subsequently determined by the

8   President of the United States to warrant as-

9   sistance by the Federal Government under the

10   Robert T. Stafford Disaster Relief and Emer-

11   gency Assistance Act.

12   "(B) DISASTER AREA.—The term 'disaster

13   area' means the area so determined to warrant

14   such assistance.".

15   (3) Section 165 is amended by striking sub-

16 section (k).

17   (4)(A) Section 165(l)(1) is amended by striking

18 "a loss described in subsection (c)(3)" and inserting

19 "an ordinary loss described in subsection (c)(2)".

20   (B) Section 165(l) is amended—

21   (i) by striking paragraph (5),

22   (ii) by redesignating paragraphs (2), (3),

23   and (4) as paragraphs (3), (4), and (5), respec-

24   tively, and

1   (iii) by inserting after paragraph (1) the

2   following new paragraph:

3   "(2) LIMITATIONS.—

4   "(A) DEPOSIT MAY NOT BE FEDERALLY

5   INSURED.—No election may be made under

6   paragraph (1) with respect to any loss on a de-

7   posit in a qualified financial institution if part

8   or all of such deposit is insured under Federal

9   law.

10   "(B) DOLLAR LIMITATION.—With respect

11   to each financial institution, the aggregate

12   amount of losses attributable to deposits in

13   such financial institution to which an election

14   under paragraph (1) may be made by the tax-

15   payer for any taxable year shall not exceed

16    $20,000 ($10,000 in the case of a separate re-

17   turn by a married individual). The limitation of

18   the preceding sentence shall be reduced by the

19   amount of any insurance proceeds under any

20   State law which can reasonably be expected to

21   be received with respect to losses on deposits in

22   such institution.".

23   (5) Section 172(b)(1)(E)(ii), prior to amend-

24   ment under title III, is amended by striking sub-

1   clause (I) and by redesignating subclauses (II) and

2   (III) as subclauses (I) and (II), respectively

3   (6) Section 172(d)(4)(C) is amended by strik-

4   ing "paragraph (2) or (3) of section 165(c)" and in-

5   serting "section 165(c)(2)".

6   (7) Section 274(f) is amended by striking

7   "Casualty Losses," in the heading thereof.

8   (8) Section 280A(b) is amended by striking

9   "Casualty Losses," in the heading thereof.

10   (9) Section 873(b), as amended by the pre-

11 ceding provisions of this Act, is amended by striking

12 paragraph (1) and by redesignating paragraphs (2)

13 and (3) as paragraphs (1) and (2), respectively.

14   (10) Section 504(b) of the Disaster Tax Relief

15 and Airport and Airway Extension Act of 2017 is

16 amended by adding at the end the following new

17 paragraph:

18   "(4) Coordination with tax reform.—This

19 subsection shall be applied without regard to the

20 amendments made by section 1306 of the Tax Cuts

21 and Jobs Act.".

22   (c) Effective Date.—The amendments made by

23 this section shall apply to taxable years beginning after

24 December 31, 2017.

110

1 **SEC. 1305. LIMITATION ON WAGERING LOSSES.**

2 (a) IN GENERAL.—Section 165(d) is amended by

3 adding at the end the following: "For purposes of the pre-

4 ceding sentence, the term 'losses from wagering trans-

5 actions' includes any deduction otherwise allowable under

6 this chapter incurred in carrying on any wagering trans-

7 action.".

8 (b) EFFECTIVE DATE.—The amendments made by

9 this section shall apply to taxable years beginning after

10 December 31, 2017.

11 **SEC. 1306. CHARITABLE CONTRIBUTIONS.**

12 (a) INCREASED LIMITATION FOR CASH CONTRIBU-

13 TIONS.—

14 (1) IN GENERAL.—Section 170(b)(1) is amend-

15 ed by redesignating subparagraph (G) as subpara-

16 graph (H) and by inserting after subparagraph (F)

17 the following new subparagraph:

18 "(G) INCREASED LIMITATION FOR CASH

19 CONTRIBUTIONS.—

20 "(i) IN GENERAL.—In the case of any

21 contribution of cash to an organization de-

22 scribed in subparagraph (A), the total

23 amount of such contributions which may

24 be taken into account under subsection (a)

25 for any taxable year shall not exceed 60

1   percent of the taxpayer's contribution base

2   for such year.

3   "(ii) CARRYOVER.—If the aggregate

4   amount of contributions described in clause

5   (i) exceeds the applicable limitation under

6   clause (i), such excess shall be treated (in

7   a manner consistent with the rules of sub-

8   section (d)(1)) as a charitable contribution

9   to which clause (i) applies in each of the

10   5 succeeding years in order of time.

11   "(iii) COORDINATION WITH SUBPARA-

12   GRAPHS (A) AND (B).—

13   "(I) IN GENERAL.—Contribu-

14   tions taken into account under this

15   subparagraph shall not be taken into

16   account under subparagraph (A).

17   "(II) LIMITATION REDUCTION.—

18   Subparagraphs (A) and (B) shall be

19   applied by reducing (but not below

20   zero) the aggregate contribution limi-

21   tation allowed for the taxable year

22   under each such subparagraph by the

23   aggregate contributions allowed under

24   this subparagraph for such taxable

25   year.".

112

1   (b) DENIAL OF DEDUCTION FOR COLLEGE ATH-
2 LETIC EVENT SEATING RIGHTS.—Section 170(l)(1) is
3 amended to read as follows:

4   "(1) IN GENERAL.—No deduction shall be al-
5   lowed under this section for any amount described in
6   paragraph (2).".

7   (c) CHARITABLE MILEAGE RATE ADJUSTED FOR IN-
8 FLATION.—Section 170(i) is amended by striking "shall
9 be 14 cents per mile" and inserting "shall be a rate which
10 takes into account the variable cost of operating an auto-
11 mobile".

12   (d) REPEAL OF SUBSTANTIATION EXCEPTION IN
13 CASE OF CONTRIBUTIONS REPORTED BY DONEE.—Sec-
14 tion 170(f)(8) is amended by striking subparagraph (D)
15 and by redesignating subparagraph (E) as subparagraph
16 (D).

17   (e) EFFECTIVE DATE.—The amendments made by
18 this section shall apply to contributions made in taxable
19 years beginning after December 31, 2017.

20 **SEC. 1307. REPEAL OF DEDUCTION FOR TAX PREPARATION**
21   **EXPENSES.**

22   (a) IN GENERAL.—Section 212 is amended by adding
23 "or" at the end of paragraph (1), by striking "; or" at
24 the end of paragraph (2) and inserting a period, and by
25 striking paragraph (3).

1   (b) EFFECTIVE DATE.—The amendments made by
2 this section shall apply to taxable years beginning after
3 December 31, 2017.

SEC. 1308. REPEAL OF MEDICAL EXPENSE DEDUCTION.

5   (a) IN GENERAL.—Part VII of subchapter B is
6 amended by striking by striking section 213 (and by strik-
7 ing the item relating to such section in the table of section
8 for such subpart).

9   (b) CONFORMING AMENDMENTS.—

10   (1)(A) Section 105(f) is amended to read as fol-
11   lows:

12   "(f) MEDICAL CARE.—For purposes of this section—

13   "(1) IN GENERAL.—The term 'medical care'
14   means amounts paid—

15   "(A) for the diagnosis, cure, mitigation,
16   treatment, or prevention of disease, or for the
17   purpose of affecting any structure or function
18   of the body,

19   "(B) for transportation primarily for and
20   essential to medical care referred to in subpara-
21   graph (A),

22   "(C) for qualified long-term care services
23   (as defined in section 7702B(c)), or

24   "(D) for insurance (including amounts
25   paid as premiums under part B of title XVIII

1   of the Social Security Act, relating to supple-

2   mentary medical insurance for the aged) cov-

3   ering medical care referred to in subparagraphs

4   (A) and (B) or for any qualified long-term care

5   insurance contract (as defined in section

6   7702B(b)).

7   In the case of a qualified long-term care insurance

8   contract (as defined in section 7702B(b)), only eligi-

9   ble long-term care premiums (as defined in para-

10   graph (7)) shall be taken into account under sub-

11   paragraph (D).

12   "(2) AMOUNTS PAID FOR CERTAIN LODGING

13   AWAY FROM HOME TREATED AS PAID FOR MEDICAL

14   CARE.—Amounts paid for lodging (not lavish or ex-

15   travagant under the circumstances) while away from

16   home primarily for and essential to medical care re-

17   ferred to in paragraph (1)(A) shall be treated as

18   amounts paid for medical care if—

19   "(A) the medical care referred to in para-

20   graph (1)(A) is provided by a physician in a li-

21   censed hospital (or in a medical care facility

22   which is related to, or the equivalent of, a li-

23   censed hospital), and

115

1   ''(B) there is no significant element of per-
2   sonal pleasure, recreation, or vacation in the
3   travel away from home.
4 The amount taken into account under the preceding
5 sentence shall not exceed $50 for each night for each
6 individual.
7   ''(3) PHYSICIAN.—The term 'physician' has the
8 meaning given to such term by section 1861(r) of
9 the Social Security Act (42 U.S.C. 1395x(r)).
10   ''(4) CONTRACTS COVERING OTHER THAN MED-
11 ICAL CARE.—In the case of an insurance contract
12 under which amounts are payable for other than
13 medical care referred to in subparagraphs (A), (B)
14 and (C) of paragraph (1)—
15   ''(A) no amount shall be treated as paid
16   for insurance to which paragraph (1)(D) applies
17   unless the charge for such insurance is either
18   separately stated in the contract, or furnished
19   to the policyholder by the insurance company in
20   a separate statement,
21   ''(B) the amount taken into account as the
22   amount paid for such insurance shall not exceed
23   such charge, and
24   ''(C) no amount shall be treated as paid
25   for such insurance if the amount specified in

1   the contract (or furnished to the policyholder by

2   the insurance company in a separate statement)

3   as the charge for such insurance is unreason-

4   ably large in relation to the total charges under

5   the contract.

6   "(5) CERTAIN PRE-PAID CONTRACTS.—Subject

7   to the limitations of paragraph (4), premiums paid

8   during the taxable year by a taxpayer before he at-

9   tains the age of 65 for insurance covering medical

10   care (within the meaning of subparagraphs (A), (B),

11   and (C) of paragraph (1)) for the taxpayer, his

12   spouse, or a dependent after the taxpayer attains the

13   age of 65 shall be treated as expenses paid during

14   the taxable year for insurance which constitutes

15   medical care if premiums for such insurance are

16   payable (on a level payment basis) under the con-

17   tract for a period of 10 years or more or until the

18   year in which the taxpayer attains the age of 65

19   (but in no case for a period of less than 5 years).

20   "(6) COSMETIC SURGERY.—

21   "(A) IN GENERAL.—The term 'medical

22   care' does not include cosmetic surgery or other

23   similar procedures, unless the surgery or proce-

24   dure is necessary to ameliorate a deformity

25   arising from, or directly related to, a congenital

1 abnormality, a personal injury resulting from
2 an accident or trauma, or disfiguring disease.

3   "(B) COSMETIC SURGERY DEFINED .—For
4 purposes of this paragraph, the term 'cosmetic
5 surgery' means any procedure which is directed
6 at improving the patient's appearance and does
7 not meaningfully promote the proper function
8 of the body or prevent or treat illness or dis-
9 ease.

10 "(7) ELIGIBLE LONG-TERM CARE PREMIUMS.—

11   "(A) IN GENERAL.—For purposes of this
12 section, the term 'eligible long-term care pre-
13 miums' means the amount paid during a tax-
14 able year for any qualified long-term care insur-
15 ance contract (as defined in section 7702B(b))
16 covering an individual, to the extent such
17 amount does not exceed the limitation deter-
18 mined under the following table:

"In the case of an individual with an attained age before the close of the taxable year of:	The limitation is:
40 or less	$200
More than 40 but not more than 50	$375
More than 50 but not more than 60	$750
More than 60 but not more than 70	$2,000
More than 70	$2,500

19   "(B) INDEXING.—

20   "(i) IN GENERAL.—In the case of any
21 taxable year beginning after 1997, each

118

1   dollar amount in subparagraph (A) shall

2   be increased by the medical care cost ad-

3   justment of such amount for such calendar

4   year. Any increase determined under the

5   preceding sentence shall be rounded to the

6   nearest multiple of $10.

7   "(ii) MEDICAL CARE COST ADJUST-

8   MENT.—For purposes of clause (i), the

9   medical care cost adjustment for any cal-

10   endar year is the adjustment prescribed by

11   the Secretary, in consultation with the Sec-

12   retary of Health and Human Services, for

13   purposes of such clause. To the extent that

14   CPI (as defined section 1(c)), or any com-

15   ponent thereof, is taken into account in de-

16   termining such adjustment, such adjust-

17   ment shall be determined by taking into

18   account C-CPI-U (as so defined), or the

19   corresponding component thereof, in lieu of

20   such CPI (or component thereof), but only

21   with respect to the portion of such adjust-

22   ment which relates to periods after Decem-

23   ber 31, 2017.

24   "(8) CERTAIN PAYMENTS TO RELATIVES

25 TREATED AS NOT PAID FOR MEDICAL CARE.—An

1   amount paid for a qualified long-term care service

2   (as defined in section 7702B(c)) provided to an indi-

3   vidual shall be treated as not paid for medical care

4   if such service is provided—

5   "(A) by the spouse of the individual or by

6   a relative (directly or through a partnership,

7   corporation, or other entity) unless the service

8   is provided by a licensed professional with re-

9   spect to such service, or

10   "(B) by a corporation or partnership which

11   is related (within the meaning of section 267(b)

12   or 707(b)) to the individual.

13   For purposes of this paragraph, the term 'relative'

14   means an individual bearing a relationship to the in-

15   dividual which is described in any of subparagraphs

16   (A) through (G) of section 7706(d)(2). This para-

17   graph shall not apply for purposes of subsection (b)

18   with respect to reimbursements through insurance.".

19   (B) Section 72(t)(2)(D)(i)(III) is amended by

20   striking "section 213(d)(1)(D)" and inserting "sec-

21   tion 105(f)(1)(D)".

22   (C) Section 104(a) is amended by striking "sec-

23   tion 213(d)(1)" in the last sentence and inserting

24   "section 105(f)(1)".

120

1   (D) Section 105(b) is amended by striking

2 "section 213(d)" and inserting "section 105(f)".

3   (E) Section 139D is amended by striking "sec-

4 tion 213" and inserting "section 223".

5   (F) Section 162(l)(2) is amended by striking

6 "section 213(d)(10)" and inserting "section

7 105(f)(7)".

8   (G) Section 220(d)(2)(A) is amended by strik-

9 ing "section 213(d)" and inserting "section 105(f)".

10   (H) Section 223(d)(2)(A) is amended by strik-

11 ing "section 213(d)" and inserting "section 105(f)".

12   (I) Section 419A(f)(2) is amended by striking

13 "section 213(d)" and inserting "section 105(f)".

14   (J) Section 501(c)(26)(A) is amended by strik-

15 ing "section 213(d)" and inserting "section 105(f)".

16   (K) Section 2503(e) is amended by striking

17 "section 213(d)" and inserting "section 105(f)".

18   (L) Section 4980B(c)(4)(B)(i)(I) is amended by

19 striking "section 213(d)" and inserting "section

20 105(f)".

21   (M) Section 6041(f) is amended by striking

22 "section 213(d)" and inserting "section 105(f)".

23   (N) Section 7702B(a)(2) is amended by strik-

24 ing "section 213(d)" and inserting "section 105(f)".

1   (O) Section 7702B(a)(4) is amended by strik-

2 ing "section 213(d)(1)(D)" and inserting "section

3 105(f)(1)(D)".

4   (P) Section 7702B(d)(5) is amended by striking

5 "section 213(d)(10)" and inserting "section

6 105(f)(7)".

7   (Q) Section 9832(d)(3) is amended by striking

8 "section 213(d)" and inserting "section 105(f)".

9   (2) Section 72(t)(2)(B) is amended to read as

10 follows:

11   "(B) MEDICAL EXPENSES.—Distributions

12   made to an individual (other than distributions

13   described in subparagraph (A), (C), or (D) to

14   the extent such distributions do not exceed the

15   excess of—

16   "(i) the expenses paid by the taxpayer

17   during the taxable year, not compensated

18   for by insurance or otherwise, for medical

19   care (as defined in 105(f)) of the taxpayer,

20   his spouse, or a dependent (as defined in

21   section 7706, determined without regard to

22   subsections (b)(1), (b)(2), and (d)(1)(B)

23   thereof), over

24   "(ii) 10 percent of the taxpayer's ad-

25   justed gross income.".

1   (3) Section 162(l) is amended by striking para-
2   graph (3).

3   (4) Section 402(l) is amended by striking para-
4   graph (7) and redesignating paragraph (8) as para-
5   graph (7).

6   (5) Section 220(f) is amended by striking para-
7   graph (6).

8   (6) Section 223(f) is amended by striking para-
9   graph (6).

10   (7) Section 7702B(e) is amended by striking
11   paragraph (2).

12   (8) Section 7706(f)(7), as redesignated by this
13   Act, is amended by striking "sections 105(b),
14   132(h)(2)(B), and 213(d)(5)" and inserting "sec-
15   tions 105(b) and 132(h)(2)(B)".

16   (c) EFFECTIVE DATE.—The amendments made by
17   this section shall apply to taxable years beginning after
18   December 31, 2017.

19   **SEC. 1309. REPEAL OF DEDUCTION FOR ALIMONY PAY-**
20   **MENTS.**

21   (a) IN GENERAL.—Part VII of subchapter B is
22   amended by striking by striking section 215 (and by strik-
23   ing the item relating to such section in the table of section
24   for such subpart).

25   (b) CONFORMING AMENDMENTS.—

1   (1) AMENDMENTS RELATING TO SECTION

2   215.—

3   (A) CORRESPONDING REPEAL OF PROVI-

4   SIONS PROVIDING FOR INCLUSION OF ALIMONY

5   IN GROSS INCOME.—

6   (i) Subsection (a) of section 61 is

7   amended by striking paragraph (8) and by

8   redesignating paragraphs (9) through (15)

9   as paragraphs (8) through (14), respec-

10   tively.

11   (ii) Part II of subchapter B of chapter

12   1 is amended by striking section 71 (and

13   by striking the item relating to such sec-

14   tion in the table of sections for such part).

15   (iii) Subpart F of part I of subchapter

16   J of chapter 1 is amended by striking sec-

17   tion 682 (and by striking the item relating

18   to such section in the table of sections for

19   such subpart).

20   (B) RELATED TO REPEAL OF SECTION

21   215.—

22   (i) Section 62(a) is amended by strik-

23   ing paragraph (10).

124

1   (ii) Section 3402(m)(1) is amended by

2   striking "(other than paragraph (10)

3   thereof)".

4   (C) RELATED TO REPEAL OF SECTION

5   71.—

6   (i) Section 121(d)(3) is amended—

7   (I) by striking "(as defined in

8   section 71(b)(2))" in subparagraph

9   (B), and

10   (II) by adding at the end the fol-

11   lowing new subparagraph:

12   "(C) DIVORCE OR SEPARATION INSTRU-

13   MENT.—For purposes of this paragraph, the

14   term 'divorce or separation instrument'

15   means—

16   "(i) a decree of divorce or separate

17   maintenance or a written instrument inci-

18   dent to such a decree,

19   "(ii) a written separation agreement,

20   or

21   "(iii) a decree (not described in clause

22   (i)) requiring a spouse to make payments

23   for the support or maintenance of the

24   other spouse.".

1   (ii) Section 220(f)(7) is amended by

2   striking "subparagraph (A) of section

3   71(b)(2)" and inserting "clause (i) of sec-

4   tion 121(d)(3)(C)".

5   (iii) Section 223(f)(7) is amended by

6   striking "subparagraph (A) of section

7   71(b)(2)" and inserting "clause (i) of sec-

8   tion 121(d)(3)(C)".

9   (iv) Section 382(l)(3)(B)(iii) is

10   amended by striking "section 71(b)(2)"

11   and inserting "section 121(d)(3)(C)".

12   (v) Section 408(d)(6) is amended by

13   striking "subparagraph (A) of section

14   71(b)(2)" and inserting "clause (i) of sec-

15   tion 121(d)(3)(C)".

16   (c) EFFECTIVE DATE.—The amendments made by

17 this section shall apply to—

18   (1) any divorce or separation instrument (as de-

19   fined in section 71(b)(2) of the Internal Revenue

20   Code of 1986 as in effect before the date of the en-

21   actment of this Act) executed after December 31,

22   2017, and

23   (2) any divorce or separation instrument (as so

24   defined) executed on or before such date and modi-

25   fied after such date if the modification expressly

126

1   provides that the amendments made by this section

2   apply to such modification.

3 **SEC. 1310. REPEAL OF DEDUCTION FOR MOVING EX-**

4   **PENSES.**

5   (a) IN GENERAL.—Part VII of subchapter B is

6 amended by striking by striking section 217 (and by strik-

7 ing the item relating to such section in the table of section

8 for such subpart).

9   (b) CONFORMING AMENDMENTS.—

10   (1) Section 62(a) is amended by striking para-

11   graph (15).

12   (2) Section 274(m)(3) is amended by striking

13   "(other than section 217)".

14   (3) Section 3121(a) is amended by striking

15   paragraph (11).

16   (4) Section 3306(b) is amended by striking

17   paragraph (9).

18   (5) Section 3401(a) is amended by striking

19   paragraph (15).

20   (6) Section 7872(f) is amended by striking

21   paragraph (11).

22   (c) EFFECTIVE DATE.—The amendments made by

23 this section shall apply to taxable years beginning after

24 December 31, 2017.

1 **SEC. 1311. TERMINATION OF DEDUCTION AND EXCLUSIONS**

2   **FOR CONTRIBUTIONS TO MEDICAL SAVINGS**

3   **ACCOUNTS.**

4   (a) TERMINATION OF INCOME TAX DEDUCTION.—

5 Section 220 is amended by adding at the end the following

6 new subsection:

7   "(k) TERMINATION.—No deduction shall be allowed

8 under subsection (a) with respect to any taxable year be-

9 ginning after December 31, 2017.".

10   (b) TERMINATION OF EXCLUSION FOR EMPLOYER-

11 PROVIDED CONTRIBUTIONS.—Section 106 is amended by

12 striking subsection (b).

13   (c) CONFORMING AMENDMENTS.—

14   (1) Section 62(a) is amended by striking para-

15   graph (16).

16   (2) Section 106(d) is amended by striking para-

17   graph (2), by redesignating paragraph (3) as para-

18   graph (6), and by inserting after paragraph (1) the

19   following new paragraphs:

20   "(2) NO CONSTRUCTIVE RECEIPT.—No amount

21   shall be included in the gross income of any em-

22   ployee solely because the employee may choose be-

23   tween the contributions referred to in paragraph (1)

24   and employer contributions to another health plan of

25   the employer.

1   ''(3) SPECIAL RULE FOR DEDUCTION OF EM-

2   PLOYER CONTRIBUTIONS.—Any employer contribu-

3   tion to a health savings account (as so defined), if

4   otherwise allowable as a deduction under this chap-

5   ter, shall be allowed only for the taxable year in

6   which paid.

7   ''(4) EMPLOYER HEALTH SAVINGS ACCOUNT

8   CONTRIBUTION REQUIRED TO BE SHOWN ON RE-

9   TURN.—Every individual required to file a return

10   under section 6012 for the taxable year shall include

11   on such return the aggregate amount contributed by

12   employers to the health savings accounts (as so de-

13   fined) of such individual or such individual's spouse

14   for such taxable year.

15   ''(5) HEALTH SAVINGS ACCOUNT CONTRIBU-

16   TIONS NOT PART OF COBRA COVERAGE.—Paragraph

17   (1) shall not apply for purposes of section 4980B.''.

18   (3) Section 223(b)(4) is amended by striking

19   subparagraph (A), by redesignating subparagraphs

20   (B) and (C) as subparagraphs (A) and (B), respec-

21   tively, and by striking the second sentence thereof.

22   (4) Section 223(b)(5) is amended by striking

23   ''under paragraph (3))'' and all that follows through

24   ''shall be divided equally between them'' and insert-

1   ing the following: "under paragraph (3)) shall be di-

2   vided equally between the spouses".

3   (5) Section 223(c) is amended by striking para-

4   graph (5).

5   (6) Section 3231(e) is amended by striking

6   paragraph (10).

7   (7) Section 3306(b) is amended by striking

8   paragraph (17).

9   (8) Section 3401(a) is amended by striking

10   paragraph (21).

11   (9) Chapter 43 is amended by striking section

12   4980E (and by striking the item relating to such

13   section in the table of sections for such chapter).

14   (10) Section 4980G is amended to read as fol-

15   lows:

16   **"SEC. 4980G. FAILURE OF EMPLOYER TO MAKE COM-**

17   **PARABLE HEALTH SAVINGS ACCOUNT CON-**

18   **TRIBUTIONS.**

19   "(a) IN GENERAL.—In the case of an employer who

20   makes a contribution to the health savings account of any

21   employee during a calendar year, there is hereby imposed

22   a tax on the failure of such employer to meet the require-

23   ments of subsection (d) for such calendar year.

24   "(b) AMOUNT OF TAX.—The amount of the tax im-

25   posed by subsection (a) on any failure for any calendar

1 year is the amount equal to 35 percent of the aggregate

2 amount contributed by the employer to health savings ac-

3 counts of employees for taxable years of such employees

4 ending with or within such calendar year.

5 "(c) WAIVER BY SECRETARY.—In the case of a fail-

6 ure which is due to reasonable cause and not to willful

7 neglect, the Secretary may waive part or all of the tax

8 imposed by subsection (a) to the extent that the payment

9 of such tax would be excessive relative to the failure in-

10 volved.

11 "(d) EMPLOYER REQUIRED TO MAKE COMPARABLE

12 HEALTH SAVINGS ACCOUNT CONTRIBUTIONS FOR ALL

13 PARTICIPATING EMPLOYEES.—

14   "(1) IN GENERAL.—An employer meets the re-

15   quirements of this subsection for any calendar year

16   if the employer makes available comparable con-

17   tributions to the health savings accounts of all com-

18   parable participating employees for each coverage

19   period during such calendar year.

20   "(2) COMPARABLE CONTRIBUTIONS.—

21   "(A) IN GENERAL.—For purposes of para-

22   graph (1), the term 'comparable contributions'

23   means contributions—

24   "(i) which are the same amount, or

1   "(ii) which are the same percentage of

2   the annual deductible limit under the high

3   deductible health plan covering the employ-

4   ees.

5   "(B) PART-YEAR EMPLOYEES.—In the

6   case of an employee who is employed by the em-

7   ployer for only a portion of the calendar year,

8   a contribution to the health savings account of

9   such employee shall be treated as comparable if

10   it is an amount which bears the same ratio to

11   the comparable amount (determined without re-

12   gard to this subparagraph) as such portion

13   bears to the entire calendar year.

14   "(3) COMPARABLE PARTICIPATING EMPLOY-

15 EES.—

16   "(A) IN GENERAL.—For purposes of para-

17   graph (1), the term 'comparable participating

18   employees' means all employees—

19   "(i) who are eligible individuals cov-

20   ered under any high deductible health plan

21   of the employer, and

22   "(ii) who have the same category of

23   coverage.

1   "(B) CATEGORIES OF COVERAGE.—For

2   purposes of subparagraph (B), the categories of

3   coverage are self-only and family coverage.

4   "(4) PART-TIME EMPLOYEES.—

5   "(A) IN GENERAL .—Paragraph (3) shall

6   be applied separately with respect to part-time

7   employees and other employees.

8   "(B) PART-TIME EMPLOYEE.—For pur-

9   poses of subparagraph (A), the term 'part-time

10   employee' means any employee who is custom-

11   arily employed for fewer than 30 hours per

12   week.

13   "(5) SPECIAL RULE FOR NON-HIGHLY COM-

14 PENSATED EMPLOYEES.—For purposes of applying

15 this section to a contribution to a health savings ac-

16 count of an employee who is not a highly com-

17 pensated employee (as defined in section 414(q)),

18 highly compensated employees shall not be treated

19 as comparable participating employees.

20   "(e) CONTROLLED GROUPS.—For purposes of this

21 section, all persons treated as a single employer under sub-

22 section (b), (c), (m), or (o) of section 414 shall be treated

23 as 1 employer.

133

1   "(f) DEFINITIONS.—Terms used in this section which

2 are also used in section 223 have the respective meanings

3 given such terms in section 223.

4   "(g) REGULATIONS.—The Secretary shall issue regu-

5 lations to carry out the purposes of this section.".

6   (11) Section 6051(a) is amended by striking

7   paragraph (11).

8   (12) Section 6051(a)(14)(A) is amended by

9   striking "paragraphs (11) and (12)" and inserting

10   "paragraph (12)".

11   (d) EFFECTIVE DATE.—The amendment made by

12 this section shall apply to taxable years beginning after

13 December 31, 2017.

14 **SEC. 1312. DENIAL OF DEDUCTION FOR EXPENSES ATTRIB-**

15 **UTABLE TO THE TRADE OR BUSINESS OF**

16 **BEING AN EMPLOYEE.**

17   (a) IN GENERAL.—Part IX of subchapter B of chap-

18 ter 1 is amended by inserting after the item relating to

19 section 262 the following new item:

20 **"SEC. 262A. EXPENSES ATTRIBUTABLE TO BEING AN EM-**

21 **PLOYEE.**

22   "(a) IN GENERAL.—Except as otherwise provided in

23 this section, no deduction shall be allowed with respect to

24 any trade or business of the taxpayer which consists of

1 the performance of services by the taxpayer as an em-
2 ployee.

3   "(b) EXCEPTION FOR ABOVE-THE-LINE DEDUC-
4 TIONS.—Subsection (a) shall not apply to any deduction
5 allowable (determined without regard to subsection (a)) in
6 determining adjusted gross income.".

7   (b) REPEAL OF CERTAIN ABOVE-THE-LINE TRADE
8 AND BUSINESS DEDUCTIONS OF EMPLOYEES.—

9   (1) IN GENERAL.—Section 62(a)(2) is amend-
10   ed—

11   (A) by striking subparagraphs (B), (C),
12   and (D), and

13   (B) by redesignating subparagraph (E) as
14   subparagraph (B).

15   (2) CONFORMING AMENDMENTS.—

16   (A) Section 62 is amended by striking sub-
17   sections (b) and (d) and by redesignating sub-
18   sections (c) and (e) as subsections (b) and (c),
19   respectively.

20   (B) Section 62(a)(20) is amended by strik-
21   ing "subsection (e)" and inserting "subsection
22   (c)".

23   (c) CONTINUED EXCLUSION OF WORKING CONDI-
24 TION FRINGE BENEFITS.—Section 132(d) is amended by

1 inserting "(determined without regard to section 262A)"

2 after "section 162".

3 (d) EFFECTIVE DATE.—The amendments made by

4 this section shall apply to taxable years beginning after

5 December 31, 2017.

Subtitle E—Simplification and Reform of Exclusions and Taxable Compensation

SEC. 1401. LIMITATION ON EXCLUSION FOR EMPLOYER-PROVIDED HOUSING.

11 (a) IN GENERAL.—Section 119 is amended by adding

12 at the end the following new subsection:

13 "(e) LIMITATION ON EXCLUSION OF LODGING.—

14 "(1) IN GENERAL.—The aggregate amount ex-

15 cluded from gross income of the taxpayer under sub-

16 sections (a) and (d) with respect to lodging for any

17 taxable year shall not exceed $50,000 (half such

18 amount in the case of a married individual filing a

19 separate return).

20 "(2) LIMITATION TO 1 HOME.—Subsections (a)

21 and (d) (separately and in combination) shall not

22 apply with respect to more than 1 residence of the

23 taxpayer at any given time. In the case of a joint re-

24 turn, the preceding sentence shall apply separately

25 to each spouse for any period during which each

1 spouse resides separate from the other spouse in a

2 residence which is provided in connection with the

3 employment of each spouse, respectively.

4 "(3) LIMITATION FOR HIGHLY COMPENSATED

5 EMPLOYEES.—

6 "(A) REDUCED FOR EXCESS COMPENSA-

7 TION.—In the case of an individual whose com-

8 pensation for the taxable year exceeds the

9 amount in effect under section 414(q)(1)(B)(i)

10 for the calendar in which such taxable year be-

11 gins, the $50,000 amount under paragraph (1)

12 shall be reduced (but not below zero) by an

13 amount equal to 50 percent of such excess. For

14 purposes of the preceding sentence, the term

15 'compensation' means wages (as defined in sec-

16 tion 3121(a) (without regard to the contribu-

17 tion and benefit base limitation in section

18 3121(a)(1)).

19 "(B) EXCLUSION DENIED FOR 5-PERCENT

20 OWNERS.—In the case of an individual who is

21 a 5-percent owner (as defined in section

22 416(i)(1)(B)(i)) of the employer at any time

23 during the taxable year, the amount under

24 paragraph (1) shall be zero.".

137

1   (b) EFFECTIVE DATE.—The amendment made by

2 this section shall apply to taxable years beginning after

3 December 31, 2017.

4 **SEC. 1402. EXCLUSION OF GAIN FROM SALE OF A PRIN-**

5   **CIPAL RESIDENCE.**

6   (a) REQUIREMENT THAT RESIDENCE BE PRINCIPAL

7 RESIDENCE FOR 5 YEARS DURING 8-YEAR PERIOD.—

8 Subsection (a) of section 121 is amended—

9   (1) by striking "5-year period" and inserting

10   "8-year period", and

11   (2) by striking "2 years" and inserting "5

12   years".

13   (b) APPLICATION TO ONLY 1 SALE OR EXCHANGE

14 EVERY 5 YEARS.—Paragraph (3) of section 121(b) is

15 amended to read as follows:

16   "(3) APPLICATION TO ONLY 1 SALE OR EX-

17   CHANGE EVERY 5 YEARS.—Subsection (a) shall not

18   apply to any sale or exchange by the taxpayer if,

19   during the 5-year period ending on the date of such

20   sale or exchange, there was any other sale or ex-

21   change by the taxpayer to which subsection (a) ap-

22   plied.".

23   (c) PHASEOUT BASED ON MODIFIED ADJUSTED

24 GROSS INCOME.—Section 121 is amended by adding at

25 the end the following new subsection:

138

1   "(h) PHASEOUT BASED ON MODIFIED ADJUSTED

2   GROSS INCOME.—

3   "(1) IN GENERAL.—If the average modified ad-

4   justed gross income of the taxpayer for the taxable

5   year and the 2 preceding taxable years exceeds

6    $250,000 (twice such amount in the case of a joint

7   return), the amount which would (but for this sub-

8   section) be excluded from gross income under sub-

9   section (a) for such taxable year shall be reduced

10   (but not below zero) by the amount of such excess.

11   "(2) MODIFIED ADJUSTED GROSS INCOME.—

12   For purposes of this subsection, the term 'modified

13   adjusted gross income' means, with respect to any

14   taxable year, adjusted gross income determined after

15   application of this section (but without regard to

16   subsection (b)(1) and this subsection).

17   "(3) SPECIAL RULE FOR JOINT RETURNS.—In

18   the case of a joint return, the average modified ad-

19   justed gross income of the taxpayer shall be deter-

20   mined without regard to any taxable year with re-

21   spect to which the taxpayer did not file a joint re-

22   turn.".

23   (d) CONFORMING AMENDMENTS.—

1   (1) The last paragraph of section 121(b) (relat-

2 ing to exclusion of gain allocated to nonqualified

3 use) is redesignated as paragraph (5).

4   (2) The following provisions of section 121 are

5 each amended by striking "5-year period" each place

6 it appears therein and inserting "8-year period":

7   (A) Subsection (b)(5)(C)(ii)(I) (as redesig-

8   nated by paragraph (1)).

9   (B) Subsection (c)(1)(B)(i)(I).

10   (C) Subsection (d)(7)(B).

11   (D) Subparagraphs (A) and (B) of sub-

12   section (d)(9).

13   (E) Subsection (d)(10)

14   (F) Subsection (d)(12)(A).

15   (3) Section 121(c)(1)(B)(ii) is amended by

16 striking "2 years" and inserting "5 years":

17 (e) EFFECTIVE DATE.—The amendments made by

18 this section shall apply to sales and exchanges after De-

19 cember 31, 2017.

20 **SEC. 1403. REPEAL OF EXCLUSION, ETC., FOR EMPLOYEE**

21   **ACHIEVEMENT AWARDS.**

22   (a) IN GENERAL.—Section 74 is amended by striking

23 subsection (c).

24   (b) REPEAL OF LIMITATION ON DEDUCTION.—Sec-

25 tion 274 is amended by striking subsection (j).

140

1   (c) CONFORMING AMENDMENTS.—

2   (1) Section 102(c)(2) is amended by striking

3   the first sentence.

4   (2) Section 414(n)(3)(C) is amended by strik-

5   ing "274(j),".

6   (3) Section 414(t)(2) is amended by striking

7   "274(j),".

8   (4) Section 3121(a)(20) is amended by striking

9   "74(c)".

10   (5) Section 3231(e)(5) is amended by striking

11   "74(c),".

12   (6) Section 3306(b)(16) is amended by striking

13   "74(c),".

14   (7) Section 3401(a)(19) is amended by striking

15   "74(c),".

16   (d) EFFECTIVE DATE.—The amendments made by

17   this section shall apply to taxable years beginning after

18   December 31, 2017.

19   **SEC. 1404. REPEAL OF EXCLUSION FOR DEPENDENT CARE**

20   **ASSISTANCE PROGRAMS.**

21   (a) IN GENERAL.—Part III of subchapter B of chap-

22   ter 1 is amended by striking section 129 (and by striking

23   the item relating to such section in the table of sections

24   for such part).

25   (b) CONFORMING AMENDMENTS.—

141

1   (1) Section 414(n)(3)(C) is amended by strik-
2 ing ", 129".

3   (2) Section 414(r)(1) is amended by striking
4 "sections 129(d)(8) and" and inserting "section".

5   (3) Section 414(t)(2) is amended by striking ",
6 129".

7   (4) Section 125(j)(6) is amended—

8   (A) by inserting "or" before "section
9 105(h)", and

10   (B) by striking ", or paragraph (2), (3),
11 (4), or (8) of section 129(d)".

12   (5) Section 3121(a)(18) is amended by striking
13 "129,".

14   (6) Section 3306(b)(13) is amended by striking
15 "129,".

16   (7) Section 3401(a)(18) is amended by striking
17 "129,".

18   (8) Section 6039D(d)(1) is amended by striking
19 ", 129".

20   (9) Section 6051(a) is amended by striking
21 paragraph (9).

22 (c) EFFECTIVE DATE.—The amendments made by
23 this section shall apply to taxable years beginning after
24 December 31, 2017.

SEC. 1405. REPEAL OF EXCLUSION FOR QUALIFIED MOVING EXPENSE REIMBURSEMENT.

(a) IN GENERAL.—Section 132(a) is amended by striking paragraph (6).

(b) CONFORMING AMENDMENTS.—

(1) Section 82 is amended by striking "Except as provided in section 132(a)(6), there" and inserting "There".

(2) Section 132 is amended by striking subsection (g).

(3) Section 132(l) is amended by striking by striking "subsections (e) and (g)" and inserting "subsection (e)".

(c) EFFECTIVE DATE.—The amendments made by this section shall apply to taxable years beginning after December 31, 2017.

SEC. 1406. REPEAL OF EXCLUSION FOR ADOPTION ASSISTANCE PROGRAMS.

(a) IN GENERAL.—Part III of subchapter B of chapter 1 is amended by striking section 137 (and by striking the item relating to such section in the table of sections for such part).

(b) CONFORMING AMENDMENTS.—

(1) Sections 414(n)(3)(C), 414(t)(2), 74(d)(2)(B), 86(b)(2)(A), 219(g)(3)(A)(ii) are each amended by striking ", 137".

1   (2) Section 1016(a), as amended by the pre-

2 ceding provision of this Act, is amended by striking

3 paragraph (26).

4   (3) Section 6039D(d)(1), as amended by the

5 preceding provisions of this Act, is amended—

6   (A) by striking ", or 137", and

7   (B) by inserting "or" before "125".

8   (c) EFFECTIVE DATE.—The amendments made by

9 this section shall apply to taxable years beginning after

10 December 31, 2017.

Subtitle F—Simplification and Reform of Savings, Pensions, Retirement

14 SEC. 1501. REPEAL OF SPECIAL RULE PERMITTING RE-

15   CHARACTERIZATION OF ROTH IRA CON-

16   TRIBUTIONS AS TRADITIONAL IRA CON-

17   TRIBUTIONS.

18   (a) IN GENERAL.—Section 408A(d) is amended by

19 striking paragraph (6) and by redesignating paragraph

20 (7) as paragraph (6).

21   (b) EFFECTIVE DATE.—The amendments made by

22 this section shall apply to taxable years beginning after

23 December 31, 2017.

144

1 **SEC. 1502. REDUCTION IN MINIMUM AGE FOR ALLOWABLE**

2 **IN-SERVICE DISTRIBUTIONS.**

3   (a) IN GENERAL.—Section 401(a)(36) is amended by

4 striking "age 62" and inserting "age 59 ½".

5   (b) APPLICATION TO GOVERNMENTAL SECTION

6 457(b) PLANS.—Clause (i) of section 457(d)(1)(A) is

7 amended by inserting "(in the case of a plan maintained

8 by an employer described in subsection (e)(1)(A), age 59

9 ½)" before the comma at the end.

10   (c) EFFECTIVE DATE.—The amendments made by

11 this section shall apply to plan years beginning after De-

12 cember 31, 2017.

13 **SEC. 1503. MODIFICATION OF RULES GOVERNING HARD-**

14 **SHIP DISTRIBUTIONS.**

15   (a) IN GENERAL.—Not later than 1 year after the

16 date of the enactment of this Act, the Secretary of the

17 Treasury shall modify Treasury Regulation section

18 1.401(k)–1(d)(3)(iv)(E) to—

19   (1) delete the 6-month prohibition on contribu-

20   tions imposed by paragraph (2) thereof, and

21   (2) make any other modifications necessary to

22   carry   out   the   purposes   of   section

23   401(k)(2)(B)(i)(IV) of the Internal Revenue Code of

24   1986.

1   (b) EFFECTIVE DATE.—The revised regulations

2 under this section shall apply to plan years beginning after

3 December 31, 2017.

4 **SEC. 1504. MODIFICATION OF RULES RELATING TO HARD-**

5   **SHIP WITHDRAWALS FROM CASH OR DE-**

6   **FERRED ARRANGEMENTS.**

7   (a) IN GENERAL.—Section 401(k) is amended by

8 adding at the end the following:

9   "(14) SPECIAL RULES RELATING TO HARDSHIP

10   WITHDRAWALS.—For purposes of paragraph

11   (2)(B)(i)(IV)—

12   "(A) AMOUNTS WHICH MAY BE WITH-

13   DRAWN.—The following amounts may be dis-

14   tributed upon hardship of the employee:

15   "(i) Contributions to a profit-sharing

16   or stock bonus plan to which section

17   402(e)(3) applies.

18   "(ii) Qualified nonelective contribu-

19   tions (as defined in subsection (m)(4)(C)).

20   "(iii) Qualified matching contributions

21   described in paragraph (3)(D)(ii)(I).

22   "(iv) Earnings on any contributions

23   described in clause (i), (ii), or (iii).

24   "(B) NO REQUIREMENT TO TAKE AVAIL-

25   ABLE LOAN.—A distribution shall not be treat-

146

1   ed as failing to be made upon the hardship of

2   an employee solely because the employee does

3   not take any available loan under the plan.".".

4   (b) CONFORMING AMENDMENT.—Section

5   401(k)(2)(B)(i)(IV) is amended to read as follows:

6   "(IV) subject to the provisions of

7   paragraph (14), upon hardship of the

8   employee, or".".

9   (c) EFFECTIVE DATE.—The amendments made by

10   this section shall apply to plan years beginning after De-

11   cember 31, 2017.

12   **SEC. 1505. EXTENDED ROLLOVER PERIOD FOR THE ROLL-**

13   **OVER OF PLAN LOAN OFFSET AMOUNTS IN**

14   **CERTAIN CASES.**

15   (a) IN GENERAL.—Paragraph (3) of section 402(c)

16   is amended by adding at the end the following new sub-

17   paragraph:

18   "(C) ROLLOVER OF CERTAIN PLAN LOAN

19   OFFSET AMOUNTS.—

20   "(i) IN GENERAL.—In the case of a

21   qualified plan loan offset amount, para-

22   graph (1) shall not apply to any transfer

23   of such amount made after the due date

24   (including extensions) for filing the return

25   of tax for the taxable year in which such

1 amount is treated as distributed from a

2 qualified employer plan.

3   "(ii) QUALIFIED PLAN LOAN OFFSET

4 AMOUNT.—For purposes of this subpara-

5 graph, the term 'qualified plan loan offset

6 amount' means a plan loan offset amount

7 which is treated as distributed from a

8 qualified employer plan to a participant or

9 beneficiary solely by reason of—

10   "(I) the termination of the quali-

11 fied employer plan, or

12   "(II) the failure to meet the re-

13 payment terms of the loan from such

14 plan because of the separation from

15 service of the participant (whether

16 due to layoff, cessation of business,

17 termination of employment, or other-

18 wise).

19   "(iii) PLAN LOAN OFFSET AMOUNT.—

20 For purposes of clause (ii), the term 'plan

21 loan offset amount' means the amount by

22 which the participant's accrued benefit

23 under the plan is reduced in order to repay

24 a loan from the plan.

148

1   "(iv) LIMITATION.—This subpara-

2   graph shall not apply to any plan loan off-

3   set amount unless such plan loan offset

4   amount relates to a loan to which section

5   72(p)(1) does not apply by reason of sec-

6   tion 72(p)(2).

7   "(v) QUALIFIED EMPLOYER PLAN.—

8   For purposes of this subsection, the term

9   'qualified employer plan' has the meaning

10   given such term by section 72(p)(4).".

11   (b) CONFORMING AMENDMENT.—Subparagraph (A)

12 of section 402(c)(3) is amended by striking "subpara-

13 graph (B)" and inserting "subparagraphs (B) and (C)".

14   (c) EFFECTIVE DATE.—The amendments made by

15 this section shall apply to taxable years beginning after

16 December 31, 2017.

17 **SEC. 1506. MODIFICATION OF NONDISCRIMINATION RULES**

18   **TO PROTECT OLDER, LONGER SERVICE PAR-**

19   **TICIPANTS.**

20   (a) IN GENERAL.—Section 401 is amended—

21   (1) by redesignating subsection (o) as sub-

22   section (p), and

23   (2) by inserting after subsection (n) the fol-

24   lowing new subsection:

1   "(o) SPECIAL RULES FOR APPLYING NON-

2 DISCRIMINATION RULES TO PROTECT OLDER, LONGER

3 SERVICE AND GRANDFATHERED PARTICIPANTS.—

4   "(1) TESTING OF DEFINED BENEFIT PLANS

5   WITH CLOSED CLASSES OF PARTICIPANTS.—

6   "(A) BENEFITS, RIGHTS, OR FEATURES

7   PROVIDED TO CLOSED CLASSES.—A defined

8 benefit plan which provides benefits, rights, or

9 features to a closed class of participants shall

10 not fail to satisfy the requirements of sub-

11 section (a)(4) by reason of the composition of

12 such closed class or the benefits, rights, or fea-

13 tures provided to such closed class, if—

14   "(i) for the plan year as of which the

15 class closes and the 2 succeeding plan

16 years, such benefits, rights, and features

17 satisfy the requirements of subsection

18 (a)(4) (without regard to this subpara-

19 graph but taking into account the rules of

20 subparagraph (I)),

21   "(ii) after the date as of which the

22 class was closed, any plan amendment

23 which modifies the closed class or the ben-

24 efits, rights, and features provided to such

25 closed class does not discriminate signifi-

1 cantly in favor of highly compensated em-

2 ployees, and

3 "(iii) the class was closed before April

4 5, 2017, or the plan is described in sub-

5 paragraph (C).

6 "(B) AGGREGATE TESTING WITH DEFINED

7 CONTRIBUTION PLANS PERMITTED ON A BENE-

8 FITS BASIS.—

9 "(i) IN GENERAL.—For purposes of

10 determining compliance with subsection

11 (a)(4) and section 410(b), a defined benefit

12 plan described in clause (iii) may be aggre-

13 gated and tested on a benefits basis with

14 1 or more defined contribution plans, in-

15 cluding with the portion of 1 or more de-

16 fined contribution plans which—

17 "(I) provides matching contribu-

18 tions (as defined in subsection

19 (m)(4)(A)),

20 "(II) provides annuity contracts

21 described in section 403(b) which are

22 purchased with matching contribu-

23 tions or nonelective contributions, or

24 "(III) consists of an employee

25 stock ownership plan (within the

151

1   meaning of section 4975(e)(7)) or a

2   tax credit employee stock ownership

3   plan (within the meaning of section

4   409(a)).

5   "(ii) SPECIAL RULES FOR MATCHING

6   CONTRIBUTIONS.—For purposes of clause

7   (i), if a defined benefit plan is aggregated

8   with a portion of a defined contribution

9   plan providing matching contributions—

10   "(I) such defined benefit plan

11   must also be aggregated with any por-

12   tion of such defined contribution plan

13   which provides elective deferrals de-

14   scribed in subparagraph (A) or (C) of

15   section 402(g)(3), and

16   "(II) such matching contribu-

17   tions shall be treated in the same

18   manner as nonelective contributions,

19   including for purposes of applying the

20   rules of subsection (l).

21   "(iii) PLANS DESCRIBED.—A defined

22   benefit plan is described in this clause if—

23   "(I) the plan provides benefits to

24   a closed class of participants,

1   "(II) for the plan year as of

2   which the class closes and the 2 suc-

3   ceeding plan years, the plan satisfies

4   the requirements of section 410(b)

5   and subsection (a)(4) (without regard

6   to this subparagraph but taking into

7   account the rules of subparagraph

8   (I)),

9   "(III) after the date as of which

10   the class was closed, any plan amend-

11   ment which modifies the closed class

12   or the benefits provided to such closed

13   class does not discriminate signifi-

14   cantly in favor of highly compensated

15   employees, and

16   "(IV) the class was closed before

17   April 5, 2017, or the plan is described

18   in subparagraph (C).

19   "(C) PLANS DESCRIBED.—A plan is de-

20   scribed in this subparagraph if, taking into ac-

21   count any predecessor plan—

22   "(i) such plan has been in effect for

23   at least 5 years as of the date the class is

24   closed, and

1   "(ii) during the 5-year period pre-

2   ceding the date the class is closed, there

3   has not been a substantial increase in the

4   coverage or value of the benefits, rights, or

5   features described in subparagraph (A) or

6   in the coverage or benefits under the plan

7   described in subparagraph (B)(iii) (which-

8   ever is applicable).

9   "(D) DETERMINATION OF SUBSTANTIAL

10 INCREASE FOR BENEFITS, RIGHTS, AND FEA-

11 TURES.—In applying subparagraph (C)(ii) for

12 purposes of subparagraph (A)(iii), a plan shall

13 be treated as having had a substantial increase

14 in coverage or value of the benefits, rights, or

15 features described in subparagraph (A) during

16 the applicable 5-year period only if, during such

17 period—

18   "(i) the number of participants cov-

19   ered by such benefits, rights, or features

20   on the date such period ends is more than

21   50 percent greater than the number of

22   such participants on the first day of the

23   plan year in which such period began, or

24   "(ii) such benefits, rights, and fea-

25   tures have been modified by 1 or more

1   plan amendments in such a way that, as of

2   the date the class is closed, the value of

3   such benefits, rights, and features to the

4   closed class as a whole is substantially

5   greater than the value as of the first day

6   of such 5-year period, solely as a result of

7   such amendments.

8   "(E) DETERMINATION OF SUBSTANTIAL

9   INCREASE FOR AGGREGATE TESTING ON BENE-

10   FITS BASIS.—In applying subparagraph (C)(ii)

11   for purposes of subparagraph (B)(iii)(IV), a

12   plan shall be treated as having had a substan-

13   tial increase in coverage or benefits during the

14   applicable 5-year period only if, during such pe-

15   riod—

16   "(i) the number of participants bene-

17   fitting under the plan on the date such pe-

18   riod ends is more than 50 percent greater

19   than the number of such participants on

20   the first day of the plan year in which such

21   period began, or

22   "(ii) the average benefit provided to

23   such participants on the date such period

24   ends is more than 50 percent greater than

25   the average benefit provided on the first

1   day of the plan year in which such period

2   began.

3   "(F) CERTAIN EMPLOYEES DIS-

4   REGARDED.—For purposes of subparagraphs

5   (D) and (E), any increase in coverage or value

6   or in coverage or benefits, whichever is applica-

7   ble, which is attributable to such coverage and

8   value or coverage and benefits provided to em-

9   ployees—

10   "(i) who became participants as a re-

11   sult of a merger, acquisition, or similar

12   event which occurred during the 7-year pe-

13   riod preceding the date the class is closed,

14   or

15   "(ii) who became participants by rea-

16   son of a merger of the plan with another

17   plan which had been in effect for at least

18   5 years as of the date of the merger,

19   shall be disregarded, except that clause (ii)

20   shall apply for purposes of subparagraph (D)

21   only if, under the merger, the benefits, rights,

22   or features under 1 plan are conformed to the

23   benefits, rights, or features of the other plan

24   prospectively.

1   "(G) RULES RELATING TO AVERAGE BEN-

2   EFIT.—For purposes of subparagraph (E)—

3   "(i) the average benefit provided to

4   participants under the plan will be treated

5   as having remained the same between the

6   2 dates described in subparagraph (E)(ii)

7   if the benefit formula applicable to such

8   participants has not changed between such

9   dates, and

10   "(ii) if the benefit formula applicable

11   to 1 or more participants under the plan

12   has changed between such 2 dates, then

13   the average benefit under the plan shall be

14   considered to have increased by more than

15   50 percent only if—

16   "(I) the total amount determined

17   under section 430(b)(1)(A)(i) for all

18   participants benefitting under the

19   plan for the plan year in which the 5-

20   year period described in subparagraph

21   (E) ends, exceeds

22   "(II) the total amount deter-

23   mined under section 430(b)(1)(A)(i)

24   for all such participants for such plan

25   year, by using the benefit formula in

1 effect for each such participant for

2 the first plan year in such 5-year pe-

3 riod, by more than 50 percent.

4 In the case of a CSEC plan (as defined in

5 section 414(y)), the normal cost of the

6 plan (as determined under section

7 433(j)(1)(B)) shall be used in lieu of the

8 amount determined under section

9 430(b)(1)(A)(i).

10 "(H) TREATMENT AS SINGLE PLAN.—For

11 purposes of subparagraphs (E) and (G), a plan

12 described in section 413(c) shall be treated as

13 a single plan rather than as separate plans

14 maintained by each participating employer.

15 "(I) SPECIAL RULES.—For purposes of

16 subparagraphs (A)(i) and (B)(iii)(II), the fol-

17 lowing rules shall apply:

18 "(i) In applying section 410(b)(6)(C),

19 the closing of the class of participants shall

20 not be treated as a significant change in

21 coverage under section 410(b)(6)(C)(i)(II).

22 "(ii) 2 or more plans shall not fail to

23 be eligible to be aggregated and treated as

24 a single plan solely by reason of having dif-

25 ferent plan years.

1   "(iii) Changes in the employee popu-

2   lation shall be disregarded to the extent at-

3   tributable to individuals who become em-

4   ployees or cease to be employees, after the

5   date the class is closed, by reason of a

6   merger, acquisition, divestiture, or similar

7   event.

8   "(iv) Aggregation and all other testing

9   methodologies otherwise applicable under

10   subsection (a)(4) and section 410(b) may

11   be taken into account.

12   The rule of clause (ii) shall also apply for pur-

13   poses of determining whether plans to which

14   subparagraph (B)(i) applies may be aggregated

15   and treated as 1 plan for purposes of deter-

16   mining whether such plans meet the require-

17   ments of subsection (a)(4) and section 410(b).

18   "(J) SPUN-OFF PLANS.—For purposes of

19   this paragraph, if a portion of a defined benefit

20   plan described in subparagraph (A) or (B)(iii)

21   is spun off to another employer and the spun-

22   off plan continues to satisfy the requirements

23   of—

24   "(i)   subparagraph   (A)(i)   or

25   (B)(iii)(II), whichever is applicable, if the

1   original plan was still within the 3-year pe-

2   riod described in such subparagraph at the

3   time of the spin off, and

4   "(ii)   subparagraph   (A)(ii)   or

5   (B)(iii)(III), whichever is applicable,

6   the treatment under subparagraph (A) or (B)

7   of the spun-off plan shall continue with respect

8   to such other employer.

9   "(2) TESTING OF DEFINED CONTRIBUTION

10   PLANS.—

11   "(A) TESTING ON A BENEFITS BASIS.—A

12   defined contribution plan shall be permitted to

13   be tested on a benefits basis if—

14   "(i) such defined contribution plan

15   provides make-whole contributions to a

16   closed class of participants whose accruals

17   under a defined benefit plan have been re-

18   duced or eliminated,

19   "(ii) for the plan year of the defined

20   contribution plan as of which the class eli-

21   gible to receive such make-whole contribu-

22   tions closes and the 2 succeeding plan

23   years, such closed class of participants sat-

24   isfies   the   requirements   of   section

1   410(b)(2)(A)(i) (determined by applying

2   the rules of paragraph (1)(I)),

3   "(iii) after the date as of which the

4   class was closed, any plan amendment to

5   the defined contribution plan which modi-

6   fies the closed class or the allocations, ben-

7   efits, rights, and features provided to such

8   closed class does not discriminate signifi-

9   cantly in favor of highly compensated em-

10   ployees, and

11   "(iv) the class was closed before April

12   5, 2017, or the defined benefit plan under

13   clause (i) is described in paragraph (1)(C)

14   (as applied for purposes of paragraph

15   (1)(B)(iii)(IV)).

16   "(B) AGGREGATION WITH PLANS INCLUD-

17   ING MATCHING CONTRIBUTIONS.—

18   "(i) IN GENERAL.—With respect to 1

19   or more defined contribution plans de-

20   scribed in subparagraph (A), for purposes

21   of determining compliance with subsection

22   (a)(4) and section 410(b), the portion of

23   such plans which provides make-whole con-

24   tributions or other nonelective contribu-

25   tions may be aggregated and tested on a

1 benefits basis with the portion of 1 or

2 more other defined contribution plans

3 which—

4   "(I) provides matching contribu-

5   tions (as defined in subsection

6   (m)(4)(A)),

7   "(II) provides annuity contracts

8   described in section 403(b) which are

9   purchased with matching contribu-

10   tions or nonelective contributions, or

11   "(III) consists of an employee

12   stock ownership plan (within the

13   meaning of section 4975(e)(7)) or a

14   tax credit employee stock ownership

15   plan (within the meaning of section

16   409(a)).

17   "(ii) SPECIAL RULES FOR MATCHING

18 CONTRIBUTIONS.—Rules similar to the

19 rules of paragraph (1)(B)(ii) shall apply

20 for purposes of clause (i).

21 "(C) SPECIAL RULES FOR TESTING DE-

22 FINED CONTRIBUTION PLAN FEATURES PRO-

23 VIDING MATCHING CONTRIBUTIONS TO CERTAIN

24 OLDER, LONGER SERVICE PARTICIPANTS.—In

25 the case of a defined contribution plan which

1   provides benefits, rights, or features to a closed

2   class of participants whose accruals under a de-

3   fined benefit plan have been reduced or elimi-

4   nated, the plan shall not fail to satisfy the re-

5   quirements of subsection (a)(4) solely by reason

6   of the composition of the closed class or the

7   benefits, rights, or features provided to such

8   closed class if the defined contribution plan and

9   defined benefit plan otherwise meet the require-

10   ments of subparagraph (A) but for the fact that

11   the make-whole contributions under the defined

12   contribution plan are made in whole or in part

13   through matching contributions.

14   "(D) SPUN-OFF PLANS.—For purposes of

15   this paragraph, if a portion of a defined con-

16   tribution plan described in subparagraph (A) or

17   (C) is spun off to another employer, the treat-

18   ment under subparagraph (A) or (C) of the

19   spun-off plan shall continue with respect to the

20   other employer if such plan continues to comply

21   with the requirements of clauses (ii) (if the

22   original plan was still within the 3-year period

23   described in such clause at the time of the spin

24   off) and (iii) of subparagraph (A), as deter-

1 mined for purposes of subparagraph (A) or (C),

2 whichever is applicable.

3 "(3) DEFINITIONS.—For purposes of this sub-

4 section—

5   "(A) MAKE-WHOLE CONTRIBUTIONS.—Ex-

6   cept as otherwise provided in paragraph (2)(C),

7   the term 'make-whole contributions' means non-

8   elective allocations for each employee in the

9   class which are reasonably calculated, in a con-

10   sistent manner, to replace some or all of the re-

11   tirement benefits which the employee would

12   have received under the defined benefit plan

13   and any other plan or qualified cash or deferred

14   arrangement under subsection (k)(2) if no

15   change had been made to such defined benefit

16   plan and such other plan or arrangement. For

17   purposes of the preceding sentence, consistency

18   shall not be required with respect to employees

19   who were subject to different benefit formulas

20   under the defined benefit plan.

21   "(B) REFERENCES TO CLOSED CLASS OF

22   PARTICIPANTS.—References to a closed class of

23   participants and similar references to a closed

24   class shall include arrangements under which 1

25   or more classes of participants are closed, ex-

164

1   cept that 1 or more classes of participants

2   closed on different dates shall not be aggre-

3   gated for purposes of determining the date any

4   such class was closed.

5   "(C) HIGHLY COMPENSATED EMPLOYEE.—

6   The term 'highly compensated employee' has

7   the meaning given such term in section

8   414(q).".".

9   (b) PARTICIPATION REQUIREMENTS.—Paragraph

10   (26) of section 401(a) is amended by adding at the end

11   the following new subparagraph:

12   "(I) PROTECTED PARTICIPANTS.—

13   "(i) IN GENERAL.—A plan shall be

14   deemed to satisfy the requirements of sub-

15   paragraph (A) if—

16   "(I) the plan is amended—

17   "(aa) to cease all benefit ac-

18   cruals, or

19   "(bb) to provide future ben-

20   efit accruals only to a closed

21   class of participants,

22   "(II) the plan satisfies subpara-

23   graph (A) (without regard to this sub-

24   paragraph) as of the effective date of

25   the amendment, and

1   "(III) the amendment was adopt-

2   ed before April 5, 2017, or the plan is

3   described in clause (ii).

4   "(ii) PLANS DESCRIBED.—A plan is

5 described in this clause if the plan would

6 be described in subsection (o)(1)(C), as ap-

7 plied   for   purposes   of   subsection

8 (o)(1)(B)(iii)(IV) and by treating the effec-

9 tive date of the amendment as the date the

10 class was closed for purposes of subsection

11 (o)(1)(C).

12   "(iii) SPECIAL RULES.—For purposes

13 of   clause   (i)(II),   in   applying   section

14 410(b)(6)(C), the amendments described in

15 clause (i) shall not be treated as a signifi-

16 cant change in coverage under section

17 410(b)(6)(C)(i)(II).

18   "(iv) SPUN-OFF PLANS.—For pur-

19 poses of this subparagraph, if a portion of

20 a plan described in clause (i) is spun off to

21 another employer, the treatment under

22 clause (i) of the spun-off plan shall con-

23 tinue with respect to the other employer.".

24   (c) EFFECTIVE DATE.—

1 (1) IN GENERAL.—Except as provided in para-
2 graph (2), the amendments made by this section
3 shall take effect on the date of the enactment of this
4 Act, without regard to whether any plan modifica-
5 tions referred to in such amendments are adopted or
6 effective before, on, or after such date of enactment.

7 (2) SPECIAL RULES.—

8   (A) ELECTION OF EARLIER APPLICA-
9 TION.—At the election of the plan sponsor, the
10 amendments made by this section shall apply to
11 plan years beginning after December 31, 2013.

12   (B) CLOSED CLASSES OF PARTICIPANTS.—
13 For purposes of paragraphs (1)(A)(iii),
14 (1)(B)(iii)(IV), and (2)(A)(iv) of section 401(o)
15 of the Internal Revenue Code of 1986 (as added
16 by this section), a closed class of participants
17 shall be treated as being closed before April 5,
18 2017, if the plan sponsor's intention to create
19 such closed class is reflected in formal written
20 documents and communicated to participants
21 before such date.

22   (C) CERTAIN POST-ENACTMENT PLAN
23 AMENDMENTS.—A plan shall not be treated as
24 failing to be eligible for the application of sec-
25 tion 401(o)(1)(A), 401(o)(1)(B)(iii), or

1   401(a)(26) of such Code (as added by this sec-

2   tion) to such plan solely because in the case

3   of—

4   (i) such section 401(o)(1)(A), the plan

5   was amended before the date of the enact-

6   ment of this Act to eliminate 1 or more

7   benefits, rights, or features, and is further

8   amended after such date of enactment to

9   provide such previously eliminated benefits,

10   rights, or features to a closed class of par-

11   ticipants, or

12   (ii) such section 401(o)(1)(B)(iii) or

13   section 401(a)(26), the plan was amended

14   before the date of the enactment of this

15   Act to cease all benefit accruals, and is

16   further amended after such date of enact-

17   ment to provide benefit accruals to a closed

18   class of participants. Any such section

19   shall only apply if the plan otherwise meets

20   the requirements of such section and in ap-

21   plying such section, the date the class of

22   participants is closed shall be the effective

23   date of the later amendment.

168

Subtitle G—Estate, Gift, and Generation-skipping Transfer Taxes

SEC. 1601. INCREASE IN CREDIT AGAINST ESTATE, GIFT, AND GENERATION-SKIPPING TRANSFER TAX.

(a) IN GENERAL.—Section 2010(c)(3) is amended by striking "$5,000,000" and inserting "$10,000,000".

(b) EFFECTIVE DATE.—The amendments made by this section shall apply to estates of decedents dying, generation-skipping transfers, and gifts made, after December 31, 2017.

SEC. 1602. REPEAL OF ESTATE AND GENERATION-SKIPPING TRANSFER TAXES.

(a) ESTATE TAX REPEAL.—

(1) IN GENERAL.—Subchapter C of chapter 11 is amended by adding at the end the following new section:

"SEC. 2210. TERMINATION.

"(a) IN GENERAL.—Except as provided in subsection (b), this chapter shall not apply to the estates of decedents dying after December 31, 2023.

"(b) CERTAIN DISTRIBUTIONS FROM QUALIFIED DOMESTIC TRUSTS.—In applying section 2056A with respect to the surviving spouse of a decedent dying on or before December 31, 2023—

1   "(1) section 2056A(b)(1)(A) shall not apply to

2 distributions made after the 10-year period begin-

3 ning on such date, and

4   "(2) section 2056A(b)(1)(B) shall not apply

5 after such date.".

6   (2) CONFORMING AMENDMENTS.—Section

7 1014(b) is amended—

8   (A) in paragraph (6), by striking "was in-

9 cludible in determining" and all that follows

10 through the end and inserting "was includible

11 (or would have been includible without regard

12 to section 2210) in determining the value of the

13 decedent's gross estate under chapter 11 of

14 subtitle B" ,

15   (B) in paragraph (9), by striking "required

16 to be included" through "Code of 1939" and

17 inserting "required to be included (or would

18 have been required to be included without re-

19 gard to section 2210) in determining the value

20 of the decedent's gross estate under chapter 11

21 of subtitle B", and

22   (C) in paragraph (10), by striking "Prop-

23 erty includible in the gross estate" and insert-

24 ing "Property includible (or which would have

1 been includible without regard to section 2210)

2 in the gross estate''.

3 (3) CLERICAL AMENDMENT.—The table of sec-

4 tions for subchapter C of chapter 11 is amended by

5 adding at the end the following new item:

"Sec. 2210. Termination.''.

6 (b) GENERATION-SKIPPING TRANSFER TAX RE-

7 PEAL.—

8 (1) IN GENERAL.—Subchapter G of chapter 13

9 of subtitle B of such Code is amended by adding at

10 the end the following new section:

11 **"SEC. 2664. TERMINATION.**

12 "This chapter shall not apply to generation-skipping

13 transfers after December 31, 2023.''.

14 (2) CLERICAL AMENDMENT.—The table of sec-

15 tions for subchapter G of chapter 13 of such Code

16 is amended by adding at the end the following new

17 item:

"Sec. 2664. Termination.''.

18 (c) CONFORMING AMENDMENTS RELATED TO GIFT

19 TAX.—

20 (1) COMPUTATION OF GIFT TAX.—Section 2502

21 is amended by adding at the end the following new

22 subsection:

23 "(d) GIFTS MADE AFTER 2023.—

1   "(1) IN GENERAL.—In the case of a gift made

2   after December 31, 2023, subsection (a) shall be ap-

3   plied by substituting 'subsection (d)(2)' for 'section

4   2001(c)' and 'such subsection' for 'such section'.

5   "(2) RATE SCHEDULE.—

"If the amount with respect to which the tentative tax to be computed is:.	The tentative tax is:
Not over $10,000	18% of such amount.
Over $10,000 but not over $20,000	$1,800, plus 20% of the excess over $10,000.
Over $20,000 but not over $40,000	$3,800, plus 22% of the excess over $20,000.
Over $40,000 but not over $60,000	$8,200, plus 24% of the excess over $40,000.
Over $60,000 but not over $80,000	$13,000, plus 26% of the excess over $60,000.
Over $80,000 but not over $100,000	$18,200, plus 28% of the excess over $80,000.
Over $100,000 but not over $150,000	$23,800, plus 30% of the excess over $100,000.
Over $150,000 but not over $250,000	$38,800, plus 32% of the excess of $150,000.
Over $250,000 but not over $500,000	$70,800, plus 34% of the excess over $250,000.
Over $500,000	$155,800, plus 35% of the excess of $500,000.".

6   (2) LIFETIME GIFT EXEMPTION.—Section 2505

7   is amended by adding at the end the following new

8   subsection:

9   "(d) GIFTS MADE AFTER 2023.—

10   "(1) IN GENERAL.—In the case of a gift made

11   after December 31, 2023, subsection (a)(1) shall be

172

1 applied by substituting 'the amount of the tentative

2 tax which would be determined under the rate sched-

3 ule set forth in section 2502(a)(2) if the amount

4 with respect to which such tentative tax is to be

5 computed were $10,000,000' for 'the applicable

6 credit amount in effect under section 2010(c) which

7 would apply if the donor died as of the end of the

8 calendar year'.

9   "(2) INFLATION ADJUSTMENT.—

10   "(A) IN GENERAL.—In the case of any cal-

11   endar year after 2023, the dollar amount in

12   subsection (a)(1) (after application of this sub-

13   section) shall be increased by an amount equal

14   to—

15   "(i) such dollar amount, multiplied by

16   "(ii) the cost-of-living adjustment de-

17   termined under section 1(f)(3) for such

18   calendar year by substituting 'calendar

19   year 2011' for 'calendar year 1992' in sub-

20   paragraph (B) thereof.

21   "(B) ROUNDING.—If any amount as ad-

22   justed under paragraph (1) is not a multiple of

23         $10,000, such amount shall be rounded to the

24   nearest multiple of $10,000.".

173

1   (3) OTHER CONFORMING AMENDMENTS RE-

2   LATED TO GIFT TAX.—Section 2801 is amended by

3   adding at the end the following new subsection:

4   striking and inserting "section 2502(a)(2)"

5   "(g) GIFTS RECEIVED AFTER 2023.—In the case of

6 a gift received after December 31, 2023, subsection (a)(1)

7 shall be applied by substituting 'section 2502(a)(2)' for

8 'section 2001(c) as in effect on the date of such receipt'.".

9   (d) EFFECTIVE DATE.—The amendments made by

10 this section shall apply to estates of decedents dying, gen-

11 eration-skipping transfers, and gifts made, after Decem-

12 ber 31, 2023.

TITLE II—ALTERNATIVE MINIMUM TAX REPEAL

15 **SEC. 2001. REPEAL OF ALTERNATIVE MINIMUM TAX.**

16   (a) IN GENERAL.—Subchapter A of chapter 1 is

17 amended by striking part VI (and by striking the item

18 relating to such part in the table of parts for subchapter

19 A).

20   (b) CREDIT FOR PRIOR YEAR MINIMUM TAX LIABIL-

21 ITY.—

22   (1) LIMITATION.—Subsection (c) of section 53

23   is amended to read as follows:

24   "(c) LIMITATION.—The credit allowable under sub-

25 section (a) shall not exceed the regular tax liability of the

174

1 taxpayer reduced by the sum of the credits allowed under
2 subparts A, B, and D.''.

3   (2) CREDITS TREATED AS REFUNDABLE.—Sec-
4 tion 53 is amended by adding at the end the fol-
5 lowing new subsection:

6   ''(e) PORTION OF CREDIT TREATED AS REFUND-
7 ABLE.—

8   ''(1) IN GENERAL.—In the case of any taxable
9 year beginning in 2019, 2020, 2021, or 2022, the
10 limitation under subsection (c) shall be increased by
11 the AMT refundable credit amount for such year.

12   ''(2) AMT REFUNDABLE CREDIT AMOUNT.—
13 For purposes of paragraph (1), the AMT refundable
14 credit amount is an amount equal to 50 percent
15 (100 percent in the case of a taxable year beginning
16 in 2022) of the excess (if any) of—

17   ''(A) the minimum tax credit determined
18 under subsection (b) for the taxable year, over

19   ''(B) the minimum tax credit allowed
20 under subsection (a) for such year (before the
21 application of this subsection for such year).

22   ''(3) CREDIT REFUNDABLE.—For purposes of
23 this title (other than this section), the credit allowed
24 by reason of this subsection shall be treated as a

1   credit allowed under subpart C (and not this sub-

2   part).

3   "(4) SHORT TAXABLE YEARS.—In the case of

4   any taxable year of less than 365 days, the AMT re-

5   fundable credit amount determined under paragraph

6   (2) with respect to such taxable year shall be the

7   amount which bears the same ratio to such amount

8   determined without regard to this paragraph as the

9   number of days in such taxable year bears to 365.".

10   (3) TREATMENT OF REFERENCES.—Section

11   53(d) is amended by adding at the end the following

12   new paragraph:

13   "(3) AMT TERM REFERENCES.—Any references

14   in this subsection to section 55, 56, or 57 shall be

15   treated as a reference to such section as in effect be-

16   fore its repeal by the Tax Cuts and Jobs Act.".

17   (c) CONFORMING AMENDMENTS RELATED TO AMT

18   REPEAL.—

19   (1) Section 2(d) is amended by striking "sec-

20   tions 1 and 55" and inserting "section 1".

21   (2) Section 5(a) is amended by striking para-

22   graph (4).

23   (3) Section 11(d) is amended by striking "the

24   taxes imposed by subsection (a) and section 55" and

25   inserting "the tax imposed by subsection (a)".

1   (4) Section 12 is amended by striking para-
2 graph (7).

3   (5) Section 26(a) is amended to read as follows:

4 "(a) LIMITATION BASED ON AMOUNT OF TAX.—The
5 aggregate amount of credits allowed by this subpart for
6 the taxable year shall not exceed the taxpayer's regular
7 tax liability for the taxable year.".

8   (6) Section 26(b)(2) is amended by striking
9 subparagraph (A).

10   (7) Section 26 is amended by striking sub-
11 section (c).

12   (8) Section 38(c) is amended—

13   (A) by striking paragraphs (1) through
14   (5),

15   (B) by redesignating paragraph (6) as
16   paragraph (2),

17   (C) by inserting before paragraph (2) (as
18   so redesignated) the following new paragraph:

19   "(1) IN GENERAL.—The credit allowed under
20 subsection (a) for any taxable year shall not exceed
21 the excess (if any) of—

22   "(A) the sum of—

23   "(i) so much of the regular tax liabil-
24   ity as does not exceed $25,000, plus

1   "(ii) 75 percent of so much of the reg-

2   ular tax liability as exceeds $25,000, over

3   "(B) the sum of the credits allowable

4   under subparts A and B of this part.", and

5   (D) by striking "subparagraph (B) of

6   paragraph (1)" each place it appears in para-

7   graph (2) (as so redesignated) and inserting

8   "clauses (i) and (ii) of paragraph (1)(A)".

9   (9) Section 39(a) is amended—

10   (A) by striking "or the eligible small busi-

11   ness credits" in paragraph (3)(A), and

12   (B) by striking paragraph (4).

13   (10) Section 45D(g)(4)(B) is amended by strik-

14   ing "or for purposes of section 55".

15   (11) Section 54(c)(1) is amended to read as fol-

16   lows:

17   "(1) regular tax liability (as defined in section

18   26(b)), over".

19   (12) Section 54A(c)(1)(A) is amended to read

20   as follows:

21   "(A) regular tax liability (as defined in

22   section 26(b)), over".

23   (13) Section 148(b)(3) is amended to read as

24   follows:

1   "(3) TAX-EXEMPT BONDS NOT TREATED AS IN-

2   VESTMENT PROPERTY.—The term 'investment prop-

3   erty' does not include any tax-exempt bond.".

4   (14) Section 168(k)(2) is amended by striking

5   subparagraph (G).

6   (15) Section 168(k) is amended by striking

7   paragraph (4).

8   (16) Section 168(k)(5) is amended by striking

9   subparagraph (E).

10   (17) Section 168(m)(2)(B)(i) is amended by

11   striking "(determined without regard to paragraph

12   (4) thereof)".

13   (18) Section 168(m)(2) is amended by striking

14   subparagraph (D).

15   (19) Section 173 is amended by striking sub-

16   section (b).

17   (20) Section 174(f) is amended to read as fol-

18   lows:

19   "(f) CROSS REFERENCE.—For adjustments to basis

20 of property for amounts allowed as deductions as deferred

21 expenses under subsection (b), see section 1016(a)(14).".

22   (21) Section 263(c) is amended by striking

23   "section 59(e) or 291" and inserting "section 291".

179

1   (22) Section 263A(c) is amended by striking

2   paragraph (6) and by redesignating paragraph (7)

3   (as amended) as paragraph (6). .

4   (23) Section 382(l) is amended by striking

5   paragraph (7) and by redesignating paragraph (8)

6   as paragraph (7).

7   (24) Section 443 is amended by striking sub-

8   section (d) and by redesignating subsection (e) as

9   subsection (d).

10   (25) Section 616 is amended by striking sub-

11   section (e).

12   (26) Section 617 is amended by striking sub-

13   section (i).

14   (27) Section 641(c) is amended—

15   (A) in paragraph (2) by striking subpara-

16   graph (B) and by redesignating subparagraphs

17   (C) and (D) as subparagraphs (B) and (C), re-

18   spectively, and

19   (B) in paragraph (3), by striking "para-

20   graph (2)(C)" and inserting "paragraph

21   (2)(B)".

22   (28) Subsections (b) and (c) of section 666 are

23   each amended by striking "(other than the tax im-

24   posed by section 55)".

1   (29) Section 848 is amended by striking sub-

2 section (i).

3   (30) Section 860E(a) is amended by striking

4 paragraph (4).

5   (31) Section 871(b)(1) is amended by striking

6 "or 55".

7   (32) Section 882(a)(1) is amended by striking

8 "55,".

9   (33) Section 897(a) is amended to read as fol-

10 lows:

11 "(a) TREATMENT AS EFFECTIVELY CONNECTED

12 WITH UNITED STATES TRADE OR BUSINESS.—For pur-

13 poses of this title, gain or loss of a nonresident alien indi-

14 vidual or a foreign corporation from the disposition of a

15 United States real property interest shall be taken into

16 account—

17   "(1) in the case of a nonresident alien indi-

18 vidual, under section 871(b)(1), or

19   "(2) in the case of a foreign corporation, under

20 section 882(a)(1),

21 as if the taxpayer were engaged in a trade or business

22 within the United States during the taxable year and as

23 if such gain or loss were effectively connected with such

24 trade or business.".

181

1   (34) Section 904(k) is amended to read as fol-

2 lows:

3   "(k) CROSS REFERENCE.—For increase of limitation

4 under subsection (a) for taxes paid with respect to

5 amounts received which were included in the gross income

6 of the taxpayer for a prior taxable year as a United States

7 shareholder with respect to a controlled foreign corpora-

8 tion, see section 960(b).".

9   (35) Section 911(f) is amended to read as fol-

10 lows:

11   "(f) DETERMINATION OF TAX LIABILITY.—

12   "(1) IN GENERAL.—If, for any taxable year,

13   any amount is excluded from gross income of a tax-

14   payer under subsection (a), then, notwithstanding

15   section 1, if such taxpayer has taxable income for

16   such taxable year, the tax imposed by section 1 for

17   such taxable year shall be equal to the excess (if

18   any) of—

19   "(A) the tax which would be imposed by

20   section 1 for such taxable year if the taxpayer's

21   taxable income were increased by the amount

22   excluded under subsection (a) for such taxable

23   year, over

24   "(B) the tax which would be imposed by

25   section 1 for such taxable year if the taxpayer's

1   taxable income were equal to the amount ex-

2   cluded under subsection (a) for such taxable

3   year.

4 For purposes of this paragraph, the amount ex-

5 cluded under subsection (a) shall be reduced by the

6 aggregate amount of any deductions or exclusions

7 disallowed under subsection (d)(6) with respect to

8 such excluded amount.

9   "(2) TREATMENT OF CAPITAL GAIN EXCESS.—

10   "(A) IN GENERAL.—In applying section

11   1(h) for purposes of determining the tax under

12   paragraph (1)(A) for any taxable year in which,

13   without regard to this subsection, the tax-

14   payer's net capital gain exceeds taxable income

15   (hereafter in this subparagraph referred to as

16   the capital gain excess)—

17   "(i) the taxpayer's net capital gain

18   (determined without regard to section

19   1(h)(11)) shall be reduced (but not below

20   zero) by such capital gain excess,

21   "(ii) the taxpayer's qualified dividend

22   income shall be reduced by so much of

23   such capital gain excess as exceeds the tax-

24   payer's net capital gain (determined with-

1   out regard to section 1(h)(11) and the re-

2   duction under clause (i)), and

3   "(iii) adjusted net capital gain,

4   unrecaptured section 1250 gain, and 28-

5   percent rate gain shall each be determined

6   after increasing the amount described in

7   section 1(h)(4)(B) by such capital gain ex-

8   cess.

9   "(B) DEFINITIONS.—Terms used in this

10   paragraph which are also used in section 1(h)

11   shall have the respective meanings given such

12   terms by section 1(h).".

13   (36) Section 962(a)(1) is amended—

14   (A) by striking "sections 1 and 55" and

15   inserting "section 1", and

16   (B) by striking "sections 11 and 55" and

17   inserting "section 11".

18   (37) Section 1016(a) is amended by striking

19   paragraph (20).

20   (38) Section 1202(a)(4) is amended by insert-

21   ing "and" at the end of subparagraph (A), by strik-

22   ing ", and" and inserting a period at the end of sub-

23   paragraph (B), and by striking subparagraph (C).

24   (39) Section 1374(b)(3)(B) is amended by

25   striking the last sentence thereof.

1   (40) Section 1561(a) is amended—

2   (A) by inserting "and" at the end of para-

3   graph (1), by striking ", and" at the end of

4   paragraph (2) and inserting a period, and by

5   striking paragraph (3), and

6   (B) by striking the last sentence.

7   (41) Section 6015(d)(2)(B) is amended by

8 striking "or 55".

9   (42) Section 6211(b)(4)(A) is amended by

10 striking", 168(k)(4)".

11   (43) Section 6425(c)(1)(A) is amended to read

12 as follows:

13   "(A) the tax imposed under section 11 or

14   subchapter L of chapter 1, whichever is applica-

15   ble, over".

16   (44) Section 6654(d)(2) is amended—

17   (A) in clause (i) of subparagraph (B), by

18   striking ", alternative minimum taxable in-

19   come,", and

20   (B) in clause (i) of subparagraph (C), by

21   striking ", alternative minimum taxable in-

22   come,".

23   (45) Section 6655(e)(2)(B)(i) is amended by

24 striking "The taxable income and alternative min-

1   imum taxable income shall" and inserting "Taxable

2   income shall".

3   (46) Section 6655(g)(1)(A) is amended by add-

4   ing "plus" at the end of clause (i), by striking clause

5   (ii), and by redesignating clause (iii) as clause (ii).

6   (47) Section 6662(e)(3)(C) is amended by strik-

7   ing "the regular tax (as defined in section 55(c))"

8   and inserting "the regular tax liability (as defined in

9   section 26(b))".

10   (d) EFFECTIVE DATES.—

11   (1) IN GENERAL.—Except as otherwise pro-

12   vided in this subsection, the amendments made by

13   this section shall apply to taxable years beginning

14   after December 31, 2017.

15   (2) PRIOR ELECTIONS WITH RESPECT TO CER-

16   TAIN TAX PREFERENCES.—So much of the amend-

17   ment made by subsection (a) as relates to the repeal

18   of section 59(e) of the Internal Revenue Code of

19   1986 shall apply to amounts paid or incurred after

20   December 31, 2017.

21   (3) TREATMENT OF NET OPERATING LOSS

22   CARRYBACKS.—For purposes of section 56(d) of the

23   Internal Revenue Code of 1986 (as in effect before

24   its repeal), the amount of any net operating loss

25   which may be carried back from a taxable year be-

1   ginning after December 31, 2017, to taxable years

2   beginning before January 1, 2018, shall be deter-

3   mined without regard to any adjustments under sec-

4   tion 56(d)(2)(A) of such Code (as so in effect).

TITLE III—BUSINESS TAX REFORM

Subtitle A—Tax Rates

SEC. 3001. REDUCTION IN CORPORATE TAX RATE.

9   (a) IN GENERAL.—Section 11(b) is amended to read

10 as follows:

11 "(b) AMOUNT OF TAX.—

12   "(1) IN GENERAL.—Except as otherwise pro-

13 vided in this subsection, the amount of the tax im-

14 posed by subsection (a) shall be 20 percent of tax-

15 able income.

16   "(2) SPECIAL RULE FOR PERSONAL SERVICE

17 CORPORATIONS.—

18   "(A) IN GENERAL.—In the case of a per-

19   sonal service corporation (as defined in section

20   448(d)(2)), the amount of the tax imposed by

21   subsection (a) shall be 25 percent of taxable in-

22   come.

23   "(B) REFERENCES TO CORPORATE

24   RATE.—Any reference to the rate imposed

25   under this section or to the highest rate in ef-

1 fect under this section (or any similar ref-

2 erence) shall be determined without regard to

3 the rate imposed with respect to personal serv-

4 ice corporations (as so defined).''.

5 (b) CONFORMING AMENDMENTS.—

6 (1)(A) Part I of subchapter P of chapter 1 is

7 amended by striking section 1201 (and by striking

8 the item relating to such section in the table of sec-

9 tions for such part).

10 (B) Section 12 is amended by striking para-

11 graph (4).

12 (C) Section 527(b) is amended—

13 (i) by striking paragraph (2), and

14 (ii) by striking all that precedes ''is hereby

15 imposed'' and inserting:

16 ''(b) TAX IMPOSED.—A tax''.

17 (D) Section 594(a) is amended by striking

18 ''taxes imposed by section 11 or 1201(a)'' and in-

19 serting ''tax imposed by section 11''.

20 (E) Section 691(c)(4) is amended by striking

21 ''1201,''.

22 (F) Section 801(a) is amended—

23 (i) by striking paragraph (2), and

24 (ii) by striking all that precedes ''is hereby

25 imposed'' and inserting:

188

1   "(a) TAX IMPOSED.—A tax".

2   (G) Section 831(e) is amended by striking para-

3   graph (1) and by redesignating paragraphs (2) and

4   (3) as paragraphs (1) and (2), respectively.

5   (H) Sections 832(c)(5) and 834(b)(1)(D) are

6   each amended by striking "sec. 1201 and fol-

7   lowing,".

8   (I) Section 852(b)(3)(A) is amended by striking

9   "section 1201(a)" and inserting "section 11(b)(1)".

10 (J) Section 857(b)(3) is amended—

11   (i) by striking subparagraph (A) and re-

12   designating subparagraphs (B) through (F) as

13   subparagraphs (A) through (E), respectively,

14   (ii) in subparagraph (C), as so redesig-

15   nated—

16   (I) by striking "subparagraph (A)(ii)"

17   in clause (i) thereof and inserting "para-

18   graph (1)",

19   (II) by striking "the tax imposed by

20   subparagraph (A)(ii)" in clauses (ii) and

21   (iv) thereof and inserting "the tax imposed

22   by paragraph (1) on undistributed capital

23   gain",

1   (iii) in subparagraph (E), as so redesig-

2   nated, by striking "subparagraph (B) or (D)"

3   and inserting "subparagraph (A) or (C)", and

4   (iv) by adding at the end the following new

5   subparagraph:

6   "(F) UNDISTRIBUTED CAPITAL GAIN.—

7   For purposes of this paragraph, the term 'un-

8   distributed capital gain' means the excess of the

9   net capital gain over the deduction for divi-

10   dends paid (as defined in section 561) deter-

11   mined with reference to capital gain dividends

12   only.".

13   (K) Section 882(a)(1) is amended by striking ",

14   or 1201(a)".

15   (L) Section 1374(b) is amended by striking

16   paragraph (4).

17   (M) Section 1381(b) is amended by striking

18   "taxes imposed by section 11 or 1201" and inserting

19   "tax imposed by section 11".

20   (N) Section 6655(g)(1)(A)(i) is amended by

21   striking "or 1201(a),".

22   (O) Section 7518(g)(6)(A) is amended by strik-

23   ing "or 1201(a)".

190

1   (2) Section 1445(e)(1) is amended by striking

2 "35 percent (or, to the extent provided in regula-

3 tions, 20 percent)" and inserting "20 percent".

4   (3) Section 1445(e)(2) is amended by striking

5 "35 percent" and inserting "20 percent".

6   (4) Section 1445(e)(6) is amended by striking

7 "35 percent (or, to the extent provided in regula-

8 tions, 20 percent)" and inserting "20 percent".

9   (5)(A) Part I of subchapter B of chapter 5 is

10 amended by striking section 1551 (and by striking

11 the item relating to such section in the table of sec-

12 tions for such part).

13   (B) Section 12 is amended by striking para-

14 graph (6).

15   (C) Section 535(c)(5) is amended to read as

16 follows:

17   "(5) CROSS REFERENCE.—For limitation on

18 credit provided in paragraph (2) or (3) in the case

19 of certain controlled corporations, see section

20 1561.".

21   (6)(A) Section 1561, as amended by the pre-

22 ceding provisions of this Act, is amended to read as

23 follows:

191

1 **"SEC. 1561. LIMITATION ON ACCUMULATED EARNINGS**

2   **CREDIT IN THE CASE OF CERTAIN CON-**

3   **TROLLED CORPORATIONS.**

4   "(a) IN GENERAL.—The component members of a

5 controlled group of corporations on a December 31 shall,

6 for their taxable years which include such December 31,

7 be limited for purposes of this subtitle to one $250,000

8 ($150,000 if any component member is a corporation de-

9 scribed in section 535(c)(2)(B)) amount for purposes of

10 computing the accumulated earnings credit under section

11 535(c)(2) and (3). Such amount shall be divided equally

12 among the component members of such group on such De-

13 cember 31 unless the Secretary prescribes regulations per-

14 mitting an unequal allocation of such amount.

15   "(b) CERTAIN SHORT TAXABLE YEARS.—If a cor-

16 poration has a short taxable year which does not include

17 a December 31 and is a component member of a controlled

18 group of corporations with respect to such taxable year,

19 then for purposes of this subtitle, the amount to be used

20 in computing the accumulated earnings credit under sec-

21 tion 535(c)(2) and (3) of such corporation for such taxable

22 year shall be the amount specified in subsection (a) with

23 respect to such group, divided by the number of corpora-

24 tions which are component members of such group on the

25 last day of such taxable year. For purposes of the pre-

192

1 ceding sentence, section 1563(b) shall be applied as if such

2 last day were substituted for December 31.''.

3   (B) The table of sections for part II of sub-

4   chapter B of chapter 5 is amended by striking the

5   item relating to section 1561 and inserting the fol-

6   lowing new item:

> "Sec. 1561. Limitation on accumulated earnings credit in the case of certain controlled corporations.''.

7   (7) Section 7518(g)(6)(A) is amended—

8   (A) by striking "With respect to the por-

9   tion" and inserting "In the case of a taxpayer

10   other than a corporation, with respect to the

11   portion", and

12   (B) by striking "(34 percent in the case of

13   a corporation)''.

14 (c) EFFECTIVE DATE.—

15   (1) IN GENERAL.—Except as otherwise pro-

16   vided in this subsection, the amendments made by

17   this section shall apply to taxable years beginning

18   after December 31, 2017.

19   (2) CERTAIN CONFORMING AMENDMENTS.—The

20   amendments made by paragraphs (2), (3), and (4)

21   of subsection (b) shall apply to distributions after

22   December 31, 2017.

23 (d) NORMALIZATION REQUIREMENTS.—

1   (1) IN GENERAL.—A normalization method of

2 accounting shall not be treated as being used with

3 respect to any public utility property for purposes of

4 section 167 or 168 of the Internal Revenue Code of

5 1986 if the taxpayer, in computing its cost of service

6 for ratemaking purposes and reflecting operating re-

7 sults in its regulated books of account, reduces the

8 excess tax reserve more rapidly or to a greater ex-

9 tent than such reserve would be reduced under the

10 average rate assumption method.

11   (2) ALTERNATIVE METHOD FOR CERTAIN TAX-

12 PAYERS.—If, as of the first day of the taxable year

13 that includes the date of enactment of this Act—

14   (A) the taxpayer was required by a regu-

15   latory agency to compute depreciation for public

16   utility property on the basis of an average life

17   or composite rate method, and

18   (B) the taxpayer's books and underlying

19   records did not contain the vintage account

20   data necessary to apply the average rate as-

21   sumption method,

22 the taxpayer will be treated as using a normalization

23 method of accounting if, with respect to such juris-

24 diction, the taxpayer uses the alternative method for

1   public utility property that is subject to the regu-

2   latory authority of that jurisdiction.

3   (3) DEFINITIONS.—For purposes of this sub-

4   section—

5   (A) EXCESS TAX RESERVE.—The term

6   "excess tax reserve" means the excess of—

7   (i) the reserve for deferred taxes (as

8   described in section 168(i)(9)(A)(ii) of the

9   Internal Revenue Code of 1986 as in effect

10   on the day before the date of the enact-

11   ment of this Act), over

12   (ii) the amount which would be the

13   balance in such reserve if the amount of

14   such reserve were determined by assuming

15   that the corporate rate reductions provided

16   in this Act were in effect for all prior peri-

17   ods.

18   (B) AVERAGE RATE ASSUMPTION METH-

19   OD.—The average rate assumption method is

20   the method under which the excess in the re-

21   serve for deferred taxes is reduced over the re-

22   maining lives of the property as used in its reg-

23   ulated books of account which gave rise to the

24   reserve for deferred taxes. Under such method,

25   if timing differences for the property reverse,

1   the amount of the adjustment to the reserve for

2   the deferred taxes is calculated by multi-

3   plying—

4   (i) the ratio of the aggregate deferred

5   taxes for the property to the aggregate

6   timing differences for the property as of

7   the beginning of the period in question, by

8   (ii) the amount of the timing dif-

9   ferences which reverse during such period.

10   (C) ALTERNATIVE METHOD.—The "alter-

11   native method" is the method in which the tax-

12   payer—

13   (i) computes the excess tax reserve on

14   all public utility property included in the

15   plant account on the basis of the weighted

16   average life or composite rate used to com-

17   pute depreciation for regulatory purposes,

18   and

19   (ii) reduces the excess tax reserve rat-

20   ably over the remaining regulatory life of

21   the property.

22   (4) TAX INCREASED FOR NORMALIZATION VIO-

23   LATION.—If, for any taxable year ending after the

24   date of the enactment of this Act, the taxpayer does

25   not use a normalization method of accounting, the

196

1   taxpayer's tax for the taxable year shall be increased

2   by the amount by which it reduces its excess tax re-

3   serve more rapidly than permitted under a normal-

4   ization method of accounting.

Subtitle B—Cost Recovery

6 **SEC. 3101. INCREASED EXPENSING.**

7   (a) 100 PERCENT EXPENSING.—Section

8 168(k)(1)(A) is amended by striking "50 percent" and in-

9 serting "100 percent".

10   (b) EXTENSION THROUGH JANUARY 1, 2023.—Sec-

11 tion 168(k)(2) is amended—

12   (1) in subparagraph (A)(iii), by striking "Janu-

13   ary 1, 2020" and inserting "January 1, 2023",

14   (2) in subparagraph (B)(i)(II), by striking

15   "January 1, 2021" and inserting "January 1,

16   2024",

17   (3) in subparagraph (B)(i)(III), by striking

18   "January 1, 2020" and inserting "January 1,

19   2023",

20   (4) in subparagraph (B)(ii), by striking "Janu-

21   ary 1, 2020" in each place it appears and inserting

22   "January 1, 2023", and

23   (5) in subparagraph (E)(i), by striking "Janu-

24   ary 1, 2020" and replacing it with "January 1,

25   2023".

1 (c) APPLICATION TO USED PROPERTY.—

2   (1) IN GENERAL.—Section 168(k)(2)(A)(ii) is

3 amended to read as follows:

4   "(ii) the original use of which begins

5   with the taxpayer or the acquisition of

6   which by the taxpayer meets the require-

7   ments of clause (ii) of subparagraph (E),

8   and".

9   (2) ACQUISITION REQUIREMENTS.—Section

10 168(k)(2)(E)(ii) is amended to read as follows:

11   "(ii) ACQUISITION REQUIREMENTS.—

12   An acquisition of property meets the re-

13   quirements of this clause if—

14   "(I) such property was not used

15   by the taxpayer at any time prior to

16   such acquisition, and

17   "(II) the acquisition of such

18   property meets the requirements of

19   paragraphs (2)(A), (2)(B), (2)(C),

20   and (3) of section 179(d).",

21   (3) ANTI-ABUSE RULES.—Section 168(k)(2)(E)

22 is further amended by amending clause (iii)(I) to

23 read as follows:

1   "(I) property is used by a lessor

2   of such property and such use is the

3   lessor's first use of such property,".

4   (d) EXCEPTION FOR CERTAIN TRADES AND BUSI-

5 NESSES NOT SUBJECT TO LIMITATION ON INTEREST EX-

6 PENSE.—Section 168(k)(2), as amended by section 2001,

7 is amended by inserting after subparagraph (F) the fol-

8 lowing new subparagraph:

9   "(G) EXCEPTION FOR CERTAIN PROPERTY

10   OF REAL PROPERTY BUSINESSES AND REGU-

11   LATED UTILITIES.—The term 'qualified prop-

12   erty' shall not include any property used in a

13   trade or business described in subparagraph

14   (B) or (C) of section 163(j)(7).".

15   (e) COORDINATION WITH SECTION 280F.—Section

16 168(k)(2)(F) is amended—

17   (1) by striking "$8,000" in clauses (i) and (iii)

18 and inserting "$16,000", and

19   (2) in clause (iii)—

20   (A) by striking "placed in service by the

21   taxpayer after December 31, 2017" and insert-

22   ing "acquired by the taxpayer before September

23   28, 2017, and placed in service by the taxpayer

24   after September 27, 2017", and

1 (B) by redesignating subclauses (I) and

2 (II) as subclauses (II) and (III) respectively,

3 and inserting before clause (II), as so redesig-

4 nated, the following new subclause:

5 "(I) in the case of a passenger

6 automobile placed in service before

7 January 1, 2018, '$8,000',".

8 (f) CONFORMING AMENDMENTS.—

9 (1) Section (k)(2)(B)(i)(III), as amended, is

10 amended by inserting "binding" before "contract".

11 (2) Section 168(k)(5) is amended by—

12 (A) by striking "January 1, 2020" in sub-

13 paragraph (A) and inserting "January 1,

14 2023",

15 (B) by striking "50 percent" in subpara-

16 graph (A)(i) and inserting "100 percent", and

17 (C) by striking subparagraph (F).

18 (3) Section 168(k)(6) is amended to read as fol-

19 lows:

20 "(6) PHASE DOWN.—In the case of qualified

21 property acquired by the taxpayer before September

22 28, 2017, and placed in service by the taxpayer after

23 September 27, 2017, paragraph (1)(A) shall be ap-

24 plied by substituting for '100 percent'—

25 "(A) '50 percent' in the case of—

1   "(i) property placed in service before

2 January 1, 2018, and

3   "(ii) property described in subpara-

4 graph (B) or (C) of paragraph (2) which

5 is placed in service in 2018,

6 "(B) '40 percent' in the case of—

7   "(i) property placed in service in 2018

8 (other than property described in subpara-

9 graph (B) or (C) of paragraph (2)), and

10   "(ii) property described in subpara-

11 graph (B) or (C) of paragraph (2) which

12 is placed in service in 2019, and

13 "(C) '30 percent' in the case of—

14   "(i) property placed in service in 2019

15 (other than property described in subpara-

16 graph (B) or (C) of paragraph (2)), and

17   "(ii) property described in subpara-

18 graph (B) or (C) of paragraph (2) which

19 is placed in service in 2020.".

20   (4) The heading of section 168(k) is amended

21 by striking "SPECIAL ALLOWANCE FOR CERTAIN

22 PROPERTY ACQUIRED AFTER DECEMBER 31, 2007,

23 AND BEFORE JANUARY 1, 2020" and inserting

24 "FULL EXPENSING OF CERTAIN PROPERTY".

1   (5) Section 460(c)(6)(B)(ii) is amended by

2   striking "January 1, 2020 (January 1, 2021 in the

3   case of property described in section 168(k)(2)(B))"

4   and inserting "January 1, 2023 (January 1, 2024 in

5   the case of property described in section

6   168(k)(2)(B))".

7   (g) EFFECTIVE DATE.—

8   (1) IN GENERAL.—Except at provided by para-

9   graph (2), the amendments made by this section

10   shall apply to property which—

11   (A) is acquired after September 27, 2017,

12   and

13   (B) is placed in service after such date.

14   For purposes of the preceding sentence, property

15   shall not be treated as acquired after the date on

16   which a written binding contract is entered into for

17   such acquisition.

18   (2) SPECIFIED PLANTS.—The amendments

19   made by subsection (f)(2) shall apply to specified

20   plants planted or grafted after September 27, 2017.

21   (3) TRANSITION RULE.—In the case of any tax-

22   payer's first taxable year ending after September 27,

23   2017, the taxpayer may elect (at such time and in

24   such form and manner as the Secretary of the

25   Treasury, or his designee, may provide) to apply sec-

1   tion 168 of the Internal Revenue Code of 1986 with-

2   out regard to the amendments made by this section.

3   (4) LIMITATION ON NET OPERATING LOSS

4   CARRYBACKS ATTRIBUTABLE TO FULL EXPENS-

5   ING.—In the case of any taxable year which includes

6   any portion of the period beginning on September

7   28, 2017, and ending on December 31, 2017, the

8   amount of any net operating loss for such taxable

9   year which may be treated as a net operating loss

10   carryback (including any such carryback attributable

11   to any specified liability loss under section

12   172(b)(1)(C), any corporate equity reduction inter-

13   est loss under section 172(b)(1)(D), any eligible loss

14   under section 172(b)(1)(E), and any farming loss

15   under section 172(b)(1)(F)) shall be determined

16   without regard to the amendments made by this sec-

17   tion. For purposes of this paragraph, terms which

18   are used in section 172 of the Internal Revenue

19   Code of 1986 (determined without regard to the

20   amendments made by section 3302) shall have the

21   same meaning as when used in such section.

Subtitle C—Small Business Reforms

24   **SEC. 3201. EXPANSION OF SECTION 179 EXPENSING.**

25   (a) INCREASED DOLLAR LIMITATIONS.—

1   (1) IN GENERAL.—Section 179(b) is amend-

2 ed—

3   (A) by inserting "($5,000,000, in the case

4 of taxable years beginning before January 1,

5 2023)" after "$500,000" in paragraph (1), and

6   (B) by inserting "($20,000,000, in the

7 case of taxable years beginning before January

8 1, 2023)" after "$2,000,000" in paragraph (2).

9   (2) INFLATION ADJUSTMENT.—Section

10 179(b)(6) is amended to read as follows:

11   "(6) INFLATION ADJUSTMENT.—

12   "(A) IN GENERAL.—In the case of a tax-

13 able year beginning after 2015 (2018 in the

14 case of the $5,000,000 and $20,000,000

15 amounts in subsection (b)), each dollar amount

16 in subsection (b) shall be increased by an

17 amount equal to such dollar amount multiplied

18 by—

19   "(i) in the case of the $500,000 and

20 $2,000,000 amounts in subsection (b), the

21 cost-of-living adjustment determined under

22 section 1(c)(2) for the calendar year in

23 which the taxable year begins, determined

24 by substituting 'calendar year 2014' for

1   'calendar year 2016' in subparagraph
2   (A)(ii) thereof, and

3   ''(ii) in the case of the $5,000,000
4   and $20,000,000 amounts in subsection
5   (b), the cost-of-living adjustment deter-
6   mined under section 1(c)(2) for the cal-
7   endar year in which the taxable year be-
8   gins, determined by substituting 'calendar
9   year 2017' for 'calendar year 2016' in sub-
10   paragraph (A)(ii) thereof.

11   ''(B) ROUNDING.—The amount of any in-
12   crease under subparagraph (A) shall be round-
13   ed to the nearest multiple of $10,000
14   ($100,000 in the case of the $5,000,000 and
15   $20,000,000 amounts in subsection (b)).''.

16   (b) APPLICATION TO QUALIFIED ENERGY EFFICIENT
17   HEATING AND AIR-CONDITIONING PROPERTY.—

18   (1) IN GENERAL.—Section 179(f)(2) is amend-
19   ed by striking ''and'' at the end of subparagraph
20   (B), by striking the period at the end of subpara-
21   graph (C) and inserting '', and'', and by adding at
22   the end the following new subparagraph:

23   ''(D) qualified energy efficient heating and
24   air-conditioning property.''.

205

1   (2) QUALIFIED ENERGY EFFICIENT HEATING

2   AND AIR-CONDITIONING PROPERTY.—Section 179(f)

3   is amended by adding at the end the following new

4   paragraph:

5   "(3) QUALIFIED ENERGY EFFICIENT HEATING

6   AND AIR-CONDITIONING PROPERTY.—For purposes

7   of this subsection—

8   "(A) IN GENERAL.—The term 'qualified

9   energy efficient heating and air-conditioning

10   property' means any section 1250 property—

11   "(i) with respect to which depreciation

12   (or amortization in lieu of depreciation) is

13   allowable,

14   "(ii) which is installed as part of a

15   building's heating, cooling, ventilation, or

16   hot water system, and

17   "(iii) which is within the scope of

18   Standard 90.1–2007 or any successor

19   standard.

20   "(B) STANDARD 90.1–2007.—The term

21   'Standard 90.1–2007' means Standard 90.1–

22   2007 of the American Society of Heating, Re-

23   frigerating and Air-Conditioning Engineers and

24   the Illuminating Engineering Society of North

25   America (as in effect on the day before the date

1   of the adoption of Standard 90.1–2010 of such

2   Societies).".

3   (c) EFFECTIVE DATE.—

4   (1) INCREASED DOLLAR LIMITATIONS.—The

5   amendments made by subsection (a) shall apply to

6   taxable years beginning after December 31, 2017.

7   (2) APPLICATION TO QUALIFIED ENERGY EFFI-

8   CIENT HEATING AND AIR-CONDITIONING PROP-

9   ERTY.—The amendments made by subsection (b)

10   shall apply to property acquired and placed in serv-

11   ice after November 2, 2017. For purposes of the

12   preceding sentence, property shall not be treated as

13   acquired after the date on which a written binding

14   contract is entered into for such acquisition.

15   **SEC. 3202. SMALL BUSINESS ACCOUNTING METHOD RE-**

16   **FORM AND SIMPLIFICATION.**

17   (a) MODIFICATION OF LIMITATION ON CASH METH-

18   OD OF ACCOUNTING.—

19   (1) INCREASED LIMITATION.—So much of sec-

20   tion 448(c) as precedes paragraph (2) is amended to

21   read as follows:

22   "(c) GROSS RECEIPTS TEST.—For purposes of this

23   section—

24   "(1) IN GENERAL.—A corporation or partner-

25   ship meets the gross receipts test of this subsection

1 for any taxable year if the average annual gross re-

2 ceipts of such entity for the 3-taxable-year period

3 ending with the taxable year which precedes such

4 taxable year does not exceed $25,000,000.''.

5   (2) APPLICATION OF EXCEPTION ON ANNUAL

6 BASIS.—Section 448(b)(3) is amended to read as fol-

7 lows:

8   ''(3) ENTITIES WHICH MEET GROSS RECEIPTS

9 TEST.—Paragraphs (1) and (2) of subsection (a)

10 shall not apply to any corporation or partnership for

11 any taxable year if such entity (or any predecessor)

12 meets the gross receipts test of subsection (c) for

13 such taxable year.''.

14   (3) INFLATION ADJUSTMENT.—Section 448(c)

15 is amended by adding at the end the following new

16 paragraph:

17   ''(4) ADJUSTMENT FOR INFLATION.—In the

18 case of any taxable year beginning after December

19 31, 2018, the dollar amount in paragraph (1) shall

20 be increased by an amount equal to—

21   ''(A) such dollar amount, multiplied by

22   ''(B) the cost-of-living adjustment deter-

23   mined under section 1(c)(2) for the calendar

24   year in which the taxable year begins, by sub-

1 stituting 'calendar year 2017' for 'calendar year

2 2016' in subparagraph (A)(ii) thereof.

3 If any amount as increased under the preceding sen-

4 tence is not a multiple of $1,000,000, such amount

5 shall be rounded to the nearest multiple of

6 $1,000,000.''.

7 (4) COORDINATION WITH SECTION 481.—Sec-

8 tion 448(d)(7) is amended to read as follows:

9 ''(7) COORDINATION WITH SECTION 481.—Any

10 change in method of accounting made pursuant to

11 this section shall be treated for purposes of section

12 481 as initiated by the taxpayer and made with the

13 consent of the Secretary.''.

14 (5) APPLICATION OF EXCEPTION TO CORPORA-

15 TIONS ENGAGED IN FARMING.—

16 (A) IN GENERAL.—Section 447(c) is

17 amended—

18 (i) by inserting ''for any taxable year''

19 after ''not being a corporation'' in the mat-

20 ter preceding paragraph (1), and

21 (ii) by amending paragraph (2) to

22 read as follows:

23 ''(2) a corporation which meets the gross re-

24 ceipts test of section 448(c) for such taxable year.''.

1   (B) COORDINATION WITH SECTION 481.—

2   Section 447(f) is amended to read as follows:

3   "(f) COORDINATION WITH SECTION 481.—Any

4 change in method of accounting made pursuant to this

5 section shall be treated for purposes of section 481 as ini-

6 tiated by the taxpayer and made with the consent of the

7 Secretary.".

8   (C) CONFORMING AMENDMENTS.—Section

9   447 is amended—

10   (i) by striking subsections (d), (e),

11   (h), and (i), and

12   (ii) by redesignating subsections (f)

13   and (g) (as amended by subparagraph (B))

14   as subsections (d) and (e), respectively.

15   (b) EXEMPTION FROM UNICAP REQUIREMENTS.—

16   (1) IN GENERAL.—Section 263A is amended by

17 redesignating subsection (i) as subsection (j) and by

18 inserting after subsection (h) the following new sub-

19 section:

20   "(i) EXEMPTION FOR CERTAIN SMALL BUSI-

21 NESSES.—

22   "(1) IN GENERAL.—In the case of any taxpayer

23 (other than a tax shelter prohibited from using the

24 cash receipts and disbursements method of account-

25 ing under section 448(a)(3)) which meets the gross

1 receipts test of section 448(c) for any taxable year,
2 this section shall not apply with respect to such tax-
3 payer for such taxable year.

4   "(2) APPLICATION OF GROSS RECEIPTS TEST
5 TO INDIVIDUALS, ETC.— In the case of any taxpayer
6 which is not a corporation or a partnership, the
7 gross receipts test of section 448(c) shall be applied
8 in the same manner as if each trade or business of
9 such taxpayer were a corporation or partnership.

10   "(3) COORDINATION WITH SECTION 481.—Any
11 change in method of accounting made pursuant to
12 this subsection shall be treated for purposes of sec-
13 tion 481 as initiated by the taxpayer and made with
14 the consent of the Secretary.".

15   (2) CONFORMING AMENDMENT.—Section
16 263A(b)(2) is amended to read as follows:

17   "(2) PROPERTY ACQUIRED FOR RESALE.—Real
18 or personal property described in section 1221(a)(1)
19 which is acquired by the taxpayer for resale.".

20   (c) EXEMPTION FROM INVENTORIES.—Section 471
21 is amended by redesignating subsection (c) as subsection
22 (d) and by inserting after subsection (b) the following new
23 subsection:

24   "(c) EXEMPTION FOR CERTAIN SMALL BUSI-
25 NESSES.—

1   "(1) IN GENERAL.—In the case of any taxpayer

2 (other than a tax shelter prohibited from using the

3 cash receipts and disbursements method of account-

4 ing under section 448(a)(3)) which meets the gross

5 receipts test of section 448(c) for any taxable year—

6   "(A) subsection (a) shall not apply with re-

7   spect to such taxpayer for such taxable year,

8   and

9   "(B) the taxpayer's method of accounting

10   for inventory for such taxable year shall not be

11   treated as failing to clearly reflect income if

12   such method either—

13   "(i) treats inventory as non-incidental

14   materials and supplies, or

15   "(ii) conforms to such taxpayer's

16   method of accounting reflected in an appli-

17   cable financial statement of the taxpayer

18   with respect to such taxable year or, if the

19   taxpayer does not have any applicable fi-

20   nancial statement with respect to such tax-

21   able year, the books and records of the

22   taxpayer prepared in accordance with the

23   taxpayer's accounting procedures.

1   "(2) APPLICABLE FINANCIAL STATEMENT.—

2   For purposes of this subsection, the term 'applicable

3   financial statement' means—

4   "(A) a financial statement which is cer-

5   tified as being prepared in accordance with gen-

6   erally accepted accounting principles and which

7   is—

8   "(i) a 10-K (or successor form), or

9   annual statement to shareholders, required

10   to be filed by the taxpayer with the United

11   States Securities and Exchange Commis-

12   sion,

13   "(ii) an audited financial statement of

14   the taxpayer which is used for—

15   "(I) credit purposes,

16   "(II) reporting to shareholders,

17   partners, or other proprietors, or to

18   beneficiaries, or

19   "(III) any other substantial

20   nontax purpose,

21   but only if there is no statement of the

22   taxpayer described in clause (i), or

23   "(iii) filed by the taxpayer with any

24   other Federal or State agency for nontax

25   purposes, but only if there is no statement

1   of the taxpayer described in clause (i) or

2   (ii), or

3   ''(B) a financial statement of the taxpayer

4   which—

5   ''(i) is used for a purpose described in

6   subclause (I), (II), or (III) of subpara-

7   graph (A)(ii), or

8   ''(ii) filed by the taxpayer with any

9   regulatory or governmental body (whether

10   domestic or foreign) specified by the Sec-

11   retary,

12   but only if there is no statement of the taxpayer

13   described in subparagraph (A).

14   ''(3) APPLICATION OF GROSS RECEIPTS TEST

15 TO INDIVIDUALS, ETC.—In the case of any taxpayer

16 which is not a corporation or a partnership, the

17 gross receipts test of section 448(c) shall be applied

18 in the same manner as if each trade or business of

19 such taxpayer were a corporation or partnership.

20   ''(4) COORDINATION WITH SECTION 481.—Any

21 change in method of accounting made pursuant to

22 this subsection shall be treated for purposes of sec-

23 tion 481 as initiated by the taxpayer and made with

24 the consent of the Secretary.''.

214

1   (d) EXEMPTION FROM PERCENTAGE COMPLETION

2 FOR LONG-TERM CONTRACTS.—

3   (1) IN GENERAL.—Section 460(e)(1)(B) is

4   amended—

5   (A) by inserting "(other than a tax shelter

6   prohibited from using the cash receipts and dis-

7   bursements method of accounting under section

8   448(a)(3))" after "taxpayer" in the matter pre-

9   ceding clause (i), and

10   (B) by amending clause (ii) to read as fol-

11   lows:

12   "(ii) who meets the gross receipts test

13   of section 448(c) for the taxable year in

14   which such contract is entered into.".

15   (2) CONFORMING AMENDMENTS.—Section

16   460(e) is amended by striking paragraphs (2) and

17   (3), by redesignating paragraphs (4), (5), and (6) as

18   paragraphs (3), (4), and (5), respectively, and by in-

19   serting after paragraph (1) the following new para-

20   graph:

21   "(2) RULES RELATED TO GROSS RECEIPTS

22   TEST.—

23   "(A) APPLICATION OF GROSS RECEIPTS

24   TEST TO INDIVIDUALS, ETC.— For purposes of

25   paragraph (1)(B)(ii), in the case of any tax-

1   payer which is not a corporation or a partner-

2   ship, the gross receipts test of section 448(c)

3   shall be applied in the same manner as if each

4   trade or business of such taxpayer were a cor-

5   poration or partnership.

6   "(B) COORDINATION WITH SECTION 481.—

7   Any change in method of accounting made pur-

8   suant to paragraph (1)(B)(ii) shall be treated

9   as initiated by the taxpayer and made with the

10   consent of the Secretary. Such change shall be

11   effected on a cut-off basis for all similarly clas-

12   sified contracts entered into on or after the

13   year of change.".

14   (e) EFFECTIVE DATE.—

15   (1) IN GENERAL.—Except as otherwise pro-

16   vided in this subsection, the amendments made by

17   this section shall apply to taxable years beginning

18   after December 31, 2017.

19   (2) PRESERVATION OF SUSPENSE ACCOUNT

20   RULES WITH RESPECT TO ANY EXISTING SUSPENSE

21   ACCOUNTS.—So much of the amendments made by

22   subsection (a)(5)(C) as relate to section 447(i) of

23   the Internal Revenue Code of 1986 shall not apply

24   with respect to any suspense account established

1 under such section before the date of the enactment

2 of this Act.

3   (3) EXEMPTION FROM PERCENTAGE COMPLE-

4 TION FOR LONG-TERM CONTRACTS.—The amend-

5 ments made by subsection (d) shall apply to con-

6 tracts entered into after December 31, 2017, in tax-

7 able years ending after such date.

8 **SEC. 3203. SMALL BUSINESS EXCEPTION FROM LIMITATION**

9   **ON DEDUCTION OF BUSINESS INTEREST.**

10 (a) IN GENERAL.—Section 163(j)(2), as amended by

11 section 3301, is amended to read as follows:

12   "(2) EXEMPTION FOR CERTAIN SMALL BUSI-

13 NESSES.—In the case of any taxpayer (other than a

14 tax shelter prohibited from using the cash receipts

15 and disbursements method of accounting under sec-

16 tion 448(a)(3)) which meets the gross receipts test

17 of section 448(c) for any taxable year, paragraph (1)

18 shall not apply to such taxpayer for such taxable

19 year. In the case of any taxpayer which is not a cor-

20 poration or a partnership, the gross receipts test of

21 section 448(c) shall be applied in the same manner

22 as if such taxpayer were a corporation or partner-

23 ship.".

217

1   (b) EFFECTIVE DATE.—The amendment made by
2 this section shall apply to taxable years beginning after
3 December 31, 2017.

Subtitle D—Reform of Business-related Exclusions, Deductions, etc.

6 **SEC. 3301. INTEREST.**

7   (a) IN GENERAL.—Section 163(j) is amended to read
8 as follows:

9   "(j) LIMITATION ON BUSINESS INTEREST.—

10   "(1) IN GENERAL.—In the case of any taxpayer
11   for any taxable year, the amount allowed as a deduc-
12   tion under this chapter for business interest shall
13   not exceed the sum of—

14   "(A) the business interest income of such
15   taxpayer for such taxable year, plus

16   "(B) 30 percent of the adjusted taxable in-
17   come of such taxpayer for such taxable year.

18 The amount determined under subparagraph (B)
19 (after any increases in such amount under para-
20 graph (3)(A)(iii)) shall not be less than zero.

21   "(2) EXEMPTION FOR CERTAIN SMALL BUSI-
22 NESSES.—For exemption for certain small busi-
23 nesses, see the amendment made by section 3204 of
24 the Tax Cuts and Jobs Act.

25   "(3) APPLICATION TO PARTNERSHIPS, ETC.—

218

1   "(A) IN GENERAL.—In the case of any

2 partnership—

3   "(i) this subsection shall be applied at

4 the partnership level and any deduction for

5 business interest shall be taken into ac-

6 count in determining the non-separately

7 stated taxable income or loss of the part-

8 nership,

9   "(ii) the adjusted taxable income of

10 each partner of such partnership shall be

11 determined without regard to such part-

12 ner's distributive share of the non-sepa-

13 rately stated taxable income or loss of such

14 partnership, and

15   "(iii) the amount determined under

16 paragraph (1)(B) with respect to each

17 partner of such partnership shall be in-

18 creased by such partner's distributive

19 share of such partnership's excess amount.

20   "(B) EXCESS AMOUNT.—The term 'excess

21 amount' means, with respect to any partner-

22 ship, the excess (if any) of—

23   "(i) 30 percent of the adjusted taxable

24 income of the partnership, over

1   "(ii) the amount (if any) by which the

2   business interest of the partnership ex-

3   ceeds the business interest income of the

4   partnership.

5   "(C) APPLICATION TO S CORPORATIONS.—

6   Rules similar to the rules of subparagraphs (A)

7   and (B) shall apply with respect to any S cor-

8   poration and its shareholders.

9   "(4) BUSINESS INTEREST.—For purposes of

10   this subsection, the term 'business interest' means

11   any interest paid or accrued on indebtedness prop-

12   erly allocable to a trade or business. Such term shall

13   not include investment interest (within the meaning

14   of subsection (d)).

15   "(5) BUSINESS INTEREST INCOME.—For pur-

16   poses of this subsection, the term 'business interest

17   income' means the amount of interest includible in

18   the gross income of the taxpayer for the taxable year

19   which is properly allocable to a trade or business.

20   Such term shall not include investment income

21   (within the meaning of subsection (d)).

22   "(6) ADJUSTED TAXABLE INCOME.—For pur-

23   poses of this subsection, the term 'adjusted taxable

24   income' means the taxable income of the taxpayer—

25   "(A) computed without regard to—

1   "(i) any item of income, gain, deduc-

2   tion, or loss which is not properly allocable

3   to a trade or business,

4   "(ii) any business interest or business

5   interest income,

6   "(iii) the amount of any net operating

7   loss deduction under section 172, and

8   "(iv) any deduction allowable for de-

9   preciation, amortization, or depletion, and

10   "(B) computed with such other adjust-

11   ments as the Secretary may provide.

12   "(7) TRADE OR BUSINESS.—For purposes of

13 this subsection, the term 'trade or business' shall not

14 include—

15   "(A) the trade or business of performing

16   services as an employee,

17   "(B) a real property trade or business (as

18   such term is defined in section 469(c)(7)(C)),

19   or

20   "(C) the trade or business of the fur-

21   nishing or sale of—

22   "(i) electrical energy, water, or sewage

23   disposal services,

24   "(ii) gas or steam through a local dis-

25   tribution system, or

1   "(iii) transportation of gas or steam

2   by pipeline, or

3   if the rates for such furnishing or sale, as the

4   case may be, have been established or approved

5   by a State or political subdivision thereof, by

6   any agency or instrumentality of the United

7   States, or by a public service or public utility

8   commission or other similar body of any State

9   or political subdivision thereof.

10   "(8) CARRYFORWARD OF DISALLOWED INTER-

11 EST.—For carryforward of interest disallowed under

12 paragraph (1), see subsection (o).".

13   (b) CARRYFORWARD OF DISALLOWED BUSINESS IN-

14 TEREST.—Section 163, after amendment by section

15 4302(a) and before amendment by section 4302(b), is

16 amended by inserting after subsection (n) the following

17 new subsection:

18   "(o) CARRYFORWARD OF DISALLOWED BUSINESS IN-

19 TEREST.—The amount of any business interest not al-

20 lowed as a deduction for any taxable year by reason of

21 subsection (j) shall be treated as business interest paid

22 or accrued in the succeeding taxable year. Business inter-

23 est paid or accrued in any taxable year (determined with-

24 out regard to the preceding sentence) shall not be carried

25 past the 5th taxable year following such taxable year, de-

1 termined by treating business interest as allowed as a de-

2 duction on a first-in, first-out basis.''.

3　(c) TREATMENT OF CARRYFORWARD OF DIS-

4 ALLOWED BUSINESS INTEREST IN CERTAIN CORPORATE

5 ACQUISITIONS.—

6　　(1) IN GENERAL.—Section 381(c) is amended

7　　by inserting after paragraph (19) the following new

8　　paragraph:

9　　　"(20) CARRYFORWARD OF DISALLOWED INTER-

10　　EST.—The carryover of disallowed interest described

11　　in section 163(o) to taxable years ending after the

12　　date of distribution or transfer.''.

13　　(2) APPLICATION OF LIMITATION.—Section

14　　382(d) is amended by adding at the end the fol-

15　　lowing new paragraph:

16　　　"(3) APPLICATION TO CARRYFORWARD OF DIS-

17　　ALLOWED INTEREST.—The term 'pre-change loss'

18　　shall include any carryover of disallowed interest de-

19　　scribed in section 163(o) under rules similar to the

20　　rules of paragraph (1).''.

21　　(3) CONFORMING AMENDMENT.—Section

22　　382(k)(1) is amended by inserting after the first

23　　sentence the following: "Such term shall include any

24　　corporation entitled to use a carryforward of dis-

25　　allowed interest described in section 381(c)(20)."

1   (d) EFFECTIVE DATE.—The amendments made by
2 this section shall apply to taxable years beginning after
3 December 31, 2017.

4 **SEC. 3302. MODIFICATION OF NET OPERATING LOSS DE-**
5   **DUCTION.**

6   (a) INDEFINITE CARRYFORWARD OF NET OPER-
7 ATING LOSSES.—Section 172(b)(1)(A)(ii) is amended by
8 striking "to each of the 20 taxable years" and inserting
9 "to each taxable year".

10   (b) REPEAL OF NET OPERATING LOSS CARRYBACKS
11 OTHER THAN 1-YEAR CARRYBACK OF ELIGIBLE DIS-
12 ASTER LOSSES.—

13   (1) IN GENERAL.—Section 172(b)(1)(A)(i) is
14   amended to read as follows:

15   "(i) in the case of any portion of a net
16   operating loss for the taxable year which is
17   an eligible disaster loss with respect to the
18   taxpayer, shall be a net operating loss
19   carryback to the taxable year preceding the
20   taxable year of such loss, and".

21   (2) CONFORMING AMENDMENTS.—

22   (A) Section 172(b)(1) is amended by strik-
23   ing subparagraphs (B) through (F) and insert-
24   ing the following:

25   "(B) ELIGIBLE DISASTER LOSS.—

1   "(i) IN GENERAL.—For purposes of

2   subparagraph (A)(i), the term 'eligible dis-

3   aster loss' means—

4   "(I) in the case of a taxpayer

5   which is a small business, net oper-

6   ating losses attributable to federally

7   declared disasters (as defined by sec-

8   tion 165(i)(5)), and

9   "(II) in the case of a taxpayer

10   engaged in the trade or business of

11   farming, net operating losses attrib-

12   utable to such federally declared dis-

13   asters.

14   "(ii) SMALL BUSINESS.—For purposes

15   of this subparagraph, the term 'small busi-

16   ness' means a corporation or partnership

17   which meets the gross receipts test of sec-

18   tion 448(c) (determined by substituting

19   '$5,000,000' for '$25,000,000' each place

20   it appears therein) for the taxable year in

21   which the loss arose (or, in the case of a

22   sole proprietorship, which would meet such

23   test if such proprietorship were a corpora-

24   tion).

225

1   "(iii) TRADE OR BUSINESS OF FARM-

2   ING.—For purposes of this subparagraph,

3   the trade or business of farming shall in-

4   clude the trade or business of—

5   "(I) operating a nursery or sod

6   farm, or

7   "(II) the raising or harvesting of

8   trees bearing fruit, nuts, or other

9   crops, or ornamental trees.

10   For purposes of subclause (II), an ever-

11   green tree which is more than 6 years old

12   at the time severed from the roots shall

13   not be treated as an ornamental tree.".

14   (B) Section 172 is amended by striking

15 subsections (f), (g), and (h).

16 (c) LIMITATION OF NET OPERATING LOSS TO 90

17 PERCENT OF TAXABLE INCOME.—

18   (1) IN GENERAL.—Section 172(a) is amended

19 to read as follows:

20 "(a) DEDUCTION ALLOWED.—There shall be allowed

21 as a deduction for the taxable year an amount equal to

22 the lesser of—

23   "(1) the aggregate of the net operating loss

24 carryovers to such year, plus the net operating loss

25 carrybacks to such year, or

1   "(2) 90 percent of taxable income computed

2   without regard to the deduction allowable under this

3   section.

4 For purposes of this subtitle, the term 'net operating loss

5 deduction' means the deduction allowed by this sub-

6 section.".

7   (2) COORDINATION OF LIMITATION WITH

8   CARRYBACKS AND CARRYOVERS.—Section 172(b)(2)

9   is amended by striking "shall be computed—" and

10   all that follows and inserting "shall—

11   "(A) be computed with the modifications

12   specified in subsection (d) other than para-

13   graphs (1), (4), and (5) thereof, and by deter-

14   mining the amount of the net operating loss de-

15   duction without regard to the net operating loss

16   for the loss year or for any taxable year there-

17   after,

18   "(B) not be considered to be less than

19   zero, and

20   "(C) not exceed the amount determined

21   under subsection (a)(2) for such prior taxable

22   year.".

23   (3) CONFORMING AMENDMENT.—Section

24   172(d)(6) is amended by striking "and" at the end

25   of subparagraph (A), by striking the period at the

1   end of subparagraph (B) and inserting "; and", and

2   by adding at the end the following new subpara-

3   graph:

4   "(C) subsection (a)(2) shall be applied by

5   substituting 'real estate investment trust tax-

6   able income (as defined in section 857(b)(2) but

7   without regard to the deduction for dividends

8   paid (as defined in section 561))' for 'taxable

9   income'.".

10   (d) ANNUAL INCREASE OF INDEFINITE CARRYOVER

11   AMOUNTS.—Section 172(b) is amended by redesignating

12   paragraph (3) as paragraph (4) and by inserting after

13   paragraph (2) the following new paragraph:

14   "(3) ANNUAL INCREASE OF INDEFINITE CARRY-

15   OVER AMOUNTS.—For purposes of paragraph (2)—

16   "(A) the amount of any indefinite net op-

17   erating loss which is carried to the next suc-

18   ceeding taxable year after the loss year (within

19   the meaning of paragraph (2)) shall be in-

20   creased by an amount equal to—

21   "(i) the amount of the loss which may

22   be so carried over to such succeeding tax-

23   able year (determined without regard to

24   this paragraph), multiplied by

25   "(ii) the sum of—

1   "(I) the annual Federal short-

2   term rate (determined under section

3   1274(d)) for the last month ending

4   before the beginning of such taxable

5   year, plus

6   "(II) 4 percentage points, and

7   "(B) the amount of any indefinite net op-

8 erating loss which is carried to any succeeding

9 taxable year (after such next succeeding taxable

10 year) shall be an amount equal to—

11   "(i) the excess of—

12   "(I) the amount of the loss car-

13   ried to the prior taxable year (after

14   any increase under this paragraph

15   with respect to such amount), over

16   "(II) the amount by which such

17   loss was reduced under paragraph (2)

18   by reason of the taxable income for

19   such prior taxable year, multiplied by

20   "(ii) a percentage equal to 100 per-

21   cent plus the percentage determined under

22   subparagraph (A)(ii) with respect to such

23   succeeding taxable year.

24 For purposes of the preceding sentence, the

25 term 'indefinite net operating loss' means any

229

1   net operating loss arising in a taxable year be-
2   ginning after December 31, 2017.''.

3   (e) EFFECTIVE DATE.—

4   (1) CARRYFORWARDS AND CARRYBACKS.—The
5   amendments made by subsections (a) and (b) shall
6   apply to net operating losses arising in taxable years
7   beginning after December 31, 2017.

8   (2) NET OPERATING LOSS LIMITED TO 90 PER-
9   CENT OF TAXABLE INCOME.—The amendments
10   made by subsection (c) shall apply to taxable years
11   beginning after December 31, 2017.

12   (3) ANNUAL INCREASE IN CARRYOVER
13   AMOUNTS.—The amendments made by subsection
14   (d) shall apply to amounts carried to taxable years
15   beginning after December 31, 2017.

16   (4) SPECIAL RULE FOR NET DISASTER
17   LOSSES.—Notwithstanding paragraph (1), the
18   amendments made by subsection (b) shall not apply
19   to the portion of the net operating loss for any tax-
20   able year which is a net disaster loss to which sec-
21   tion 504(b) of the Disaster Tax Relief and Airport
22   and Airway Extension Act of 2017 applies.

1 **SEC. 3303. LIKE-KIND EXCHANGES OF REAL PROPERTY.**

2   (a) IN GENERAL.—Section 1031(a)(1) is amended by

3 striking "property" each place it appears and inserting

4 "real property".

5   (b) CONFORMING AMENDMENTS.—

6   (1) Paragraph (2) of section 1031(a) is amend-

7   ed to read as follows:

8   "(2) EXCEPTION FOR REAL PROPERTY HELD

9   FOR SALE.—This subsection shall not apply to any

10   exchange of real property held primarily for sale.".

11   (2) Section 1031 is amended by striking sub-

12   sections (e) and (i).

13   (3) Section 1031, as amended by paragraph

14   (2), is amended by inserting after subsection (d) the

15   following new subsection:

16   "(e) APPLICATION TO CERTAIN PARTNERSHIPS.—

17 For purposes of this section, an interest in a partnership

18 which has in effect a valid election under section 761(a)

19 to be excluded from the application of all of subchapter

20 K shall be treated as an interest in each of the assets of

21 such partnership and not as an interest in a partnership.".

22   (4) Section 1031(h) is amended to read as fol-

23   lows:

24   "(h) SPECIAL RULES FOR FOREIGN REAL PROP-

25 ERTY.—Real property located in the United States and

1 real property located outside the United States are not

2 property of a like kind.''.

3   (5) The heading of section 1031 is amended by

4 striking "**PROPERTY**" and inserting "**REAL PROP-**

5 **ERTY**".

6   (6) The table of sections for part III of sub-

7 chapter O of chapter 1 is amended by striking the

8 item relating to section 1031 and inserting the fol-

9 lowing new item:

"Sec. 1031. Exchange of real property held for productive use or investment.''.

10   (c) EFFECTIVE DATE.—

11   (1) IN GENERAL.—Except as otherwise pro-

12 vided in this subsection, the amendments made by

13 this section shall apply to exchanges completed after

14 December 31, 2017.

15   (2) TRANSITION RULE.—The amendments

16 made by this section shall not apply to any exchange

17 if—

18   (A) the property disposed of by the tax-

19   payer in the exchange is disposed of on or be-

20   fore December 31 2017, or

21   (B) the property received by the taxpayer

22   in the exchange is received on or before Decem-

23   ber 31, 2017.

1 **SEC. 3304. REVISION OF TREATMENT OF CONTRIBUTIONS**
2 **TO CAPITAL.**

3 (a) INCLUSION OF CONTRIBUTIONS TO CAPITAL.—
4 Part II of subchapter B of chapter 1 is amended by insert-
5 ing after section 75 the following new section:

6 **"SEC. 76. CONTRIBUTIONS TO CAPITAL.**

7 "(a) IN GENERAL.—Gross income includes any con-
8 tribution to the capital of any entity.

9 "(b) TREATMENT OF CONTRIBUTIONS IN EXCHANGE
10 FOR STOCK, ETC.—

11 "(1) IN GENERAL.—In the case of any con-
12 tribution of money or other property to a corpora-
13 tion in exchange for stock of such corporation—

14 "(A) such contribution shall not be treated
15 for purposes of subsection (a) as a contribution
16 to the capital of such corporation (and shall not
17 be includible in the gross income of such cor-
18 poration), and

19 "(B) no gain or loss shall be recognized to
20 such corporation upon the issuance of such
21 stock.

22 "(2) TREATMENT LIMITED TO VALUE OF
23 STOCK.—For purposes of this subsection, a contribu-
24 tion of money or other property to a corporation
25 shall be treated as being in exchange for stock of
26 such corporation only to the extent that the fair

1   market value of such money and other property does

2   not exceed the fair market value of such stock.

3   "(3) APPLICATION TO ENTITIES OTHER THAN

4   CORPORATIONS.—In the case of any entity other

5   than a corporation, rules similar to the rules of

6   paragraphs (1) and (2) shall apply in the case of

7   any contribution of money or other property to such

8   entity in exchange for any interest in such entity.

9   "(c) TREASURY STOCK TREATED AS STOCK.—Any

10 reference in this section to stock shall be treated as includ-

11 ing a reference to treasury stock.".

12 (b) BASIS OF CORPORATION IN CONTRIBUTED PROP-

13 ERTY.—

14   (1) CONTRIBUTIONS TO CAPITAL.—Subsection

15 (c) of section 362 is amended to read as follows:

16 "(c) CONTRIBUTIONS TO CAPITAL.—If property

17 other than money is transferred to a corporation as a con-

18 tribution to the capital of such corporation (within the

19 meaning of section 76) then the basis of such property

20 shall be the greater of—

21   "(1) the basis determined in the hands of the

22 transferor, increased by the amount of gain recog-

23 nized to the transferor on such transfer, or

234

1   "(2) the amount included in gross income by

2 such corporation under section 76 with respect to

3 such contribution.".

4   (2) CONTRIBUTIONS IN EXCHANGE FOR

5 STOCK.—Paragraph (2) of section 362(a) is amend-

6 ed by striking "contribution to capital" and insert-

7 ing "contribution in exchange for stock of such cor-

8 poration (determined under rules similar to the rules

9 of paragraphs (2) and (3) of section 76(b))".

10   (c) CONFORMING AMENDMENTS.—

11   (1) Section 108(e) is amended by striking para-

12 graph (6).

13   (2) Part III of subchapter B of chapter 1 is

14 amended by striking section 118 (and by striking

15 the item relating to such section in the table of sec-

16 tions for such part).

17   (3) The table of sections for part II of sub-

18 chapter B of chapter 1 is amended by inserting after

19 the item relating to section 75 the following new

20 item:

"Sec. 76. Contributions to capital.".

21   (d) EFFECTIVE DATE.—The amendments made by

22 this section shall apply to contributions made, and trans-

23 actions entered into, after the date of the enactment of

24 this Act.

1 **SEC. 3305. REPEAL OF DEDUCTION FOR LOCAL LOBBYING**

2 **EXPENSES.**

3 (a) IN GENERAL.—Section 162(e) is amended by

4 striking paragraphs (2) and (7) and by redesignating

5 paragraphs (3), (4), (5), (6), and (8) as paragraphs (2),

6 (3), (4), (5), and (6), respectively.

7 (b) CONFORMING AMENDMENT.—Section

8 6033(e)(1)(B)(ii) is amended by striking "section

9 162(e)(5)(B)(ii)" and inserting "section

10 162(e)(4)(B)(ii)".

11 (c) EFFECTIVE DATE.—The amendments made by

12 this section shall apply to amounts paid or incurred after

13 December 31, 2017.

14 **SEC. 3306. REPEAL OF DEDUCTION FOR INCOME ATTRIB-**

15 **UTABLE TO DOMESTIC PRODUCTION ACTIVI-**

16 **TIES.**

17 (a) IN GENERAL.—Part VI of subchapter B of chap-

18 ter 1 is amended by striking section 199 (and by striking

19 the item relating to such section in the table of sections

20 for such part).

21 (b) CONFORMING AMENDMENTS.—

22 (1) Sections 74(d)(2)(B), 86(b)(2)(A),

23 137(b)(3)(A), and 246(b)(1) are each amended by

24 striking "199,".

25 (2) Section 170(b)(2)(D), as amended by the

26 preceding provisions of this Act, is amended by

236

1 striking clause (iv), by redesignating clause (v) as

2 clause (iv), and by inserting "and" at the end of

3 clause (iii).

4 (3) Section 172(d) is amended by striking para-

5 graph (7).

6 (4) Section 613(a) is amended by striking "and

7 without the deduction under section 199".

8 (5) Section 613A(d)(1) is amended by striking

9 subparagraph (B) and by redesignating subpara-

10 graphs (C), (D), and (E) as subparagraphs (B), (C),

11 and (D), respectively.

12 (6) Section 1402(a) is amended by adding

13 "and" at the end of paragraph (15) and by striking

14 paragraph (16).

15 (c) EFFECTIVE DATE.—The amendments made by

16 this section shall apply to taxable years beginning after

17 December 31, 2017.

18 **SEC. 3307. ENTERTAINMENT, ETC. EXPENSES.**

19 (a) DENIAL OF DEDUCTION.—Subsection (a) of sec-

20 tion 274 is amended to read as follows:

21 "(a) ENTERTAINMENT, AMUSEMENT, RECREATION,

22 AND OTHER FRINGE BENEFITS .—

23 "(1) IN GENERAL.—No deduction otherwise al-

24 lowable under this chapter shall be allowed for

237

1   amounts paid or incurred for any of the following

2   items:

3   "(A) ACTIVITY.—With respect to an activ-

4   ity which is of a type generally considered to

5   constitute entertainment, amusement, or recre-

6   ation.

7   "(B) MEMBERSHIP DUES.—With respect

8   to membership in any club organized for busi-

9   ness, pleasure, recreation or other social pur-

10   poses.

11   "(C) AMENITY.—With respect to a de

12   minimis fringe (as defined in section 132(e)(1))

13   that is primarily personal in nature and involv-

14   ing property or services that are not directly re-

15   lated to the taxpayer's trade or business.

16   "(D) FACILITY.—With respect to a facility

17   or portion thereof used in connection with an

18   activity referred to in subparagraph (A), mem-

19   bership dues or similar amounts referred to in

20   subparagraph (B), or an amenity referred to in

21   subparagraph (C).

22   "(E)   QUALIFIED   TRANSPORTATION

23   FRINGE AND PARKING FACILITY.—Which is a

24   qualified transportation fringe (as defined in

25   section 132(f)) or which is a parking facility

238

1   used in connection with qualified parking (as

2   defined in section 132(f)(5)(C)).

3   "(F) ON-PREMISES ATHLETIC FACILITY.—

4   Which is an on-premises athletic facility as de-

5   fined in section 132(j)(4)(B).

6   "(2) SPECIAL RULES.—For purposes of apply-

7 ing paragraph (1), an activity described in section

8 212 shall be treated as a trade or business.

9   "(3) REGULATIONS.—Under the regulations

10 prescribed to carry out this section, the Secretary

11 shall include regulations—

12   "(A) defining entertainment, amenities,

13   recreation, amusement, and facilities for pur-

14   poses of this subsection,

15   "(B) providing for the appropriate alloca-

16   tion of depreciation and other costs with respect

17   to facilities used for parking or for on-premises

18   athletic facilities, and

19   "(C) specifying arrangements a primary

20   purpose of which is the avoidance of this sub-

21   section.".

22   (b) EXCEPTION FOR CERTAIN EXPENSES INCLUD-

23 IBLE IN INCOME OF RECIPIENT.—

239

1   (1) EXPENSES TREATED AS COMPENSATION.—

2   Paragraph (2) of section 274(e) is amended to read

3   as follows:

4   "(2) EXPENSES TREATED AS COMPENSATION.—

5   Expenses for goods, services, and facilities, to the

6   extent that the expenses do not exceed the amount

7   of the expenses which are treated by the taxpayer,

8   with respect to the recipient of the entertainment,

9   amusement, or recreation, as compensation to an

10   employee on the taxpayer's return of tax under this

11   chapter and as wages to such employee for purposes

12   of chapter 24 (relating to withholding of income tax

13   at source on wages).".

14   (2) EXPENSES INCLUDIBLE IN INCOME OF PER-

15   SONS WHO ARE NOT EMPLOYEES.—Paragraph (9) of

16   section 274(e) is amended by striking "to the extent

17   that the expenses" and inserting "to the extent that

18   the expenses do not exceed the amount of the ex-

19   penses that".

20   (c) EXCEPTIONS FOR REIMBURSED EXPENSES.—

21 Paragraph (3) of section 274(e) is amended to read as

22 follows:

23   "(3) REIMBURSED EXPENSES.—

24   "(A) IN GENERAL.—Expenses paid or in-

25   curred by the taxpayer, in connection with the

1 performance by him of services for another per-
2 son (whether or not such other person is the
3 taxpayer's employer), under a reimbursement or
4 other expense allowance arrangement with such
5 other person, but this paragraph shall apply—

6   "(i) where the services are performed
7   for an employer, only if the employer has
8   not treated such expenses in the manner
9   provided in paragraph (2), or

10   "(ii) where the services are performed
11   for a person other than an employer, only
12   if the taxpayer accounts (to the extent pro-
13   vided by subsection (d)) to such person.

14   "(B) EXCEPTION.—Except as provided by
15 the Secretary, subparagraph (A) shall not
16 apply—

17   "(i) in the case of an arrangement in
18   which the person other than the employer
19   is an entity described in section
20   168(h)(2)(A), or

21   "(ii) to any other arrangement des-
22   ignated by the Secretary as having the ef-
23   fect of avoiding the limitation under sub-
24   paragraph (A).".

241

1 (d) 50 PERCENT LIMITATION ON MEALS AND EN-

2 TERTAINMENT EXPENSES.—Subsection (n) of section 274

3 is amended to read as follows:

4 "(n) LIMITATION ON CERTAIN EXPENSES.—

5   "(1) IN GENERAL.—The amount allowable as a

6 deduction under this chapter for any expense for

7 food or beverages (pursuant to subsection (e)(1)) or

8 business meals (pursuant to subsection (k)(1)) shall

9 not exceed 50 percent of the amount of such expense

10 or item which would (but for this paragraph) be al-

11 lowable as a deduction under this chapter.

12   "(2) EXCEPTIONS.—Paragraph (1) shall not

13 apply to any expense if—

14   "(A) such expense is described in para-

15   graph (2), (3), (6), (7), or (8) of subsection (e),

16   "(B) in the case of an expense for food or

17   beverages, such expense is excludable from the

18   gross income of the recipient under section 132

19   by reason of subsection (e) thereof (relating to

20   de minimis fringes) or under section 119 (relat-

21   ing to meals and lodging furnished for conven-

22   ience of employer), or

23   "(C) in the case of an employer who pays

24   or reimburses moving expenses of an employee,

242

1   such expenses are includible in the income of

2   the employee under section 82.

3   "(3) SPECIAL RULE FOR INDIVIDUALS SUBJECT

4   TO FEDERAL HOURS OF SERVICE.—In the case of

5   any expenses for food or beverages consumed while

6   away from home (within the meaning of section

7   162(a)(2)) by an individual during, or incident to,

8   the period of duty subject to the hours of service

9   limitations of the Department of Transportation,

10   paragraph (1) shall be applied by substituting '80

11   percent' for '50 percent'.".

12   (e) CONFORMING AMENDMENTS.—

13   (1) Section 274(d) is amended—

14   (A) by striking paragraph (2) and redesig-

15   nating paragraphs (3) and (4) as paragraphs

16   (2) and (3), respectively, and

17   (B) in the flush material following para-

18   graph (3) (as so redesignated)—

19   (i) by striking ", entertainment,

20   amusement, recreation, or" in item (B),

21   and

22   (ii) by striking "(D) the business rela-

23   tionship to the taxpayer of persons enter-

24   tained, using the facility or property, or re-

25   ceiving the gift" and inserting "(D) the

1   business relationship to the taxpayer of the

2   person receiving the benefit".

3   (2) Section 274(e) is amended by striking para-

4   graph (4) and redesignating paragraphs (5), (6),

5   (7), (8), and (9) as paragraphs (4), (5), (6), (7),

6   and (8), respectively.

7   (3) Section 274(k)(2)(A) is amended by strik-

8   ing "(4), (7), (8), or (9)" and inserting "(6), (7), or

9   (8)".

10   (4) Section 274 is amended by striking sub-

11   section (l).

12   (5) Section 274(m)(1)(B)(ii) is amended by

13   striking "(4), (7), (8), or (9)" and inserting "(6),

14   (7), or (8)".

15   (f) EFFECTIVE DATE.—The amendments made by

16 this section shall apply to amounts paid or incurred after

17 December 31, 2017.

18 **SEC. 3308. UNRELATED BUSINESS TAXABLE INCOME IN-**

19   **CREASED BY AMOUNT OF CERTAIN FRINGE**

20   **BENEFIT EXPENSES FOR WHICH DEDUCTION**

21   **IS DISALLOWED.**

22   (a) IN GENERAL.—Section 512(a) is amended by

23 adding at the end the following new paragraph:

24   "(6) INCREASE IN UNRELATED BUSINESS TAX-

25   ABLE INCOME BY DISALLOWED FRINGE.—Unrelated

1 business taxable income of an organization shall be

2 increased by any amount for which a deduction is

3 not allowable under this chapter by reason of section

4 274 and which is paid or incurred by such organiza-

5 tion for any qualified transportation fringe (as de-

6 fined in section 132(f)), any parking facility used in

7 connection with qualified parking (as defined in sec-

8 tion 132(f)(5)(C)), or any on-premises athletic facil-

9 ity (as defined in section 132(j)(4)(B)). The pre-

10 ceding sentence shall not apply to the extent the

11 amount paid or incurred is directly connected with

12 an unrelated trade or business which is regularly

13 carried on by the organization. The Secretary may

14 issue such regulations or other guidance as may be

15 necessary or appropriate to carry out the purposes

16 of this paragraph, including regulations or other

17 guidance providing for the appropriate allocation of

18 depreciation and other costs with respect to facilities

19 used for parking or for on-premises athletic facili-

20 ties.

21 ''.

22 (b) EFFECTIVE DATE.—The amendment made by

23 this section shall apply to amounts paid or incurred after

24 December 31, 2017.

SEC. 3309. LIMITATION ON DEDUCTION FOR FDIC PREMIUMS.

(a) IN GENERAL.—Section 162 is amended by redesignating subsection (q) as subsection (r) and by inserting after subsection (p) the following new subsection:

"(q) DISALLOWANCE OF FDIC PREMIUMS PAID BY CERTAIN LARGE FINANCIAL INSTITUTIONS.—

"(1) IN GENERAL.—No deduction shall be allowed for the applicable percentage of any FDIC premium paid or incurred by the taxpayer.

"(2) EXCEPTION FOR SMALL INSTITUTIONS.—Paragraph (1) shall not apply to any taxpayer for any taxable year if the total consolidated assets of such taxpayer (determined as of the close of such taxable year) do not exceed $10,000,000,000.

"(3) APPLICABLE PERCENTAGE.—For purposes of this subsection, the term 'applicable percentage' means, with respect to any taxpayer for any taxable year, the ratio (expressed as a percentage but not greater than 100 percent) which—

"(A) the excess of—

"(i) the total consolidated assets of such taxpayer (determined as of the close of such taxable year), over

"(ii) $10,000,000,000, bears to

"(B) $40,000,000,000.

1   "(4) FDIC PREMIUMS.—For purposes of this

2 subsection, the term 'FDIC premium' means any as-

3 sessment imposed under section 7(b) of the Federal

4 Deposit Insurance Act (12 U.S.C. 1817(b)).

5   "(5) TOTAL CONSOLIDATED ASSETS.—For pur-

6 poses of this subsection, the term 'total consolidated

7 assets' has the meaning given such term under sec-

8 tion 165 of the Dodd-Frank Wall Street Reform and

9 Consumer Protection Act (12 U.S.C. 5365).

10   "(6) AGGREGATION RULE.—

11   "(A) IN GENERAL.—Members of an ex-

12 panded affiliated group shall be treated as a

13 single taxpayer for purposes of applying this

14 subsection.

15   "(B) EXPANDED AFFILIATED GROUP.—

16 For purposes of this paragraph, the term 'ex-

17 panded affiliated group' means an affiliated

18 group as defined in section 1504(a), deter-

19 mined—

20   "(i) by substituting 'more than 50

21 percent' for 'at least 80 percent' each place

22 it appears, and

23   "(ii) without regard to paragraphs (2)

24 and (3) of section 1504(b).

1   A partnership or any other entity (other than a

2   corporation) shall be treated as a member of an

3   expanded affiliated group if such entity is con-

4   trolled (within the meaning of section

5   954(d)(3)) by members of such group (includ-

6   ing any entity treated as a member of such

7   group by reason of this sentence).''.

8   (b) EFFECTIVE DATE.—The amendments made by

9 this section shall apply to taxable years beginning after

10 December 31, 2017.

11 **SEC. 3310. REPEAL OF ROLLOVER OF PUBLICLY TRADED**

12   **SECURITIES GAIN INTO SPECIALIZED SMALL**

13   **BUSINESS INVESTMENT COMPANIES.**

14   (a) IN GENERAL.—Part III of subchapter O of chap-

15 ter 1 is amended by striking section 1044 (and by striking

16 the item relating to such section in the table of sections

17 of such part).

18   (b)   CONFORMING   AMENDMENTS.—Section

19 1016(a)(23) is amended—

20   (1) by striking "1044,", and

21   (2) by striking "1044(d),".

22   (c) EFFECTIVE DATE.—The amendments made by

23 this section shall apply to sales after December 31, 2017.

SEC. 3311. CERTAIN SELF-CREATED PROPERTY NOT TREAT-ED AS A CAPITAL ASSET.

(a) PATENTS, ETC.—Section 1221(a)(3) is amended by inserting "a patent, invention, model or design (whether or not patented), a secret formula or process," before "a copyright".

(b) SELF-CREATED MUSICAL WORKS.—Section 1221(b) is amended by striking paragraph (3) and redesignating paragraph (4) as paragraph (3).

(c) CONFORMING AMENDMENTS.—

(1) Section 170(e)(1)(A) is amended by striking "(determined without regard to section 1221(b)(3))".

(2) Section 1231(b)(1)(C) is amended by inserting "a patent, invention, model or design (whether or not patented), a secret formula or process," before "a copyright".

(d) EFFECTIVE DATE.—The amendments made by this section shall apply to dispositions after December 31, 2017.

SEC. 3312. REPEAL OF SPECIAL RULE FOR SALE OR EXCHANGE OF PATENTS.

(a) IN GENERAL.—Part IV of subchapter P of chapter 1 is amended by striking section 1235 (and by striking the item relating to such section in the table of sections of such part).

249

1   (b) CONFORMING AMENDMENTS.—

2   (1) Section 483(d) is amended by striking para-

3 graph (4).

4   (2) Section 901(l)(5) is amended by striking

5 "without regard to section 1235 or any similar rule"

6 and inserting "without regard to any provision

7 which treats a disposition as a sale or exchange of

8 a capital asset held for more than 1 year or any

9 similar provision".

10   (3) Section 1274(c)(3) is amended by striking

11 subparagraph (E) and redesignating subparagraph

12 (F) as subparagraph (E).

13   (c) EFFECTIVE DATE.—The amendments made by

14 this section shall apply to dispositions after December 31,

15 2017.

16 **SEC. 3313. REPEAL OF TECHNICAL TERMINATION OF PART-**

17   **NERSHIPS.**

18   (a) IN GENERAL.—Paragraph (1) of section 708(b)

19 is amended—

20   (1) by striking ", or" at the end of subpara-

21 graph (A) and all that follows and inserting a pe-

22 riod, and

23   (2) by striking "only if—" and all that follows

24 through "no part of any business" and inserting the

25 following: "only if no part of any business".

250

1   (b) EFFECTIVE DATE.—The amendments made by

2 this section shall apply to partnership taxable years begin-

3 ning after December 31, 2017.

4   ## Subtitle E—Reform of Business

5   ## Credits

6 **SEC. 3401. REPEAL OF CREDIT FOR CLINICAL TESTING EX-**

7   **PENSES FOR CERTAIN DRUGS FOR RARE DIS-**

8   **EASES OR CONDITIONS.**

9   (a) IN GENERAL.—Subpart D of part IV of sub-

10 chapter A of chapter 1 is amended by striking section 45C

11 (and by striking the item relating to such section in the

12 table of sections for such subpart).

13   (b) CONFORMING AMENDMENTS.—

14   (1) Section 38(b) is amended by striking para-

15   graph (12).

16   (2) Section 280C is amended by striking sub-

17   section (b).

18   (3) Section 6501(m) is amended by striking

19   "45C(d)(4),".

20   (c) EFFECTIVE DATE.—The amendments made by

21 this section shall apply to amounts paid or incurred in tax-

22 able years beginning after December 31, 2017.

SEC. 3402. REPEAL OF EMPLOYER-PROVIDED CHILD CARE CREDIT.

(a) IN GENERAL.—Subpart D of part IV of subchapter A of chapter 1 is amended by striking section 45F (and by striking the item relating to such section in the table of sections for such subpart).

(b) CONFORMING AMENDMENTS.—

(1) Section 38(b) is amended by striking paragraph (15).

(2) Section 1016(a) is amended by striking paragraph (28).

(c) EFFECTIVE DATE.—

(1) IN GENERAL.—Except as otherwise provided in this subsection, the amendments made by this section shall apply to taxable years beginning after December 31, 2017.

(2) BASIS ADJUSTMENTS.—The amendment made by subsection (b)(2) shall apply to credits determined for taxable years beginning after December 31, 2017.

SEC. 3403. REPEAL OF REHABILITATION CREDIT.

(a) IN GENERAL.—Subpart E of part IV of subchapter A of chapter 1 is amended by striking section 47 (and by striking the item relating to such section in the table of sections for such subpart).

(b) CONFORMING AMENDMENTS.—

1   (1) Section 170(f)(14)(A) is amended by insert-

2   ing "(as in effect before its repeal by the Tax Cuts

3   and Jobs Act)" after "section 47".

4   (2) Section 170(h)(4) is amended—

5   (A) by striking "(as defined in section

6   47(c)(3)(B))" in subparagraph (C)(ii), and

7   (B) by adding at the end the following new

8   subparagraph:

9   "(D) REGISTERED HISTORIC DISTRICT.—

10   The term 'registered historic district' means—

11   "(i) any district listed in the National

12   Register, and

13   "(ii) any district—

14   "(I) which is designated under a

15   statute of the appropriate State or

16   local government, if such statute is

17   certified by the Secretary of the Inte-

18   rior to the Secretary as containing cri-

19   teria which will substantially achieve

20   the purpose of preserving and reha-

21   bilitating buildings of historic signifi-

22   cance to the district, and

23   "(II) which is certified by the

24   Secretary of the Interior to the Sec-

25   retary as meeting substantially all of

1   the requirements for the listing of dis-

2   tricts in the National Register.''.

3 (3) Section 469(i)(3) is amended by striking

4 subparagraph (B).

5 (4) Section 469(i)(6)(B) is amended—

6   (A) by striking ''in the case of—'' and all

7   that follows and inserting ''in the case of any

8   credit determined under section 42 for any tax-

9   able year.'', and

10   (B) by striking '', REHABILITATION CRED-

11   IT,'' in the heading thereof.

12 (5) Section 469(k)(1) is amended by striking '',

13 or any rehabilitation credit determined under section

14 47,''.

15 (c) EFFECTIVE DATE.—

16 (1) IN GENERAL.—Except as provided in para-

17 graph (2), the amendments made by this section

18 shall apply to amounts paid or incurred after De-

19 cember 31, 2017.

20 (2) TRANSITION RULE.—In the case of quali-

21 fied rehabilitation expenditures (within the meaning

22 of section 47 of the Internal Revenue Code of 1986

23 as in effect before its repeal) with respect to any

24 building—

1   (A) owned or leased (as permitted by sec-

2   tion 47 of the Internal Revenue Code of 1986

3   as in effect before its repeal) by the taxpayer at

4   all times after December 31, 2017, and

5   (B) with respect to which the 24-month

6   period selected by the taxpayer under section

7   47(c)(1)(C) of such Code begins not later than

8   the end of the 180-day period beginning on the

9   date of the enactment of this Act,

10 the amendments made by this section shall apply to

11 such expenditures paid or incurred after the end of

12 the taxable year in which the 24-month period re-

13 ferred to in subparagraph (B) ends.

14 **SEC. 3404. REPEAL OF WORK OPPORTUNITY TAX CREDIT.**

15   (a) IN GENERAL.—Subpart F of part IV of sub-

16 chapter A of chapter 1 is amended by striking section 51

17 (and by striking the item relating to such section in the

18 table of sections for such subpart).

19   (b) CLERICAL AMENDMENT.—The heading of such

20 subpart F (and the item relating to such subpart in the

21 table of subparts for part IV of subchapter A of chapter

22 1) are each amended by striking "Rules for Computing

23 Work Opportunity Credit" and inserting "Special Rules".

24   (c) EFFECTIVE DATE.—The amendments made by

25 this section shall apply to amounts paid or incurred to

255

1 individuals who begin work for the employer after Decem-

2 ber 31, 2017.

SEC. 3405. REPEAL OF DEDUCTION FOR CERTAIN UNUSED

BUSINESS CREDITS.

5 (a) IN GENERAL.—Part VI of subchapter B of chap-

6 ter 1 is amended by striking section 196 (and by striking

7 the item relating to such section in the table of sections

8 for such part).

9 (b) EFFECTIVE DATE.—The amendments made by

10 this section shall apply to taxable years beginning after

11 December 31, 2017.

SEC. 3406. TERMINATION OF NEW MARKETS TAX CREDIT.

13 (a) IN GENERAL.—Section 45D(f) is amended—

14 (1) by striking "2019" in paragraph (1)(G) and

15 inserting "2017", and

16 (2) by striking "2024" in paragraph (3) and in-

17 serting "2022".

18 (b) EFFECTIVE DATE.—The amendments made by

19 this section shall apply to calendar years beginning after

20 December 31, 2017.

SEC. 3407. REPEAL OF CREDIT FOR EXPENDITURES TO

PROVIDE ACCESS TO DISABLED INDIVID-

UALS.

24 (a) IN GENERAL.—Subpart D of part IV of sub-

25 chapter A of chapter 1 is amended by striking section 44

1 (and by striking the item relating to such section in the

2 table of sections for such subpart).

3 (b) CONFORMING AMENDMENT.—Section 38(b) is

4 amended by striking paragraph (7).

5 (c) EFFECTIVE DATE.—The amendments made by

6 this section shall apply to taxable years beginning after

7 December 31, 2017.

SEC. 3408. MODIFICATION OF CREDIT FOR PORTION OF EM-PLOYER SOCIAL SECURITY TAXES PAID WITH RESPECT TO EMPLOYEE TIPS.

11 (a) CREDIT DETERMINED WITH RESPECT TO MIN-

12 IMUM WAGE AS IN EFFECT.—Section 45B(b)(1)(B) is

13 amended by striking "as in effect on January 1, 2007,

14 and".

15 (b) INFORMATION RETURN REQUIREMENT.—Section

16 45B is amended by redesignating subsections (c) and (d)

17 as subsections (d) and (e), respectively, and by inserting

18 after subsection (b) the following new subsection:

19 "(c) INFORMATION RETURN REQUIREMENT.—

20 "(1) IN GENERAL.—No credit shall be deter-

21 mined under subsection (a) with respect to any food

22 or beverage establishment of any taxpayer for any

23 taxable year unless such taxpayer has, with respect

24 to the calendar year which ends in or with such tax-

25 able year—

1   "(A) made a report to the Secretary show-

2   ing the information described in section

3   6053(c)(1) with respect to such food or bev-

4   erage establishment, and

5   "(B) furnished written statements to each

6   employee of such food or beverage establish-

7   ment showing the information described in sec-

8   tion 6053(c)(2).

9   "(2) ALLOCATION OF 10 PERCENT OF GROSS

10   RECEIPTS.—For purposes of determining the infor-

11   mation referred to in subparagraphs (A) and (B),

12   section 6053(c)(3)(A)(i) shall be applied by sub-

13   stituting '10 percent' for '8 percent'. For purposes

14   of section 6053(c)(5), any reference to section

15   6053(c)(3)(B) contained therein shall be treated as

16   including a reference to this paragraph.

17   "(3) FOOD OR BEVERAGE ESTABLISHMENT.—

18   For purposes of this subsection, the term 'food or

19   beverage establishment' means any trade or business

20   (or portion thereof) which would be a large food or

21   beverage establishment (as defined in section

22   6053(c)(4)) if such section were applied without re-

23   gard to subparagraph (C) thereof.".

258

1   (c) EFFECTIVE DATE.—The amendments made by
2 this section shall apply to taxable years beginning after
3 December 31, 2017.

Subtitle F—Energy Credits

SEC. 3501. MODIFICATIONS TO CREDIT FOR ELECTRICITY PRODUCED FROM CERTAIN RENEWABLE RESOURCES.

8   (a) TERMINATION OF INFLATION ADJUSTMENT.—
9 Section 45(b)(2) is amended—

10   (1) by striking "The 1.5 cent amount" and in-
11   serting the following:

12   "(A) IN   GENERAL.—The   1.5   cent
13   amount", and

14   (2) by adding at the end the following new sub-
15   paragraph:

16   "(B) TERMINATION.—Subparagraph (A)
17   shall not apply with respect to any electricity or
18   refined coal produced at a facility the construc-
19   tion of which begins after the date of the enact-
20   ment of this subparagraph.".

21   (b) SPECIAL RULE FOR DETERMINATION OF BEGIN-
22 NING OF CONSTRUCTION.—Section 45(e) is amended by
23 adding at the end the following new paragraph:

24   "(12) SPECIAL RULE FOR DETERMINING BE-
25   GINNING OF CONSTRUCTION.—For purposes of sub-

1   section (d), the construction of any facility, modi-

2   fication, improvement, addition, or other property

3   shall not be treated as beginning before any date un-

4   less there is a continuous program of construction

5   which begins before such date and ends on the date

6   that such property is placed in service.''.

7   (c) EFFECTIVE DATES.—

8   (1) TERMINATION OF INFLATION ADJUST-

9   MENT.—The amendments made by subsection (a)

10   shall apply to taxable years ending after the date of

11   the enactment of this Act.

12   (2) SPECIAL RULE FOR DETERMINATION OF

13   BEGINNING OF CONSTRUCTION.—The amendment

14   made by subsection (b) shall apply to taxable years

15   beginning before, on, or after the date of the enact-

16   ment of this Act.

17 **SEC. 3502. MODIFICATION OF THE ENERGY INVESTMENT**

18   **TAX CREDIT.**

19   (a) EXTENSION OF SOLAR ENERGY PROPERTY.—

20 Section 48(a)(3)(A)(ii) is amended by striking "periods

21 ending before January 1, 2017" and inserting "property

22 the construction of which begins before January 1, 2022".

23   (b) EXTENSION OF QUALIFIED FUEL CELL PROP-

24 ERTY.—Section 48(c)(1)(D) is amended by striking "for

25 any period after December 31, 2016" and inserting "the

1 construction of which does not begin before January 1,

2 2022".

3   (c) EXTENSION OF QUALIFIED MICROTURBINE

4 PROPERTY.—Section 48(c)(2)(D) is amended by striking

5 "for any period after December 31, 2016" and inserting

6 "the construction of which does not begin before January

7 1, 2022".

8   (d) EXTENSION OF COMBINED HEAT AND POWER

9 SYSTEM PROPERTY.—Section 48(c)(3)(A)(iv) is amended

10 by striking "which is placed in service before January 1,

11 2017" and inserting "the construction of which begins be-

12 fore January 1, 2022".

13   (e) EXTENSION OF QUALIFIED SMALL WIND EN-

14 ERGY PROPERTY.—Section 48(c)(4)(C) is amended by

15 striking "for any period after December 31, 2016" and

16 inserting "the construction of which does not begin before

17 January 1, 2022".

18   (f) EXTENSION OF THERMAL ENERGY PROPERTY.—

19 Section 48(a)(3)(A)(vii) is amended by striking "periods

20 ending before January 1, 2017" and inserting "property

21 the construction of which begins before January 1, 2022".

22   (g) PHASEOUT OF 30 PERCENT CREDIT RATE FOR

23 FUEL CELL AND SMALL WIND ENERGY PROPERTY.—

24 Section 48(a) is amended by adding at the end the fol-

25 lowing new paragraph:

1   "(7) PHASEOUT FOR QUALIFIED FUEL CELL

2 PROPERTY AND QUALIFIED SMALL WIND ENERGY

3 PROPERTY.—

4   "(A) IN GENERAL.—In the case of quali-

5 fied fuel cell property or qualified small wind

6 energy property, the construction of which be-

7 gins before January 1, 2022, the energy per-

8 centage determined under paragraph (2) shall

9 be equal to—

10   "(i) in the case of any property the

11 construction of which begins after Decem-

12 ber 31, 2019, and before January 1, 2021,

13 26 percent, and

14   "(ii) in the case of any property the

15 construction of which begins after Decem-

16 ber 31, 2020, and before January 1, 2022,

17 22 percent.

18   "(B) PLACED IN SERVICE DEADLINE.—In

19 the case of any qualified fuel cell property or

20 qualified small wind energy property, the con-

21 struction of which begins before January 1,

22 2022, and which is not placed in service before

23 January 1, 2024, the energy percentage deter-

24 mined under paragraph (2) shall be equal to 10

25 percent.".

1   (h) PHASEOUT FOR FIBER-OPTIC SOLAR ENERGY

2 PROPERTY.—Subparagraphs (A) and (B) of section

3 48(a)(6) are each amended by inserting "or (3)(A)(ii)"

4 after "paragraph (3)(A)(i)".

5   (i) TERMINATION OF SOLAR ENERGY PROPERTY.—

6 Section 48(a)(3)(A)(i) is amended by inserting ", the con-

7 struction of which begins before January 1, 2028, and"

8 after "equipment".

9   (j) TERMINATION OF GEOTHERMAL ENERGY PROP-

10 ERTY.—Section 48(a)(3)(A)(iii) is amended by inserting

11 ", the construction of which begins before January 1,

12 2028, and" after "equipment".

13   (k) SPECIAL RULE FOR DETERMINATION OF BEGIN-

14 NING OF CONSTRUCTION.—Section 48(c) is amended by

15 adding at the end the following new paragraph:

16   "(5) SPECIAL RULE FOR DETERMINING BEGIN-

17   NING OF CONSTRUCTION.—The construction of any

18   facility, modification, improvement, addition, or

19   other property shall not be treated as beginning be-

20   fore any date unless there is a continuous program

21   of construction which begins before such date and

22   ends on the date that such property is placed in

23   service.".

24   (l) EFFECTIVE DATE.—

1   (1) IN GENERAL.—Except as otherwise pro-

2 vided in this subsection, the amendments made by

3 this section shall apply to periods after December

4 31, 2016, under rules similar to the rules of section

5 48(m) of the Internal Revenue Code of 1986 (as in

6 effect on the day before the date of the enactment

7 of the Revenue Reconciliation Act of 1990).

8   (2) EXTENSION OF COMBINED HEAT AND

9 POWER SYSTEM PROPERTY.—The amendment made

10 by subsection (d) shall apply to property placed in

11 service after December 31, 2016.

12   (3) PHASEOUTS AND TERMINATIONS.—The

13 amendments made by subsections (g), (h), (i), and

14 (j) shall take effect on the date of the enactment of

15 this Act.

16   (4) SPECIAL RULE FOR DETERMINATION OF

17 BEGINNING OF CONSTRUCTION.—The amendment

18 made by subsection (k) shall apply to taxable years

19 beginning before, on, or after the date of the enact-

20 ment of this Act.

21 **SEC. 3503. EXTENSION AND PHASEOUT OF RESIDENTIAL**

22   **ENERGY EFFICIENT PROPERTY.**

23 (a) EXTENSION.—Section 25D(h) is amended by

24 striking "December 31, 2016 (December 31, 2021, in the

25 case of any qualified solar electric property expenditures

264

1 and qualified solar water heating property expenditures)"

2 and inserting "December 31, 2021".

3   (b) PHASEOUT.—

4   (1) IN GENERAL.—Paragraphs (3), (4), and (5)

5   of section 25D(a) are amended by striking "30 per-

6   cent" each place it appears and inserting "the appli-

7   cable percentage".

8   (2) CONFORMING AMENDMENT.—Section

9   25D(g) of such Code is amended by striking "para-

10   graphs (1) and (2) of".

11   (c) EFFECTIVE DATE.—The amendments made by

12 this section shall apply to property placed in service after

13 December 31, 2016.

14 **SEC. 3504. REPEAL OF ENHANCED OIL RECOVERY CREDIT.**

15   (a) IN GENERAL.—Subpart D of part IV of sub-

16 chapter A of chapter 1 is amended by striking section 43

17 (and by striking the item relating to such section in the

18 table of sections for such subpart).

19   (b) CONFORMING AMENDMENTS.—

20   (1) Section 38(b) is amended by striking para-

21   graph (6).

22   (2) Section 6501(m) is amended by striking

23   "43,".

265

1   (c) EFFECTIVE DATE.—The amendments made by
2 this section shall apply to taxable years beginning after
3 December 31, 2017.

4 SEC. 3505. REPEAL OF CREDIT FOR PRODUCING OIL AND

5   GAS FROM MARGINAL WELLS.

6   (a) IN GENERAL.—Subpart D of part IV of sub-
7 chapter A of chapter 1 is amended by striking section 45I
8 (and by striking the item relating to such section in the
9 table of sections for such subpart).

10   (b) CONFORMING AMENDMENT.—Section 38(b) is
11 amended by striking paragraph (19).

12   (c) EFFECTIVE DATE.—The amendments made by
13 this section shall apply to taxable years beginning after
14 December 31, 2017.

15 SEC. 3506. MODIFICATIONS OF CREDIT FOR PRODUCTION

16   FROM ADVANCED NUCLEAR POWER FACILI-

17   TIES.

18   (a) TREATMENT OF UNUTILIZED LIMITATION
19 AMOUNTS.—Section 45J(b) is amended—

20   (1) in paragraph (4), by inserting "or any
21   amendment to" after "enactment of"; and

22   (2) by adding at the end the following new
23   paragraph:

24   "(5) ALLOCATION OF UNUTILIZED LIMITA-
25   TION.—

266

1   "(A) IN GENERAL.—Any unutilized na-

2 tional megawatt capacity limitation shall be al-

3 located by the Secretary under paragraph (3)

4 as rapidly as is practicable after December 31,

5 2020—

6   "(i) first to facilities placed in service

7 on or before such date to the extent that

8 such facilities did not receive an allocation

9 equal to their full nameplate capacity; and

10   "(ii) then to facilities placed in service

11 after such date in the order in which such

12 facilities are placed in service.

13   "(B) UNUTILIZED NATIONAL MEGAWATT

14 CAPACITY LIMITATION.—The term 'unutilized

15 national megawatt capacity limitation' means

16 the excess (if any) of—

17   "(i) 6,000 megawatts, over

18   "(ii) the aggregate amount of national

19 megawatt capacity limitation allocated by

20 the Secretary before January 1, 2021, re-

21 duced by any amount of such limitation

22 which was allocated to a facility which was

23 not placed in service before such date.

24   "(C) COORDINATION WITH OTHER PROVI-

25 SIONS.—In the case of any unutilized national

1   megawatt capacity limitation allocated by the

2   Secretary pursuant to this paragraph—

3   "(i) such allocation shall be treated

4   for purposes of this section in the same

5   manner as an allocation of national mega-

6   watt capacity limitation; and

7   "(ii) subsection (d)(1)(B) shall not

8   apply to any facility which receives such al-

9   location.".

10   (b) TRANSFER OF CREDIT BY CERTAIN PUBLIC EN-

11 TITIES.—

12   (1) IN GENERAL.—Section 45J is amended—

13   (A) by redesignating subsection (e) as sub-

14   section (f); and

15   (B) by inserting after subsection (d) the

16   following new subsection:

17   "(e) TRANSFER OF CREDIT BY CERTAIN PUBLIC EN-

18 TITIES.—

19   "(1) IN GENERAL.—If, with respect to a credit

20   under subsection (a) for any taxable year—

21   "(A) the taxpayer would be a qualified

22   public entity; and

23   "(B) such entity elects the application of

24   this paragraph for such taxable year with re-

268

1   spect to all (or any portion specified in such

2   election) of such credit,

3   the eligible project partner specified in such election

4   (and not the qualified public entity) shall be treated

5   as the taxpayer for purposes of this title with re-

6   spect to such credit (or such portion thereof).

7   "(2) DEFINITIONS.—For purposes of this sub-

8   section—

9   "(A) QUALIFIED PUBLIC ENTITY.—The

10   term 'qualified public entity' means—

11   "(i) a Federal, State, or local govern-

12   ment entity, or any political subdivision,

13   agency, or instrumentality thereof;

14   "(ii) a mutual or cooperative electric

15   company described in section 501(c)(12) or

16   section 1381(a)(2); or

17   "(iii) a not-for-profit electric utility

18   which has or had received a loan or loan

19   guarantee under the Rural Electrification

20   Act of 1936.

21   "(B) ELIGIBLE PROJECT PARTNER.—The

22   term 'eligible project partner' means—

23   "(i) any person responsible for, or

24   participating in, the design or construction

25   of the advanced nuclear power facility to

1 which the credit under subsection (a) re-
2 lates;

3 "(ii) any person who participates in
4 the provision of the nuclear steam supply
5 system to the advanced nuclear power fa-
6 cility to which the credit under subsection
7 (a) relates;

8 "(iii) any person who participates in
9 the provision of nuclear fuel to the ad-
10 vanced nuclear power facility to which the
11 credit under subsection (a) relates; or

12 "(iv) any person who has an owner-
13 ship interest in such facility.

14 "(3) SPECIAL RULES.—

15 "(A) APPLICATION TO PARTNERSHIPS.—In
16 the case of a credit under subsection (a) which
17 is determined at the partnership level—

18 "(i) for purposes of paragraph (1)(A),
19 a qualified public entity shall be treated as
20 the taxpayer with respect to such entity's
21 distributive share of such credit; and

22 "(ii) the term 'eligible project partner'
23 shall include any partner of the partner-
24 ship.

1   "(B) TAXABLE YEAR IN WHICH CREDIT

2   TAKEN INTO ACCOUNT.—In the case of any

3   credit (or portion thereof) with respect to which

4   an election is made under paragraph (1), such

5   credit shall be taken into account in the first

6   taxable year of the eligible project partner end-

7   ing with, or after, the qualified public entity's

8   taxable year with respect to which the credit

9   was determined.

10   "(C) TREATMENT OF TRANSFER UNDER

11   PRIVATE USE RULES.—For purposes of section

12   141(b)(1), any benefit derived by an eligible

13   project partner in connection with an election

14   under this subsection shall not be taken into ac-

15   count as a private business use.".

16   (2) SPECIAL RULE FOR PROCEEDS OF TRANS-

17   FERS FOR MUTUAL OR COOPERATIVE ELECTRIC

18   COMPANIES.—Section 501(c)(12) of such Code is

19   amended by adding at the end the following new

20   subparagraph:

21   "(I) In the case of a mutual or cooperative

22   electric company described in this paragraph or

23   an organization described in section 1381(a)(2),

24   income received or accrued in connection with

25   an election under section 45J(e)(1) shall be

1   treated as an amount collected from members

2   for the sole purpose of meeting losses and ex-

3   penses.''.

4   (c) EFFECTIVE DATES.—

5   (1) TREATMENT OF UNUTILIZED LIMITATION

6   AMOUNTS.—The amendment made by subsection (a)

7   shall take effect on the date of the enactment of this

8   Act.

9   (2) TRANSFER OF CREDIT BY CERTAIN PUBLIC

10   ENTITIES.—The amendments made by subsection

11   (b) shall apply to taxable years beginning after the

12   date of the enactment of this Act.

Subtitle G—Bond Reforms

SEC. 3601. TERMINATION OF PRIVATE ACTIVITY BONDS.

15   (a) IN GENERAL.—Paragraph (1) of section 103(b)

16 is amended—

17   (1) by striking "which is not a qualified bond

18   (within the meaning of section 141)", and

19   (2) by striking "WHICH IS NOT A QUALIFIED

20   BOND" in the heading thereof.

21   (b) CONFORMING AMENDMENTS.—

22   (1) Subpart A of part IV of subchapter B of

23   chapter 1 is amended by striking sections 142, 143,

24   144, 145, 146, and 147 (and by striking each of the

1   items relating to such sections in the table of sec-

2   tions for such subpart).

3   (2) Section 25 is amended by adding at the end

4   the following new subsection:

5   "(j) COORDINATION WITH REPEAL OF PRIVATE AC-

6   TIVITY BONDS.—Any reference to section 143, 144, or

7   146 shall be treated as a reference to such section as in

8   effect before its repeal by the Tax Cuts and Jobs Act.".

9   (3) Section 26(b)(2) is amended by striking

10   subparagraph (D).

11   (4) Section 141(b) is amended by striking para-

12   graphs (5) and (9).

13   (5) Section 141(d) is amended by striking para-

14   graph (5).

15   (6) Section 141 is amended by striking sub-

16   section (e).

17   (7) Section 148(f)(4) is amended—

18   (A) by striking "(determined in accordance

19   with section 147(b)(2)(A))" in the flush matter

20   following subparagraph (A)(ii) and inserting

21   "(determined by taking into account the respec-

22   tive issue prices of the bonds issued as part of

23   the issue)", and

24   (B) by striking the last sentence of sub-

25   paragraph (D)(v).

273

(8) Clause (iv) of section 148(f)(4)(C) is amended to read as follows:

"(iv) CONSTRUCTION ISSUE.—For purposes of this subparagraph—

"(I) IN GENERAL.—The term 'construction issue' means any issue if at least 75 percent of the available construction proceeds of such issue are to be used for construction expenditures.

"(II) CONSTRUCTION.—The term 'construction' includes reconstruction and rehabilitation''.

(9) Section 149(b)(3) is amended by striking subparagraph (C).

(10) Section 149(e)(2) is amended—

(A) by striking subparagraphs (C), (D), and (F) and by redesignating subparagraphs (E) and (G) as subparagraphs (C) and (D), respectively, and

(B) by striking the second sentence.

(11) Section 149(f)(6) is amended—

(A) by striking subparagraph (B), and

(B) by striking "For purposes of this subsection" and all that follows through "The

1 term" and inserting the following: "For pur-
2 poses of this subsection, the term".

3 (12) Section 150(e)(3) is amended to read as
4 follows:

5 "(3) PUBLIC APPROVAL REQUIREMENT.—A
6 bond shall not be treated as part of an issue which
7 meets the requirements of paragraph (1) unless such
8 bond satisfies the requirements of section 147(f)(2)
9 (as in effect before its repeal by the Tax Cuts and
10 Jobs Act).".

11 (13) Section 269A(b)(3) is amended by striking
12 "144(a)(3)" and inserting "414(n)(6)(A)".

13 (14) Section 414(m)(5) is amended by striking
14 "section 144(a)(3)" and inserting "subsection
15 (n)(6)(A)".

16 (15) Section 414(n)(6)(A) is amended to read
17 as follows:

18 "(A) RELATED PERSONS.—A person is a
19 related person to another person if—

20 "(i) the relationship between such per-
21 sons would result in a disallowance of
22 losses under section 267 or 707(b), or

23 "(ii) such persons are members of the
24 same controlled group of corporations (as
25 defined in section 1563(a), except that

'more than 50 percent' shall be substituted for 'at least 80 percent' each place it appears therein).".

(16) Section 6045(e)(4)(B) is amended by inserting "(as in effect before its repeal by the Tax Cuts and Jobs Act)" after "section 143(m)(3)".

(17) Section 6654(f)(1) is amended by inserting "(as in effect before its repeal by the Tax Cuts and Jobs Act)" after "section 143(m)".

(18) Section 7871(c) is amended—

(A) by striking paragraphs (2) and (3), and

(B) by striking "TAX-EXEMPT BONDS.—" and all that follows through "Subsection (a) of section 103" and inserting the following: "TAX-EXEMPT BONDS.—Subsection (a) of section 103".

(c) EFFECTIVE DATE.—The amendments made by this section shall apply to bonds issued after December 31, 2017.

SEC. 3602. REPEAL OF ADVANCE REFUNDING BONDS.

(a) IN GENERAL.—Paragraph (1) of section 149(d) is amended by striking "as part of an issue described in paragraph (2), (3), or (4)." and inserting "to advance refund another bond.".

276

1 (b) CONFORMING AMENDMENTS.—

2 (1) Section 149(d) is amended by striking para-

3 graphs (2), (3), (4), and (6) and by redesignating

4 paragraphs (5) and (7) as paragraphs (2) and (3).

5 (2) Section 148(f)(4)(C) is amended by striking

6 clause (xiv) and by redesignating clauses (xv) to

7 (xvii) as clauses (xiv) to (xvi).

8 (c) EFFECTIVE DATE.—The amendments made by

9 this section shall apply to advance refunding bonds issued

10 after December 31, 2017.

11 **SEC. 3603. REPEAL OF TAX CREDIT BONDS.**

12 (a) IN GENERAL.—Part IV of subchapter A of chap-

13 ter 1 is amended by striking subparts H, I, and J (and

14 by striking the items relating to such subparts in the table

15 of subparts for such part).

16 (b) PAYMENTS TO ISSUERS.—Subchapter B of chap-

17 ter 65 is amended by striking section 6431 (and by strik-

18 ing the item relating to such section in the table of sec-

19 tions for such subchapter).

20 (c) CONFORMING AMENDMENTS.—

21 (1) Part IV of subchapter U of chapter 1 is

22 amended by striking section 1397E (and by striking

23 the item relating to such section in the table of sec-

24 tions for such part).

277

1   (2) Section 54(l)(3)(B) is amended by inserting

2 "(as in effect before its repeal by the Tax Cuts and

3 Jobs Act)" after "section 1397E(I)".

4   (3) Section 6211(b)(4)(A) is amended by strik-

5 ing ", and 6431" and inserting "and" before

6 "36B".

7   (4) Section 6401(b)(1) is amended by striking

8 "G, H, I, and J" and inserting "and G".

9   (d) EFFECTIVE DATE.—The amendments made by

10 this section shall apply to bonds issued after December

11 31, 2017.

12 **SEC. 3604. NO TAX EXEMPT BONDS FOR PROFESSIONAL**

13   **STADIUMS.**

14   (a) IN GENERAL.—Section 103(b), as amended by

15 this Act, is further amended by adding at the end the fol-

16 lowing new paragraph:

17   "(4) PROFESSIONAL STADIUM BOND.—Any pro-

18   fessional stadium bond.".

19   (b) PROFESSIONAL STADIUM BOND DEFINED.—Sub-

20 section (c) of section 103 is amended by adding at the

21 end the following new paragraph:

22   "(3) PROFESSIONAL STADIUM BOND.—The

23   term 'professional stadium bond' means any bond

24   issued as part of an issue any proceeds of which are

25   used to finance or refinance capital expenditures al-

1 locable to a facility (or appurtenant real property)

2 which, during at least 5 days during any calendar

3 year, is used as a stadium or arena for professional

4 sports exhibitions, games, or training.".

5 (c) EFFECTIVE DATE.—The amendments made by

6 this section shall apply to bonds issued after November

7 2, 2017.

Subtitle H—Insurance

SEC. 3701. NET OPERATING LOSSES OF LIFE INSURANCE COMPANIES.

11 (a) IN GENERAL.—Section 805(b) is amended by

12 striking paragraph (4) and by redesignating paragraph

13 (5) as paragraph (4).

14 (b) CONFORMING AMENDMENTS.—

15 (1) Part I of subchapter L of chapter 1 is

16 amended by striking section 810 (and by striking

17 the item relating to such section in the table of sec-

18 tions for such part).

19 (2) Part III of subchapter L of chapter 1 is

20 amended by striking section 844 (and by striking

21 the item relating to such section in the table of sec-

22 tions for such part).

23 (3) Section 381 is amended by striking sub-

24 section (d).

279

1   (4) Section 805(a)(4)(B)(ii) is amended to read

2 as follows:

3   "(ii) the deduction allowed under sec-

4   tion 172,".

5   (5) Section 805(a) is amended by striking para-

6 graph (5).

7   (6) Section 953(b)(1)(B) is amended to read as

8 follows:

9   "(B) So much of section 805(a)(8) as re-

10   lates to the deduction allowed under section

11   172.".

12   (c) EFFECTIVE DATE.—The amendments made by

13 this section shall apply to losses arising in taxable years

14 beginning after December 31, 2017.

15 **SEC. 3702. REPEAL OF SMALL LIFE INSURANCE COMPANY**

16   **DEDUCTION.**

17   (a) IN GENERAL.—Part I of subchapter L of chapter

18 1 is amended by striking section 806 (and by striking the

19 item relating to such section in the table of sections for

20 such part).

21   (b) CONFORMING AMENDMENTS.—

22   (1) Section 453B(e) is amended—

23   (A) by striking "(as defined in section

24   806(b)(3))" in paragraph (2)(B), and

1 (B) by adding at the end the following new

2 paragraph:

3 "(3) NONINSURANCE BUSINESS.—

4 "(A) IN GENERAL.—For purposes of this

5 subsection, the term 'noninsurance business'

6 means any activity which is not an insurance

7 business.

8 "(B) CERTAIN ACTIVITIES TREATED AS IN-

9 SURANCE BUSINESSES.—For purposes of sub-

10 paragraph (A), any activity which is not an in-

11 surance business shall be treated as an insur-

12 ance business if—

13 "(i) it is of a type traditionally carried

14 on by life insurance companies for invest-

15 ment purposes, but only if the carrying on

16 of such activity (other than in the case of

17 real estate) does not constitute the active

18 conduct of a trade or business, or

19 "(ii) it involves the performance of ad-

20 ministrative services in connection with

21 plans providing life insurance, pension, or

22 accident and health benefits.".

23 (2) Section 465(c)(7)(D)(v)(II) is amended by

24 striking "section 806(b)(3)" and inserting "section

25 453B(e)(3)".

1   (3) Section 801(a)(2) is amended by striking

2 subparagraph (C).

3   (4) Section 804 is amended by striking

4 "means—" and all that follows and inserting

5 "means the general deductions provided in section

6 805.".

7   (5) Section 805(a)(4)(B), as amended by sec-

8 tion 3701, is amended by striking clause (i) and by

9 redesignating clauses (ii), (iii), and (iv) as clauses

10 (i), (ii), and (iii), respectively.

11   (6) Section 805(b)(2)(A) is amended by strik-

12 ing clause (iii) and by redesignating clauses (iv) and

13 (v) as clauses (iii) and (iv), respectively.

14   (7) Section 842(c) is amended by striking para-

15 graph (1) and by redesignating paragraphs (2) and

16 (3) as paragraphs (1) and (2), respectively.

17   (8) Section 953(b)(1), as amended by section

18 3701, is amended by striking subparagraph (A) and

19 by redesignating subparagraphs (B) and (C) as sub-

20 paragraphs (A) and (B), respectively.

21   (c) EFFECTIVE DATE.—The amendments made by

22 this section shall apply to taxable years beginning after

23 December 31, 2017.

1 **SEC. 3703. COMPUTATION OF LIFE INSURANCE TAX RE-**

2   **SERVES.**

3   (a) IN GENERAL.—Section 807 is amended by strik-

4 ing subsections (c), (d), and (e) and inserting the following

5 new subsections:

6   "(c) ITEMS DESCRIBED.—The items described in this

7 subsection are the reserves for future unaccrued claims

8 defined in subsection (e) as determined by applying the

9 method of computing the reserves in subsection (d).

10   "(d) METHOD OF COMPUTING RESERVES FOR PUR-

11 POSES OF DETERMINING INCOME.—For purposes of this

12 part (other than section 816), the amount of the reserves

13 for future unaccrued claims shall be 76.5 percent of the

14 amount of such reserves as defined in subsection (e).

15   "(e) DEFINITIONS AND SPECIAL RULES.—For pur-

16 poses of this section—

17   "(1) RESERVES FOR FUTURE UNACCRUED

18   CLAIMS.—The term 'reserves for future unaccrued

19   claims' means—

20   "(A) life insurance reserves (as defined in

21   section 816(b)) determined in accordance with

22   the method prescribed by the National Associa-

23   tion of Insurance Commissioners and reported

24   by the taxpayer on its annual statement for the

25   calendar year that is the taxable year,

1   "(B) unpaid losses included in total re-

2   serves under section 816(c)(2), and

3   "(C) the amount (not included in subpara-

4   graph (A) or (B)) of reserves solely for claims

5   with respect to insurance risks which are deter-

6   mined in accordance with the method prescribed

7   by the National Association of Insurance Com-

8   missioners and reported by the taxpayer on its

9   annual statement for the calendar year that is

10   the taxable year,

11   but not including any amount of asset adequacy re-

12   serves, contingency reserves, unearned premium re-

13   serves, or any other amount not constituting re-

14   serves for future unaccrued claims as provided in

15   guidance by the Secretary. For purposes of subpara-

16   graph (B) and section 805(a)(1), the amount of the

17   unpaid losses (other than losses on life insurance

18   contracts) shall be the amount of the discounted un-

19   paid losses as defined in section 846.

20   "(2) REPORTING RULES.—The Secretary shall

21   require reporting (at such time and in such manner

22   as the Secretary shall prescribe) with respect to the

23   opening balance and closing balance of reserves and

24   with respect to the method of computing reserves for

25   purposes of determining income.".

1   (b) CONFORMING AMENDMENTS.—

2   (1) Section 808 is amended by adding at the

3   end the following new subsection:

4   "(g) PREVAILING STATE ASSUMED INTEREST

5   RATE.—For purposes of this subchapter—

6   "(1) IN GENERAL.—The term 'prevailing State

7   assumed interest rate' means, with respect to any

8   contract, the highest assumed interest rate per-

9   mitted to be used in computing life insurance re-

10   serves for insurance contracts or annuity contracts

11   (as the case may be) under the insurance laws of at

12   least 26 States. For purposes of the preceding sen-

13   tence, the effect of nonforfeiture laws of a State on

14   interest rates for reserves shall not be taken into ac-

15   count.

16   "(2) WHEN RATE DETERMINED.—The pre-

17   vailing State assumed interest rate with respect to

18   any contract shall be determined as of the beginning

19   of the calendar year in which the contract was

20   issued.".

21   (2) Paragraph (1) of section 811(d) is amended

22   by striking "the greater of the prevailing State as-

23   sumed interest rate or applicable Federal interest

24   rate in effect under section 807" and inserting "the

25   interest rate in effect under section 808(g)".

1   (3) Subparagraph (A) of section 846(f)(6) is

2   amended by striking "except that" and all that fol-

3   lows and inserting "except that the limitation of

4   subsection (a)(3) shall apply, and".

5   (4) Subparagraph (B) of section 954(i)(5) is

6   amended by striking "shall apply, and".

7   (c) EFFECTIVE DATE.—

8   (1) IN GENERAL.—The amendments made by

9   this section shall apply to taxable years beginning

10   after December 31, 2017.

11   (2) TRANSITION RULE.—For the first taxable

12   year beginning after December 31, 2017, the reserve

13   with respect to any contract (as determined under

14   section 807(d)(2) of the Internal Revenue Code of

15   1986) at the end of the preceding taxable year shall

16   be determined as if the amendments made by this

17   section had applied to such reserve in such preceding

18   taxable year.

19   (3) TRANSITION RELIEF.—

20   (A) IN GENERAL.—If—

21   (i) the reserve determined under sec-

22   tion 807(d)(2) of the Internal Revenue

23   Code of 1986 (determined without regard

24   to the amendments made by this section)

25   with respect to any contract as of the close

1   of the year preceding the first taxable year

2   beginning after December 31, 2017, differs

3   from

4   (ii) the reserve which would have been

5   determined with respect to such contract

6   as of the close of such taxable year under

7   such section determined without regard to

8   paragraph (2),

9   then the difference between the amount of the

10   reserve described in clause (i) and the amount

11   of the reserve described in clause (ii) shall be

12   taken into account under the method provided

13   in subparagraph (B).

14   (B) METHOD.—The method provided in

15   this subparagraph is as follows:

16   (i) if the amount determined under

17   subparagraph (A)(i) exceeds the amount

18   determined under subparagraph (A)(ii), 1/8

19   of such excess shall be taken into account,

20   for each of the 8 succeeding taxable years,

21   as a deduction under section 805(a)(2) of

22   such Code, or

23   (ii) if the amount determined under

24   subparagraph (A)(ii) exceeds the amount

25   determined under subparagraph (A)(i), 1/8

1   of such excess shall be included in gross in-

2   come, for each of the 8 succeeding taxable

3   years, under section 803(a)(2) of such

4   Code.

5 **SEC. 3704. ADJUSTMENT FOR CHANGE IN COMPUTING RE-**

6   **SERVES.**

7   (a) IN GENERAL.—Paragraph (1) of section 807(f)

8 is amended to read as follows:

9   "(1) TREATMENT AS CHANGE IN METHOD OF

10   ACCOUNTING.—If the basis for determining any item

11   referred to in subsection (c) as of the close of any

12   taxable year differs from the basis for such deter-

13   mination as of the close of the preceding taxable

14   year, then so much of the difference between—

15   "(A) the amount of the item at the close

16   of the taxable year, computed on the new basis,

17   and

18   "(B) the amount of the item at the close

19   of the taxable year, computed on the old basis,

20   as is attributable to contracts issued before the tax-

21   able year shall be taken into account under section

22   481 as adjustments attributable to a change in

23   method of accounting initiated by the taxpayer and

24   made with the consent of the Secretary.".

288

1   (b) EFFECTIVE DATE.—The amendments made by

2 this section shall apply to taxable years beginning after

3 December 31, 2017.

4 **SEC. 3705. MODIFICATION OF RULES FOR LIFE INSURANCE**

5   **PRORATION FOR PURPOSES OF DETER-**

6   **MINING THE DIVIDENDS RECEIVED DEDUC-**

7   **TION.**

8   (a) IN GENERAL.—Section 812 is amended to read

9 as follows:

10 **"SEC. 812. DEFINITION OF COMPANY'S SHARE AND POLICY-**

11   **HOLDER'S SHARE.**

12   "(a) COMPANY'S SHARE.—For purposes of section

13 805(a)(4), the term 'company's share' means, with respect

14 to any taxable year beginning after December 31, 2017,

15 40 percent.

16   "(b) POLICYHOLDER'S SHARE.—For purposes of sec-

17 tion 807, the term 'policyholder's share' means, with re-

18 spect to any taxable year beginning after December 31,

19 2017, 60 percent.".

20   (b) CONFORMING AMENDMENT.—Section 817A(e)(2)

21 is amended by striking ", 807(d)(2)(B), and 812" and in-

22 serting "and 807(d)(2)(B)".

23   (c) EFFECTIVE DATE.—The amendments made by

24 this section shall apply to taxable years beginning after

25 December 31, 2017.

SEC. 3706. REPEAL OF SPECIAL RULE FOR DISTRIBUTIONS TO SHAREHOLDERS FROM PRE-1984 POLICY-HOLDERS SURPLUS ACCOUNT.

(a) IN GENERAL.—Subpart D of part I of subchapter L is amended by striking section 815 (and by striking the item relating to such section in the table of sections for such subpart).

(b) CONFORMING AMENDMENT.—Section 801 is amended by striking subsection (c).

(c) EFFECTIVE DATE.—The amendments made by this section shall apply to taxable years beginning after December 31, 2017.

(d) PHASED INCLUSION OF REMAINING BALANCE OF POLICYHOLDERS SURPLUS ACCOUNTS.—In the case of any stock life insurance company which has a balance (determined as of the close of such company's last taxable year beginning before January 1, 2018) in an existing policyholders surplus account (as defined in section 815 of the Internal Revenue Code of 1986, as in effect before its repeal), the tax imposed by section 801 of such Code for the first 8 taxable years beginning after December 31, 2017, shall be the amount which would be imposed by such section for such year on the sum of—

(1) life insurance company taxable income for such year (within the meaning of such section 801 but not less than zero), plus

1   (2) ⅛ of such balance.

2 **SEC. 3707. MODIFICATION OF PRORATION RULES FOR**

3   **PROPERTY AND CASUALTY INSURANCE COM-**

4   **PANIES.**

5   (a) IN GENERAL.—Section 832(b)(5)(B) is amended

6 by striking "15 percent" and inserting "26.25 percent".

7   (b) EFFECTIVE DATE.—The amendment made by

8 this section shall apply to taxable years beginning after

9 December 31, 2017.

10 **SEC. 3708. MODIFICATION OF DISCOUNTING RULES FOR**

11   **PROPERTY AND CASUALTY INSURANCE COM-**

12   **PANIES.**

13   (a) MODIFICATION OF RATE OF INTEREST USED TO

14 DISCOUNT UNPAID LOSSES.—Paragraph (2) of section

15 846(c) is amended to read as follows:

16   "(2) DETERMINATION OF ANNUAL RATE.—The

17   annual rate determined by the Secretary under this

18   paragraph for any calendar year shall be a rate de-

19   termined on the basis of the corporate bond yield

20   curve (as defined in section 430(h)(2)(D)(i)).".

21   (b) MODIFICATION OF COMPUTATIONAL RULES FOR

22 LOSS PAYMENT PATTERNS.—Section 846(d)(3) is amend-

23 ed by striking subparagraphs (B) through (G) and insert-

24 ing the following new subparagraphs:

1   "(B) TREATMENT OF CERTAIN LOSSES.—

2   Losses which would have been treated as paid

3   in the last year of the period applicable under

4   subparagraph (A)(i) or (A)(ii) shall be treated

5   as paid in the following manner:

6   "(i) 3-YEAR LOSS PAYMENT PAT-

7   TERN.—

8   "(I) IN GENERAL.—The period

9   taken into account under subpara-

10   graph (A)(i) shall be extended to the

11   extent required under subclause (II).

12   "(II) COMPUTATION OF EXTEN-

13   SION.—The amount of losses which

14   would have been treated as paid in the

15   3d year after the accident year shall

16   be treated as paid in such 3d year

17   and each subsequent year in an

18   amount equal to the average of the

19   losses treated as paid in the 1st and

20   2d years after the accident year (or, if

21   lesser, the portion of the unpaid losses

22   not theretofore taken into account).

23   To the extent such unpaid losses have

24   not been treated as paid before the

25   18th year after the accident year, they

1   shall be treated as paid in such 18th

2   year.

3   "(ii) 10-YEAR LOSS PAYMENT PAT-

4   TERN.—

5   "(I) IN GENERAL.—The period

6   taken into account under subpara-

7   graph (A)(ii) shall be extended to the

8   extent required under subclause (II).

9   "(II) COMPUTATION OF EXTEN-

10   SION.—The amount of losses which

11   would have been treated as paid in the

12   10th year after the accident year shall

13   be treated as paid in such 10th year

14   and each subsequent year in an

15   amount equal to the amount of the

16   average of the losses treated as paid

17   in the 7th, 8th, and 9th years after

18   the accident year (or, if lesser, the

19   portion of the unpaid losses not there-

20   tofore taken into account). To the ex-

21   tent such unpaid losses have not been

22   treated as paid before the 25th year

23   after the accident year, they shall be

24   treated as paid in such 25th year.".

1   (c) REPEAL OF HISTORICAL PAYMENT PATTERN

2 ELECTION.—Section 846 is amended by striking sub-

3 section (e) and by redesignating subsections (f) and (g)

4 as subsections (e) and (f), respectively.

5   (d) EFFECTIVE DATE.—The amendments made by

6 this section shall apply to taxable years beginning after

7 December 31, 2017.

8   (e) TRANSITIONAL RULE.—For the first taxable year

9 beginning after December 31, 2017—

10   (1) the unpaid losses and the expenses unpaid

11   (as defined in paragraphs (5)(B) and (6) of section

12   832(b) of the Internal Revenue Code of 1986) at the

13   end of the preceding taxable year, and

14   (2) the unpaid losses as defined in sections

15   807(c)(2) and 805(a)(1) of such Code at the end of

16   the preceding taxable year,

17 shall be determined as if the amendments made by this

18 section had applied to such unpaid losses and expenses

19 unpaid in the preceding taxable year and by using the in-

20 terest rate and loss payment patterns applicable to acci-

21 dent years ending with calendar year 2018, and any ad-

22 justment shall be taken into account ratably in such first

23 taxable year and the 7 succeeding taxable years. For sub-

24 sequent taxable years, such amendments shall be applied

25 with respect to such unpaid losses and expenses unpaid

1 by using the interest rate and loss payment patterns appli-

2 cable to accident years ending with calendar year 2018.

3 SEC. 3709. REPEAL OF SPECIAL ESTIMATED TAX PAY-

4   MENTS.

5   (a) IN GENERAL.—Part III of subchapter L of chap-

6 ter 1 is amended by striking section 847 (and by striking

7 the item relating to such section in the table of sections

8 for such part).

9   (b) EFFECTIVE DATE.—The amendments made by

10 this section shall apply to taxable years beginning after

11 December 31, 2017.

12 SEC. 3710. CAPITALIZATION OF CERTAIN POLICY ACQUISI-

13   TION EXPENSES.

14   (a) IN GENERAL.—Paragraph (1) of section 848(c)

15 is amended by striking subparagraphs (A), (B), and (C)

16 and inserting the following new subparagraphs:

17   "(A) 4 percent of the net premiums for

18   such taxable year on specified insurance con-

19   tracts which are group contracts, and

20   "(B) 11 percent of the net premiums for

21   such taxable year on specified insurance con-

22   tracts not described in subparagraph (A).".

23   (b) GROUP CONTRACTS.—So much of paragraph (2)

24 of section 848(e) as precedes subparagraph (A) thereof is

25 amended to read as follows:

1   ''(2) GROUP CONTRACT.—The term 'group con-

2   tract' means any specified insurance contract—''.

3   (c) CONFORMING AMENDMENTS.—Section 848(e) is

4   amended by striking paragraphs (3) and (6) and by redes-

5   ignating paragraphs (4) and (5) as paragraphs (3) and

6   (4), respectively.

7   (d) EFFECTIVE DATE.—The amendments made by

8   this section shall apply to taxable years beginning after

9   December 31, 2017.

Subtitle I—Compensation

11 **SEC. 3801. NONQUALIFIED DEFERRED COMPENSATION.**

12 (a) IN GENERAL.—Subpart A of part I of subchapter

13 D of chapter 1 is amended by adding at the end the fol-

14 lowing new section:

15 **''SEC. 409B. NONQUALIFIED DEFERRED COMPENSATION.**

16 ''(a) IN GENERAL.—Any compensation which is de-

17 ferred under a nonqualified deferred compensation plan

18 shall be includible in the gross income of the person who

19 performed the services to which such compensation relates

20 when there is no substantial risk of forfeiture of the rights

21 of such person to such compensation.

22 ''(b) DEFINITIONS.—For purposes of this section—

23 ''(1) SUBSTANTIAL RISK OF FORFEITURE.—The

24 rights of a person to compensation shall be treated

25 as subject to a substantial risk of forfeiture only if

1   such person's rights to such compensation are condi-

2   tioned upon the future performance of substantial

3   services by any person. Such rights shall not be

4   treated as subject to a substantial risk of forfeiture

5   solely by reason of a covenant not to compete or the

6   occurrence of a condition related to a purpose of the

7   compensation other than the future performance of

8   services .

9   "(2) NONQUALIFIED DEFERRED COMPENSA-

10   TION PLAN.—For purposes of this section:

11   "(A) NONQUALIFIED DEFERRED COM-

12   PENSATION PLAN.—The term 'nonqualified de-

13   ferred compensation plan' means any plan that

14   provides for the deferral of compensation, other

15   than—

16   "(i) a qualified employer plan,

17   "(ii) any bona fide vacation leave, sick

18   leave, compensatory time, disability pay, or

19   death benefit plan, and

20   "(iii) any other plan or arrangement

21   designated by the Secretary consistent with

22   the purposes of this section.

23   "(B) EQUITY-BASED COMPENSATION.—

24   The term 'nonqualified deferred compensation

25   plan' shall include any plan that provides—

1   "(i) a right to compensation based on

2   the value of, or appreciation in value of, a

3   specified number of equity units of the

4   service recipient, whether paid in cash or

5   equity, or

6   "(ii) stock appreciation rights or stock

7   options.

8   Such term shall not include that portion of any

9 plan which consists of a transfer of property de-

10 scribed in section 83 (other than stock options)

11 or which consists of a trust to which section

12 402(b) applies.

13   "(3) QUALIFIED EMPLOYER PLAN.—The term

14 'qualified employer plan' means any plan, contract,

15 pension, account, or trust described in section

16 408(p)(2)(D)(ii) or a simple retirement account

17 (within the meaning of section 408(p)).

18   "(4) PLAN INCLUDES ARRANGEMENTS, ETC.—

19 The term 'plan' includes any agreement or arrange-

20 ment, including an agreement or arrangement that

21 includes one person.

22   "(5) EXCEPTION.—Compensation shall not be

23 treated as deferred for purposes of this section if the

24 service provider receives payment of such compensa-

25 tion not later than 2 ½ months after the end of the

1   taxable year of the service recipient during which the

2   right to the payment of such compensation is no

3   longer subject to a substantial risk of forfeiture.

4   "(6) TREATMENT OF EARNINGS.—References to

5   deferred compensation shall be treated as including

6   references to income (whether actual or notional) at-

7   tributable to such compensation or such income.

8   "(7) AGGREGATION RULES.—Except as pro-

9   vided by the Secretary, rules similar to the rules of

10   subsections (b) and (c) of section 414 shall apply.

11   "(c) NO INFERENCE ON EARLIER INCOME INCLU-

12   SION OR REQUIREMENT OF LATER INCLUSION.—Nothing

13   in this section shall be construed to prevent the inclusion

14   of amounts in gross income under any other provision of

15   this chapter or any other rule of law earlier than the time

16   provided in this section. Any amount included in gross in-

17   come under this section shall not be required to be in-

18   cluded in gross income under any other provision of this

19   chapter or any other rule of law later than the time pro-

20   vided in this section.

21   "(d) APPLICATION TO EXISTING DEFERRALS.—In

22   the case of any amount deferred to which this section does

23   not otherwise apply solely by reason of the fact that the

24   amount is attributable to services performed before Janu-

25   ary 1, 2018, to the extent such amount is not includible

1 in gross income in a taxable year beginning before 2026,

2 such amounts shall be includible in gross income in the

3 later of—

4   "(1) the last taxable year beginning before

5   2026, or

6   "(2) the taxable year in which there is no sub-

7   stantial risk of forfeiture of the rights to such com-

8   pensation.

9   "(e) REGULATIONS.—The Secretary shall prescribe

10 such regulations as may be necessary or appropriate to

11 carry out the purposes of this section, including regula-

12 tions disregarding a substantial risk of forfeiture in cases

13 where necessary to carry out the purposes of this sec-

14 tion.".

15   (b) REPORTING AND WITHHOLDING REQUIRE-

16 MENTS.—

17   (1) WAGE WITHHOLDING.—The flush sentence

18   at the end of section 3401(a) is amended by insert-

19   ing "or 409B" after "409A".

20   (2) WITHHOLDING OF TAX ON NONRESIDENT

21   ALIENS.—Section 1441(c)(4) is amended by insert-

22   ing "(other than under a nonqualified deferred com-

23   pensation plan (within the meaning of section

24   409B(b))" after "compensation for personal serv-

25   ices".

1   (3) INFORMATION REPORTING.—Section

2   6041(g) is amended—

3   (A) by inserting "or 409B(b)" after

4   "409A(d)" in paragraph (1), and

5   (B) by inserting "or 409B" after "409A"

6   in paragraph (2).

7   (4) RECEIPTS FOR EMPLOYEES.—Section

8   6051(a)(13), as amended by the preceding provi-

9   sions of this Act, is amended by inserting "or

10   409B(b)" after "409A(d)".

11   (c) TERMINATION OF CERTAIN OTHER NON-

12 QUALIFIED DEFERRED COMPENSATION RULES.—

13   (1) NONQUALIFIED DEFERRED COMPENSA-

14   TION.—

15   (A) IN GENERAL.—Subpart A of part I of

16   subchapter D of chapter 1 is amended by strik-

17   ing section 409A (and by striking the item re-

18   lating to such section in the table of sections

19   for such subpart).

20   (B) CONFORMING AMENDMENT.—Section

21   26(b)(2) is amended by striking subparagraph

22   (V).

23   (2) 457(b) PLANS OF TAX EXEMPT ORGANIZA-

24   TIONS.—Section 457 is amended by adding at the

25   end the following new subsection:

301

1   "(h) TERMINATION OF CERTAIN PLANS.—

2   "(1) TAX-EXEMPT ORGANIZATION PLANS.—

3   This section shall not apply to amounts deferred

4   which are attributable to services performed after

5   December 31, 2017, under a plan maintained by an

6   employer described in subsection (e)(1)(B).

7   "(2) INELIGIBLE DEFERRED COMPENSATION

8   PLANS.—Subsection (f) shall not apply to amounts

9   deferred which are attributable to services performed

10 after December 31, 2017.".

11   (3) NONQUALIFIED DEFERRED COMPENSATION

12 FROM CERTAIN TAX INDIFFERENT PARTIES.—

13   (A) IN GENERAL.—Subpart B of part II of

14   subchapter E of chapter 1 is amended by strik-

15   ing section 457A (and by striking the item re-

16   lating to such section in the table of sections

17   for such subpart).

18   (B) CONFORMING AMENDMENT.—Section

19   26(b)(2) is amended by striking subparagraph

20   (X).

21 (d) CLERICAL AMENDMENT.—The table of sections

22 for part I of subchapter D of chapter 1 is amended by

23 adding at the end the following new item:

"Sec. 409B. Nonqualified deferred compensation.".

24 (e) EFFECTIVE DATE.—

1   (1) IN GENERAL.—Except as otherwise pro-
2 vided in this subsection and section 409B(d) of the
3 Internal Revenue Code of 1986 (as added by this
4 Act), the amendments made by this section shall
5 apply to amounts which are attributable to services
6 performed after December 31, 2017.

7   (2) ACCELERATED PAYMENTS.—No later than
8 120 days after the date of the enactment of this Act,
9 the Secretary shall issue guidance providing a lim-
10 ited period of time during which a nonqualified de-
11 ferred compensation arrangement attributable to
12 services performed on or before December 31, 2017,
13 may, without violating the requirements of section
14 409A of the Internal Revenue Code of 1986, be
15 amended to conform the date of distribution to the
16 date the amounts are required to be included in in-
17 come.

18   (3) CERTAIN BACK-TO-BACK ARRANGEMENTS.—
19 If the taxpayer is also a service recipient and main-
20 tains one or more nonqualified deferred compensa-
21 tion arrangements for its service providers under
22 which any amount is attributable to services per-
23 formed on or before December 31, 2017, the guid-
24 ance issued under paragraph (3) shall permit such
25 arrangements to be amended to conform the dates of

1 distribution under such arrangement to the date

2 amounts are required to be included in the income

3 of such taxpayer under this subsection.

4   (4) ACCELERATED PAYMENT NOT TREATED AS

5 MATERIAL MODIFICATION.—Any amendment to a

6 nonqualified deferred compensation arrangement

7 made pursuant to paragraph (3) or (4) shall not be

8 treated as a material modification of the arrange-

9 ment for purposes of section 409A of the Internal

10 Revenue Code of 1986.

11 **SEC. 3802. MODIFICATION OF LIMITATION ON EXCESSIVE**

12   **EMPLOYEE REMUNERATION.**

13 (a) REPEAL OF PERFORMANCE-BASED COMPENSA-

14 TION AND COMMISSION EXCEPTIONS FOR LIMITATION ON

15 EXCESSIVE EMPLOYEE REMUNERATION.—

16   (1) IN GENERAL.—Section 162(m)(4) is amend-

17 ed by striking subparagraphs (B) and (C) and by re-

18 designating subparagraphs (D), (E), (F), and (G) as

19 subparagraphs (B), (C), (D), and (E), respectively.

20   (2) CONFORMING AMENDMENTS.—

21   (A) Paragraphs (5)(E) and (6)(D) of sec-

22   tion 162(m) are each amended by striking

23   "subparagraphs (B), (C), and (D)" and insert-

24   ing "subparagraph (B)".

1   (B) Paragraphs (5)(G) and (6)(G) of sec-

2   tion 162(m) are each amended by striking "(F)

3   and (G)" and inserting "(D) and (E)".

4   (b) EXPANSION OF APPLICABLE EMPLOYER.—Sec-

5 tion 162(m)(2) is amended to read as follows:

6   "(2) PUBLICLY HELD CORPORATION.—For pur-

7   poses of this subsection, the term 'publicly held cor-

8   poration' means any corporation which is an issuer

9   (as defined in section 3 of the Securities Exchange

10   Act of 1934 (15 U.S.C. 78c))—

11   "(A) the securities of which are required to

12   be registered under section 12 of such Act (15

13   U.S.C. 78l), or

14   "(B) that is required to file reports under

15   section 15(d) of such Act (15 U.S.C. 78o(d)).".

16   (c) MODIFICATION OF DEFINITION OF COVERED EM-

17 PLOYEES.—Section 162(m)(3) is amended—

18   (1) in subparagraph (A), by striking "as of the

19   close of the taxable year, such employee is the chief

20   executive officer of the taxpayer or is" and inserting

21   "such employee is the principal executive officer or

22   principal financial officer of the taxpayer at any

23   time during the taxable year, or was",

24   (2) in subparagraph (B)—

25   (A) by striking "4" and inserting "3", and

1   (B) by striking "(other than the chief exec-

2   utive officer)" and inserting "(other than the

3   principal executive officer)", and

4   (3) by striking "or" at the end of subparagraph

5   (A), by striking the period at the end of subpara-

6   graph (B) and inserting ", or", and by adding at the

7   end the following:

8   "(C) was a covered employee of the tax-

9   payer (or any predecessor) for any preceding

10   taxable year beginning after December 31,

11   2016.

12   Such term shall include any employee who would be

13   described in subparagraph (B) if the reporting de-

14   scribed in such subparagraph were required as so

15   described.".

16   (d) SPECIAL RULE FOR REMUNERATION PAID TO

17 BENEFICIARIES, ETC.—Section 162(m)(4), as amended by

18 subsection (a), is amended by adding at the end the fol-

19 lowing new subparagraph:

20   "(F) SPECIAL RULE FOR REMUNERATION

21   PAID TO BENEFICIARIES, ETC.—Remuneration

22   shall not fail to be applicable employee remu-

23   neration merely because it is includible in the

24   income of, or paid to, a person other than the

1   covered employee, including after the death of

2   the covered employee.".

3   (e) EFFECTIVE DATE.—The amendments made by

4 this section shall apply to taxable years beginning after

5 December 31, 2017.

6 **SEC. 3803. EXCISE TAX ON EXCESS TAX-EXEMPT ORGANIZA-**

7   **TION EXECUTIVE COMPENSATION.**

8   (a) IN GENERAL.—Subchapter D of chapter 42 is

9 amended by adding at the end the following new section:

10 **"SEC. 4960. TAX ON EXCESS TAX-EXEMPT ORGANIZATION**

11   **EXECUTIVE COMPENSATION.**

12   "(a) TAX IMPOSED.—There is hereby imposed a tax

13 equal to 20 percent of the sum of—

14   "(1) so much of the remuneration paid (other

15   than any excess parachute payment) by an applica-

16   ble tax-exempt organization for the taxable year with

17   respect to employment of any covered employee in

18   excess of $1,000,000, plus

19   "(2) any excess parachute payment paid by

20   such an organization to any covered employee.

21   "(b) LIABILITY FOR TAX.—The employer shall be lia-

22 ble for the tax imposed under subsection (a).

23   "(c) DEFINITIONS AND SPECIAL RULES.—For pur-

24 poses of this section—

1   "(1) APPLICABLE TAX-EXEMPT ORGANIZA-

2 TION.—The term 'applicable tax-exempt organiza-

3 tion' means any organization that for the taxable

4 year—

5   "(A) is exempt from taxation under section

6   501(a),

7   "(B) is a farmers' cooperative organization

8   described in section 521(b)(1),

9   "(C) has income excluded from taxation

10   under section 115(1), or

11   "(D) is a political organization described in

12   section 527(e)(1).

13   "(2) COVERED EMPLOYEE.—For purposes of

14 this section, the term 'covered employee' means any

15 employee (including any former employee) of an ap-

16 plicable tax-exempt organization if the employee—

17   "(A) is one of the 5 highest compensated

18   employees of the organization for the taxable

19   year, or

20   "(B) was a covered employee of the organi-

21   zation (or any predecessor) for any preceding

22   taxable year beginning after December 31,

23   2016.

24   "(3) REMUNERATION.—For purposes of this

25 section, the term 'remuneration' means wages (as

1 defined in section 3401(a)), except that such term

2 shall not include any designated Roth contribution

3 (as defined in section 402A(c)).

4   "(4) REMUNERATION FROM RELATED ORGANI-

5 ZATIONS.—

6   "(A) IN GENERAL.—Remuneration of a

7   covered employee paid by an applicable tax-ex-

8   empt organization shall include any remunera-

9   tion paid with respect to employment of such

10   employee by any related person or governmental

11   entity.

12   "(B) RELATED ORGANIZATIONS.—A per-

13   son or governmental entity shall be treated as

14   related to an applicable tax-exempt organization

15   if such person or governmental entity—

16   "(i) controls, or is controlled by, the

17   organization,

18   "(ii) is controlled by one or more per-

19   sons that control the organization,

20   "(iii) is a supported organization (as

21   defined in section 509(f)(2)) during the

22   taxable year with respect to the organiza-

23   tion,

24   "(iv) is a supporting organization de-

25   scribed in section 509(a)(3) during the

1   taxable year with respect to the organiza-

2   tion, or

3   "(v) in the case of an organization

4   that is a voluntary employees' beneficiary

5   association described in section 501(a)(9),

6   establishes, maintains, or makes contribu-

7   tions to such voluntary employees' bene-

8   ficiary association.

9   "(C) LIABILITY FOR TAX.—In any case in

10   which remuneration from more than one em-

11   ployer is taken into account under this para-

12   graph in determining the tax imposed by sub-

13   section (a), each such employer shall be liable

14   for such tax in an amount which bears the

15   same ratio to the total tax determined under

16   subsection (a) with respect to such remunera-

17   tion as—

18   "(i) the amount of remuneration paid

19   by such employer with respect to such em-

20   ployee, bears to

21   "(ii) the amount of remuneration paid

22   by all such employers to such employee.

23   "(5) EXCESS PARACHUTE PAYMENT.—For pur-

24   poses determining the tax imposed by subsection

25   (a)(2)—

1   "(A) IN GENERAL.—The term 'excess

2   parachute payment' means an amount equal to

3   the excess of any parachute payment over the

4   portion of the base amount allocated to such

5   payment.

6   "(B) PARACHUTE PAYMENT.—The term

7   'parachute payment' means any payment in the

8   nature of compensation to (or for the benefit

9   of) a covered employee if—

10   "(i) such payment is contingent on

11   such employee's separation from employ-

12   ment with the employer, and

13   "(ii) the aggregate present value of

14   the payments in the nature of compensa-

15   tion to (or for the benefit of) such indi-

16   vidual which are contingent on such sepa-

17   ration equals or exceeds an amount equal

18   to 3 times the base amount.

19   Such term does not include any payment de-

20   scribed in section 280G(b)(6) (relating to ex-

21   emption for payments under qualified plans) or

22   any payment made under or to an annuity con-

23   tract described in section 403(b) or a plan de-

24   scribed in section 457(b).

1   "(C) BASE AMOUNT.—Rules similar to the

2   rules of 280G(b)(3) shall apply for purposes of

3   determining the base amount.

4   "(D) PROPERTY TRANSFERS; PRESENT

5   VALUE.—Rules similar to the rules of para-

6   graphs (3) and (4) of section 280G(d) shall

7   apply.

8   "(6) COORDINATION WITH DEDUCTION LIMITA-

9 TION.—Remuneration the deduction for which is not

10 allowed by reason of section 162(m) shall not be

11 taken into account for purposes of this section.

12   "(d) REGULATIONS.—The Secretary shall prescribe

13 such regulations as may be necessary to prevent avoidance

14 of the purposes of this section through the performance

15 of services other than as an employee.".

16   (b) CLERICAL AMENDMENT.—The table of sections

17 for subchapter D of chapter 42 is amended by adding at

18 the end the following new item:

"Sec. 4960. Tax on excess exempt organization executive compensation.".

19   (c) EFFECTIVE DATE.—The amendments made by

20 this section shall apply to taxable years beginning after

21 December 31, 2017.

312

1 **TITLE IV—TAXATION OF FOR-**
2 **EIGN INCOME AND FOREIGN**
3 **PERSONS**
4 **Subtitle A—Establishment of Par-**
5 **ticipation Exemption System for**
6 **Taxation of Foreign Income**

7 **SEC. 4001. DEDUCTION FOR FOREIGN-SOURCE PORTION OF**
8 **DIVIDENDS RECEIVED BY DOMESTIC COR-**
9 **PORATIONS FROM SPECIFIED 10-PERCENT**
10 **OWNED FOREIGN CORPORATIONS.**

11 (a) IN GENERAL.—Part VIII of subchapter B of
12 chapter 1 is amended by inserting after section 245 the
13 following new section:

14 **"SEC. 245A. DEDUCTION FOR FOREIGN-SOURCE PORTION**
15 **OF DIVIDENDS RECEIVED BY DOMESTIC COR-**
16 **PORATIONS FROM SPECIFIED 10-PERCENT**
17 **OWNED FOREIGN CORPORATIONS.**

18 "(a) IN GENERAL.—In the case of any dividend re-
19 ceived from a specified 10-percent owned foreign corpora-
20 tion by a domestic corporation which is a United States
21 shareholder with respect to such foreign corporation, there
22 shall be allowed as a deduction an amount equal to the
23 foreign-source portion of such dividend.

24 "(b) SPECIFIED 10-PERCENT OWNED FOREIGN COR-
25 PORATION.—For purposes of this section, the term 'speci-

1 fied 10-percent owned foreign corporation' means any for-

2 eign corporation with respect to which any domestic cor-

3 poration is a United States shareholder. Such term shall

4 not include any passive foreign investment company (with-

5 in the meaning of subpart D of part VI of subchapter P)

6 that is not a controlled foreign corporation.

7   "(c) FOREIGN-SOURCE PORTION.—For purposes of

8 this section—

9   "(1) IN GENERAL.—The foreign-source portion

10   of any dividend is an amount which bears the same

11   ratio to such dividend as—

12   "(A) the post-1986 undistributed foreign

13   earnings of the specified 10-percent owned for-

14   eign corporation, bears to

15   "(B) the total post-1986 undistributed

16   earnings of such foreign corporation.

17   "(2) POST-1986 UNDISTRIBUTED EARNINGS.—

18   The term 'post-1986 undistributed earnings' means

19   the amount of the earnings and profits of the speci-

20   fied 10-percent owned foreign corporation (computed

21   in accordance with sections 964(a) and 986) accu-

22   mulated in taxable years beginning after December

23   31, 1986—

314

1   "(A) as of the close of the taxable year of

2   the specified 10-percent owned foreign corpora-

3   tion in which the dividend is distributed, and

4   "(B) without diminution by reason of divi-

5   dends distributed during such taxable year.

6   "(3) POST-1986 UNDISTRIBUTED FOREIGN

7   EARNINGS.—The term 'post-1986 undistributed for-

8   eign earnings' means the portion of the post-1986

9   undistributed earnings which is attributable to nei-

10   ther—

11   "(A) income described in subparagraph (A)

12   of section 245(a)(5), nor

13   "(B) dividends described in subparagraph

14   (B) of such section (determined without regard

15   to section 245(a)(12)).

16   "(4) TREATMENT OF DISTRIBUTIONS FROM

17   EARNINGS BEFORE 1987.—

18   "(A) IN GENERAL.—In the case of any div-

19   idend paid out of earnings and profits of the

20   specified 10-percent owned foreign corporation

21   (computed in accordance with sections 964(a)

22   and 986) accumulated in taxable years begin-

23   ning before January 1, 1987—

1   "(i) paragraphs (1), (2), and (3) shall

2   be applied without regard to the phrase

3   'post-1986' each place it appears, and

4   "(ii) paragraph (2) shall be applied by

5   substituting 'after the date specified in sec-

6   tion 316(a)(1)' for 'in taxable years begin-

7   ning after December 31, 1986'.

8   "(B) DIVIDENDS PAID FIRST OUT OF

9   POST-1986 EARNINGS.—Dividends shall be treat-

10   ed as paid out of post-1986 undistributed earn-

11   ings to the extent thereof.

12   "(5) TREATMENT OF CERTAIN DIVIDENDS IN

13   EXCESS OF UNDISTRIBUTED EARNINGS.—In the case

14   of any dividend from the specified 10-percent owned

15   foreign corporation which is in excess of undistrib-

16   uted earnings (as determined under paragraph (2)

17   after taking into account the modifications described

18   in clauses (i) and (ii) of paragraph (4)(A)), the for-

19   eign-source portion of such dividend is an amount

20   which bears the same ratio to such dividend as—

21   "(A) the portion of the earnings and prof-

22   its described in subparagraph (B) which is at-

23   tributable to neither income described in para-

24   graph (3)(A) nor dividends described in para-

25   graph (3)(B), bears to

316

"(B) the earnings and profits of such corporation for the taxable year in which such distribution is made (computed as of the close of the taxable year without diminution by reason of any distributions made during the taxable year).

"(d) DISALLOWANCE OF FOREIGN TAX CREDIT, ETC.—

"(1) IN GENERAL.—No credit shall be allowed under section 901 for any taxes paid or accrued (or treated as paid or accrued) with respect to any dividend for which a deduction is allowed under this section.

"(2) DENIAL OF DEDUCTION.—No deduction shall be allowed under this chapter for any tax for which credit is not allowable under section 901 by reason of paragraph (1) (determined by treating the taxpayer as having elected the benefits of subpart A of part III of subchapter N).

"(e) REGULATIONS.—The Secretary may prescribe such regulations or other guidance as may be necessary or appropriate to carry out the provisions of this section.".

(b) APPLICATION OF HOLDING PERIOD REQUIREMENT.—Section 246(c) is amended—

317

1   (1) by striking "or 245" in paragraph (1) and

2   inserting "245, or 245A", and

3   (2) by adding at the end the following new

4   paragraph:

5   "(5) SPECIAL RULES FOR FOREIGN SOURCE

6   PORTION OF DIVIDENDS RECEIVED FROM SPECIFIED

7   10-PERCENT OWNED FOREIGN CORPORATIONS.—

8   "(A) 6-MONTH HOLDING PERIOD REQUIRE-

9   MENT.—For purposes of section 245A—

10   "(i) paragraph (1)(A) shall be ap-

11   plied—

12   "(I) by substituting '180 days'

13   for '45 days'each place it appears, and

14   "(II) by substituting '361-day pe-

15   riod' for '91-day period', and

16   "(ii) paragraph (2) shall not apply.

17   "(B) STATUS MUST BE MAINTAINED DUR-

18   ING HOLDING PERIOD.—For purposes of apply-

19   ing paragraph (1) with respect to section 245A,

20   the taxpayer shall be treated as holding the

21   stock referred to in paragraph (1) for any pe-

22   riod only if—

23   "(i) the specified 10-percent owned

24   foreign corporation referred to in section

318

1   245A(a) is a specified 10-percent owned

2   foreign corporation for such period, and

3   "(ii) the taxpayer is a United States

4   shareholder with respect to such specified

5   10-percent owned foreign corporation for

6   such period.".

7   (c) APPLICATION OF RULES GENERALLY APPLICA-

8 BLE TO DEDUCTIONS FOR DIVIDENDS RECEIVED.—

9   (1) TREATMENT OF DIVIDENDS FROM CERTAIN

10   CORPORATIONS.—Section 246(a)(1) is amended by

11   striking "and 245" and inserting "245, and 245A".

12   (2) COORDINATION WITH SECTION 1059.—Sec-

13   tion 1059(b)(2)(B) is amended by striking "or 245"

14   and inserting "245, or 245A".

15   (d) COORDINATION WITH FOREIGN TAX CREDIT

16 LIMITATION.—Section 904(b) is amended by adding at

17 the end the following new paragraph:

18   "(5) TREATMENT OF DIVIDENDS FOR WHICH

19   DEDUCTION IS ALLOWED UNDER SECTION 245A.—

20   For purposes of subsection (a), in the case of a

21   United States shareholder with respect to a specified

22   10-percent owned foreign corporation, such share-

23   holder's taxable income from sources without the

24   United States (and entire taxable income) shall be

25   determined without regard to—

1   ''(A) the foreign-source portion of any divi-

2   dend received from such foreign corporation,

3   and

4   ''(B) any deductions properly allocable or

5   apportioned to—

6   ''(i) income (other than subpart F in-

7   come (as defined in section 952) and for-

8   eign high return amounts (as defined in

9   section 951A(b)) with respect to stock of

10   such specified 10-percent owned foreign

11   corporation, or

12   ''(ii) such stock (to the extent income

13   with respect to such stock is other than

14   subpart F income (as so defined) or for-

15   eign high return amounts (as so defined)).

16 Any term which is used in section 245A and in this

17 paragraph shall have the same meaning for purposes

18 of this paragraph as when used in such section.''.

19 (e) CONFORMING AMENDMENTS.—

20   (1) Section 245(a)(4) is amended by striking

21 ''section 902(c)(1)'' and inserting ''section

22 245A(c)(2) applied by substituting 'qualified 10-per-

23 cent owned foreign corporation' for 'specified 10-per-

24 cent owned foreign corporation' each place it ap-

25 pears''.

1   (2) Section 951(b) is amended by striking "sub-

2 part" and inserting "title".

3   (3) Section 957(a) is amended by striking "sub-

4 part" in the matter preceding paragraph (1) and in-

5 serting "title".

6   (4) The table of sections for part VIII of sub-

7 chapter B of chapter 1 is amended by inserting after

8 section 245 the following new item:

"Sec. 245A. Deduction for foreign-source portion of dividends received by domestic corporations from specified 10-percent owned foreign
corporations.".

9   (f) EFFECTIVE DATE.—The amendments made by

10 this section shall apply to distributions made after (and,

11 in the case of the amendments made by subsection (d),

12 deductions with respect to taxable years ending after) De-

13 cember 31, 2017.

14 **SEC. 4002. APPLICATION OF PARTICIPATION EXEMPTION**

15   **TO INVESTMENTS IN UNITED STATES PROP-**

16   **ERTY.**

17   (a) IN GENERAL.—Section 956(a) is amended in the

18 matter preceding paragraph (1) by inserting "(other than

19 a corporation)" after "United States shareholder".

20   (b) REGULATORY AUTHORITY TO PREVENT

21 ABUSE.—Section 956(e) is amended by striking "includ-

22 ing regulations to prevent" and inserting "including regu-

23 lations—

1   "(1) to address United States shareholders that

2   are partnerships with corporate partners, and

3   "(2) to prevent".

4   (c) EFFECTIVE DATE.—The amendments made by

5 this section shall apply to taxable years of foreign corpora-

6 tions beginning after December 31, 2017.

7 **SEC. 4003. LIMITATION ON LOSSES WITH RESPECT TO**

8   **SPECIFIED 10-PERCENT OWNED FOREIGN**

9   **CORPORATIONS.**

10   (a) BASIS IN SPECIFIED 10-PERCENT OWNED FOR-

11 EIGN CORPORATION REDUCED BY NONTAXED PORTION

12 OF DIVIDEND FOR PURPOSES OF DETERMINING LOSS.—

13   (1) IN GENERAL.—Section 961 is amended by

14   adding at the end the following new subsection:

15   "(d) BASIS IN SPECIFIED 10-PERCENT OWNED FOR-

16 EIGN CORPORATION REDUCED BY NONTAXED PORTION

17 OF DIVIDEND FOR PURPOSES OF DETERMINING LOSS.—

18 If a domestic corporation received a dividend from a speci-

19 fied 10-percent owned foreign corporation (as defined in

20 section 245A) in any taxable year, solely for purposes of

21 determining loss on any disposition of stock of such for-

22 eign corporation in such taxable year or any subsequent

23 taxable year, the basis of such domestic corporation in

24 such stock shall be reduced (but not below zero) by the

25 amount of any deduction allowable to such domestic cor-

322

1 poration under section 245A with respect to such stock

2 except to the extent such basis was reduced under section

3 1059 by reason of a dividend for which such a deduction

4 was allowable.''.

5   (2) EFFECTIVE DATE.—The amendments made

6   by this subsection shall apply to distributions made

7   after December 31, 2017.

8   (b) TREATMENT OF FOREIGN BRANCH LOSSES

9 TRANSFERRED TO SPECIFIED 10-PERCENT OWNED FOR-

10 EIGN CORPORATIONS.—

11   (1) IN GENERAL.—Part II of subchapter B of

12   chapter 1 is amended by adding at the end the fol-

13   lowing new section:

14 **"SEC. 91. CERTAIN FOREIGN BRANCH LOSSES TRANS-**

15   **FERRED TO SPECIFIED 10-PERCENT OWNED**

16   **FOREIGN CORPORATIONS.**

17   "(a) IN GENERAL.—If a domestic corporation trans-

18 fers substantially all of the assets of a foreign branch

19 (within the meaning of section 367(a)(3)(C)) to a specified

20 10-percent owned foreign corporation (as defined in sec-

21 tion 245A) with respect to which it is a United States

22 shareholder after such transfer, such domestic corporation

23 shall include in gross income for the taxable year which

24 includes such transfer an amount equal to the transferred

25 loss amount with respect to such transfer.

1   "(b) TRANSFERRED LOSS AMOUNT.—For purposes

2 of this section, the term 'transferred loss amount' means,

3 with respect to any transfer of substantially all of the as-

4 sets of a foreign branch, the excess (if any) of—

5   "(1) the sum of losses—

6   "(A) which were incurred by the foreign

7   branch after December 31, 2017, and before

8   the transfer, and

9   "(B) with respect to which a deduction was

10   allowed to the taxpayer, over

11   "(2) the sum of—

12   "(A) any taxable income of such branch

13   for a taxable year after the taxable year in

14   which the loss was incurred and through the

15   close of the taxable year of the transfer, and

16   "(B) any amount which is recognized

17   under section 904(f)(3) on account of the trans-

18   fer.

19   "(c) REDUCTION FOR RECOGNIZED GAINS.—

20   "(1) IN GENERAL.—In the case of a transfer

21   not described in section 367(a)(3)(C), the trans-

22   ferred loss amount shall be reduced (but not below

23   zero) by the amount of gain recognized by the tax-

24   payer on account of the transfer (other than

324

1 amounts taken into account under subsection

2 (c)(2)(B)).

3 "(2) COORDINATION WITH RECOGNITION

4 UNDER SECTION 367.—In the case of a transfer de-

5 scribed in section 367(a)(3)(C), the transferred loss

6 amount shall not exceed the excess (if any) of—

7 "(A) the excess of the amount described in

8 section 367(a)(3)(C)(i) over the amount de-

9 scribed in section 367(a)(3)(C)(ii) with respect

10 to such transfer, over

11 "(B) the amount of gain recognized under

12 section 367(a)(3)(C) with respect to such trans-

13 fer.

14 "(d) SOURCE OF INCOME.—Amounts included in

15 gross income under this section shall be treated as derived

16 from sources within the United States.

17 "(e) BASIS ADJUSTMENTS.—Consistent with such

18 regulations or other guidance as the Secretary may pre-

19 scribe, proper adjustments shall be made in the adjusted

20 basis of the taxpayer's stock in the specified 10-percent

21 owned foreign corporation to which the transfer is made,

22 and in the transferee's adjusted basis in the property

23 transferred, to reflect amounts included in gross income

24 under this section.".

1   (2) AMOUNTS RECOGNIZED UNDER SECTION 367

2   ON TRANSFER OF FOREIGN BRANCH WITH PRE-

3   VIOUSLY DEDUCTED LOSSES TREATED AS UNITED

4   STATES SOURCE.—Section 367(a)(3)(C) is amended

5   by striking "outside" in the last sentence and insert-

6   ing "within".

7   (3) CLERICAL AMENDMENT.—The table of sec-

8   tions for part II of subchapter B of chapter 1 is

9   amended by adding at the end the following new

10   item:

"Sec. 91. Certain foreign branch losses transferred to specified 10-percent
        owned foreign corporations.".

11   (4) EFFECTIVE DATE.—The amendments made

12   by this subsection shall apply to transfers after De-

13   cember 31, 2017.

14 **SEC. 4004. TREATMENT OF DEFERRED FOREIGN INCOME**

15   **UPON TRANSITION TO PARTICIPATION EX-**

16   **EMPTION SYSTEM OF TAXATION.**

17   (a) IN GENERAL.—Section 965 is amended to read

18   as follows:

19 **"SEC. 965. TREATMENT OF DEFERRED FOREIGN INCOME**

20   **UPON TRANSITION TO PARTICIPATION EX-**

21   **EMPTION SYSTEM OF TAXATION.**

22   "(a) TREATMENT OF DEFERRED FOREIGN INCOME

23 AS SUBPART F INCOME.—In the case of the last taxable

24 year of a deferred foreign income corporation which begins

326

1 before January 1, 2018, the subpart F income of such

2 foreign corporation (as otherwise determined for such tax-

3 able year under section 952) shall be increased by the

4 greater of—

5   "(1) the accumulated post-1986 deferred for-

6   eign income of such corporation determined as of

7   November 2, 2017, or

8   "(2) the accumulated post-1986 deferred for-

9   eign income of such corporation determined as of

10   December 31, 2017.

11 "(b) REDUCTION IN AMOUNTS INCLUDED IN GROSS

12 INCOME OF UNITED STATES SHAREHOLDERS OF SPECI-

13 FIED FOREIGN CORPORATIONS WITH DEFICITS IN EARN-

14 INGS AND PROFITS.—

15   "(1) IN GENERAL.—In the case of a taxpayer

16   which is a United States shareholder with respect to

17   at least one deferred foreign income corporation and

18   at least one E&P deficit foreign corporation, the

19   amount which would (but for this subsection) be

20   taken into account under section 951(a)(1) by rea-

21   son of subsection (a) as such United States share-

22   holder's pro rata share of the subpart F income of

23   each deferred foreign income corporation shall be re-

24   duced (but not below zero) by the amount of such

25   United States shareholder's aggregate foreign E&P

327

1   deficit which is allocated under paragraph (2) to

2   such deferred foreign income corporation.

3   "(2) ALLOCATION OF AGGREGATE FOREIGN E&P

4   DEFICIT.—The aggregate foreign E&P deficit of any

5   United States shareholder shall be allocated among

6   the deferred foreign income corporations of such

7   United States shareholder in an amount which bears

8   the same proportion to such aggregate as—

9   "(A) such United States shareholder's pro

10   rata share of the accumulated post-1986 de-

11   ferred foreign income of each such deferred for-

12   eign income corporation, bears to

13   "(B) the aggregate of such United States

14   shareholder's pro rata share of the accumulated

15   post-1986 deferred foreign income of all de-

16   ferred foreign income corporations of such

17   United States shareholder.

18   "(3) DEFINITIONS RELATED TO E&P DEFI-

19   CITS.—For purposes of this subsection—

20   "(A) AGGREGATE FOREIGN E&P DEF-

21   ICIT.—The term 'aggregate foreign E&P deficit'

22   means, with respect to any United States share-

23   holder, the aggregate of such shareholder's pro

24   rata shares of the specified E&P deficits of the

328

1   E&P deficit foreign corporations of such share-

2   holder.

3   "(B) E&P DEFICIT FOREIGN CORPORA-

4   TION.—The term 'E&P deficit foreign corpora-

5   tion' means, with respect to any taxpayer, any

6   specified foreign corporation with respect to

7   which such taxpayer is a United States share-

8   holder, if—

9   "(i) such specified foreign corporation

10   has a deficit in post-1986 earnings and

11   profits, and

12   "(ii) as of November 2, 2017—

13   "(I) such corporation was a spec-

14   ified foreign corporation, and

15   "(II) such taxpayer was a United

16   States shareholder of such corpora-

17   tion.

18   "(C) SPECIFIED E&P DEFICIT.—The term

19   'specified E&P deficit' means, with respect to

20   any E&P deficit foreign corporation, the

21   amount of the deficit referred to in subpara-

22   graph (B).

23   "(4) NETTING AMONG UNITED STATES SHARE-

24   HOLDERS IN SAME AFFILIATED GROUP.—

1   "(A) IN GENERAL.—In the case of any af-
2   filiated group which includes at least one E&P
3   net surplus shareholder and one E&P net def-
4   icit shareholder, the amount which would (but
5   for this paragraph) be taken into account under
6   section 951(a)(1) by reason of subsection (a) by
7   each such E&P net surplus shareholder shall be
8   reduced (but not below zero) by such share-
9   holder's applicable share of the affiliated
10   group's aggregate unused E&P deficit.

11   "(B) E&P NET SURPLUS SHARE-
12   HOLDER.—For purposes of this paragraph, the
13   term 'E&P net surplus shareholder' means any
14   United States shareholder which would (deter-
15   mined without regard to this paragraph) take
16   into account an amount greater than zero
17   under section 951(a)(1) by reason of subsection
18   (a).

19   "(C) E&P NET DEFICIT SHAREHOLDER.—
20   For purposes of this paragraph, the term 'E&P
21   net deficit shareholder' means any United
22   States shareholder if—

23   "(i) the aggregate foreign E&P deficit
24   with respect to such shareholder (as de-
25   fined in paragraph (3)(A)), exceeds

1   "(ii) the amount which would (but for

2   this subsection) be taken into account by

3   such shareholder under section 951(a)(1)

4   by reason of subsection (a).

5   "(D) AGGREGATE UNUSED E&P DEFICIT.—

6   For purposes of this paragraph—

7   "(i) IN GENERAL.—The term 'aggre-

8   gate unused E&P deficit' means, with re-

9   spect to any affiliated group, the lesser

10   of—

11   "(I) the sum of the excesses de-

12   scribed in subparagraph (C), deter-

13   mined with respect to each E&P net

14   deficit shareholder in such group, or

15   "(II) the amount determined

16   under subparagraph (E)(ii).

17   "(ii) REDUCTION WITH RESPECT TO

18   E&P NET DEFICIT SHAREHOLDERS WHICH

19   ARE NOT WHOLLY OWNED BY THE AFFILI-

20   ATED GROUP.—If the group ownership per-

21   centage of any E&P net deficit shareholder

22   is less than 100 percent, the amount of the

23   excess described in subparagraph (C)

24   which is taken into account under clause

25   (i)(I) with respect to such E&P net deficit

1 shareholder shall be such group ownership
2 percentage of such amount.

3 "(E) APPLICABLE SHARE.—For purposes
4 of this paragraph, the term 'applicable share'
5 means, with respect to any E&P net surplus
6 shareholder in any affiliated group, the amount
7 which bears the same proportion to such
8 group's aggregate unused E&P deficit as—

9 "(i) the product of—

10 "(I) such shareholder's group
11 ownership percentage, multiplied by

12 "(II) the amount which would
13 (but for this paragraph) be taken into
14 account under section 951(a)(1) by
15 reason of subsection (a) by such
16 shareholder, bears to

17 "(ii) the aggregate amount deter-
18 mined under clause (i) with respect to all
19 E&P net surplus shareholders in such
20 group.

21 "(F) GROUP OWNERSHIP PERCENTAGE.—
22 For purposes of this paragraph, the term
23 'group ownership percentage' means, with re-
24 spect to any United States shareholder in any
25 affiliated group, the percentage of the value of

1   the stock of such United States shareholder

2   which is held by other includible corporations in

3   such affiliated group. Notwithstanding the pre-

4   ceding sentence, the group ownership percent-

5   age of the common parent of the affiliated

6   group is 100 percent. Any term used in this

7   subparagraph which is also used in section

8   1504 shall have the same meaning as when

9   used in such section.

10   "(c) APPLICATION OF PARTICIPATION EXEMPTION

11   TO INCLUDED INCOME.—

12   "(1) IN GENERAL.—In the case of a United

13   States shareholder of a deferred foreign income cor-

14   poration, there shall be allowed as a deduction for

15   the taxable year in which an amount is included in

16   the gross income of such United States shareholder

17   under section 951(a)(1) by reason of this section an

18   amount equal to the sum of—

19   "(A) the United States shareholder's 5

20   percent rate equivalent percentage of the excess

21   (if any) of—

22   "(i) the amount so included as gross

23   income, over

1   ''(ii) the amount of such United

2   States shareholder's aggregate foreign cash

3   position, plus

4   ''(B) the United States shareholder's 12

5   percent rate equivalent percentage of so much

6   of the amount described in subparagraph (A)(ii)

7   as does not exceed the amount described in sub-

8   paragraph (A)(i).

9   ''(2) 5 AND 12 PERCENT RATE EQUIVALENT

10   PERCENTAGES.—For purposes of this subsection—

11   ''(A) 5 PERCENT RATE EQUIVALENT PER-

12   CENTAGE.—The term '5 percent rate equivalent

13   percentage' means, with respect to any United

14   States shareholder for any taxable year, the

15   percentage which would result in the amount to

16   which such percentage applies being subject to

17   a 5 percent rate of tax determined by only tak-

18   ing into account a deduction equal to such per-

19   centage of such amount and the highest rate of

20   tax specified in section 11 for such taxable

21   year. In the case of any taxable year of a

22   United States shareholder to which section 15

23   applies, the highest rate of tax under section 11

24   before the effective date of the change in rates

25   and the highest rate of tax under section 11

1   after the effective date of such change shall

2   each be taken into account under the preceding

3   sentence in the same proportions as the portion

4   of such taxable year which is before and after

5   such effective date, respectively.

6   "(B) 12 PERCENT RATE EQUIVALENT PER-

7   CENTAGE.—The term '12 percent rate equiva-

8   lent percentage' means, with respect to any

9   United States shareholder for any taxable year,

10   the percentage determined under subparagraph

11   (A) applied by substituting '12 percent rate of

12   tax' for '5 percent rate of tax'.

13   "(3) AGGREGATE FOREIGN CASH POSITION.—

14   For purposes of this subsection—

15   "(A) IN GENERAL.—The term 'aggregate

16   foreign cash position' means, with respect to

17   any United States shareholder, one-third of the

18   sum of—

19   "(i) the aggregate of such United

20   States shareholder's pro rata share of the

21   cash position of each specified foreign cor-

22   poration of such United States shareholder

23   determined as of November 2, 2017,

24   "(ii) the aggregate described in clause

25   (i) determined as of the close of the last

1   taxable year of each such specified foreign

2   corporation which ends before November 2,

3   2017, and

4   "(iii) the aggregate described in

5   clause (i) determined as of the close of the

6   taxable year of each such specified foreign

7   corporation which precedes the taxable

8   year referred to in clause (ii).

9   In the case of any foreign corporation which did

10   not exist as of the determination date described

11   in clause (ii) or (iii), this subparagraph shall be

12   applied separately to such foreign corporation

13   by not taking into account such clause and by

14   substituting 'one-half (100 percent in the case

15   that both clauses (ii) and (iii) are disregarded)'

16   for 'one-third'.

17   "(B) CASH POSITION.—For purposes of

18   this paragraph, the cash position of any speci-

19   fied foreign corporation is the sum of—

20   "(i) cash held by such foreign cor-

21   poration,

22   "(ii) the net accounts receivable of

23   such foreign corporation, plus

24   "(iii) the fair market value of the fol-

25   lowing assets held by such corporation:

1   "(I) Actively traded personal

2   property for which there is an estab-

3   lished financial market.

4   "(II) Commercial paper, certifi-

5   cates of deposit, the securities of the

6   Federal government and of any State

7   or foreign government.

8   "(III) Any foreign currency.

9   "(IV) Any obligation with a term

10   of less than one year.

11   "(V) Any asset which the Sec-

12   retary identifies as being economically

13   equivalent to any asset described in

14   this subparagraph.

15   "(C) NET ACCOUNTS RECEIVABLE.—For

16 purposes of this paragraph, the term 'net ac-

17 counts receivable' means, with respect to any

18 specified foreign corporation, the excess (if any)

19 of—

20   "(i) such corporation's accounts re-

21   ceivable, over

22   "(ii) such corporation's accounts pay-

23   able (determined consistent with the rules

24   of section 461).

1   "(D) PREVENTION OF DOUBLE COUNT-

2   ING.—

3   "(i) IN GENERAL.—The applicable

4   percentage of each specified cash position

5   of a specified foreign corporation shall not

6   be taken into account by—

7   "(I) the United States share-

8   holder referred to in clause (ii) with

9   respect to such position, or

10   "(II) any United States share-

11   holder which is an includible corpora-

12   tion in the same affiliated group as

13   such United States shareholder re-

14   ferred to in clause (ii).

15   "(ii) SPECIFIED CASH POSITION.—For

16   purposes of this subparagraph, the term

17   'specified cash position' means—

18   "(I) amounts described in sub-

19   paragraph (B)(ii) to the extent such

20   amounts are receivable from another

21   specified foreign corporation with re-

22   spect to any United States share-

23   holder,

24   "(II) amounts described in sub-

25   paragraph (B)(iii)(I) to the extent

338

1 such amounts consist of an equity in-

2 terest in another specified foreign cor-

3 poration with respect to any United

4 States shareholder, and

5 ''(III) amounts described in sub-

6 paragraph (B)(iii)(IV) to the extent

7 that another specified foreign corpora-

8 tion with respect to any United States

9 shareholder is obligated to repay such

10 amount.

11 ''(iii) APPLICABLE PERCENTAGE.—

12 For purposes of this subparagraph, the

13 term 'applicable percentage' means—

14 ''(I) with respect to each speci-

15 fied cash position described in sub-

16 clause (I) or (III) of clause (ii), the

17 pro rata share of the United States

18 shareholder referred to in clause (ii)

19 with respect to the specified foreign

20 corporation referred to in such clause,

21 and

22 ''(II) with respect to each speci-

23 fied cash position described in clause

24 (ii)(II), the ratio (expressed as a per-

25 centage and not in excess of 100 per-

1   cent) of the United States share-

2   holder's pro rata share of the cash po-

3   sition of the specified foreign corpora-

4   tion referred to in such clause divided

5   by the amount of such specified cash

6   position.

7   For purposes of this subparagraph, a sepa-

8   rate applicable percentage shall be deter-

9   mined under each of subclauses (I) and

10   (II) with respect to each specified foreign

11   corporation referred to in clause (ii) with

12   respect to which a specified cash position

13   is determined for the specified foreign cor-

14   poration referred to in clause (i).

15   "(iv) REDUCTION WITH RESPECT TO

16   AFFILIATED GROUP MEMBERS NOT WHOL-

17   LY OWNED BY THE AFFILIATED GROUP.—

18   For purposes of clause (i)(II), in the case

19   of an includible corporation the group own-

20   ership percentage of which is less than 100

21   percent (as determined under subsection

22   (b)(4)(F)), the amount not take into ac-

23   count by reason of such clause shall be the

24   group ownership percentage of such

1   amount (determined without regard to this

2   clause).

3   ''(E) CERTAIN BLOCKED ASSETS NOT

4   TAKEN INTO ACCOUNT.—A cash position of a

5   specified foreign corporation shall not be taken

6   into account under subparagraph (A) if such

7   position could not (as of the date that it would

8   otherwise have been taken into account under

9   clause (i), (ii), or (iii) of subparagraph (A))

10   have been distributed by such specified foreign

11   corporation to United States shareholders of

12   such specified foreign corporation because of

13   currency or other restrictions or limitations im-

14   posed under the laws of any foreign country

15   (within the meaning of section 964(b)).

16   ''(F) CASH POSITIONS OF CERTAIN NON-

17   CORPORATE ENTITIES TAKEN INTO ACCOUNT.—

18   An entity (other than a domestic corporation)

19   shall be treated as a specified foreign corpora-

20   tion of a United States shareholder for pur-

21   poses of determining such United States share-

22   holder's aggregate foreign cash position if any

23   interest in such entity is held by a specified for-

24   eign corporation of such United States share-

25   holder (determined after application of this sub-

1 paragraph) and such entity would be a specified

2 foreign corporation of such United States

3 shareholder if such entity were a foreign cor-

4 poration

5   "(G) TIME OF CERTAIN DETERMINA-

6 TIONS.—For purposes of this paragraph, the

7 determination of whether a person is a United

8 States shareholder, whether a person is a speci-

9 fied foreign corporation, and the pro rata share

10 of a United States shareholder with respect to

11 a specified foreign corporation, shall be deter-

12 mined as of the end of the taxable year de-

13 scribed in subsection (a).

14   "(H) ANTI-ABUSE.—If the Secretary de-

15 termines that the principal purpose of any

16 transaction was to reduce the aggregate foreign

17 cash position taken into account under this sub-

18 section, such transaction shall be disregarded

19 for purposes of this subsection.

20 "(d) DEFERRED FOREIGN INCOME CORPORATION;

21 ACCUMULATED POST-1986 DEFERRED FOREIGN IN-

22 COME.—For purposes of this section—

23   "(1) DEFERRED FOREIGN INCOME CORPORA-

24 TION.—The term 'deferred foreign income corpora-

25 tion' means, with respect to any United States

1 shareholder, any specified foreign corporation of

2 such United States shareholder which has accumu-

3 lated post-1986 deferred foreign income (as of the

4 date referred to in paragraph (1) or (2) of sub-

5 section (a), whichever is applicable with respect to

6 such foreign corporation) greater than zero.

7   "(2) ACCUMULATED POST-1986 DEFERRED FOR-

8 EIGN INCOME.—The term 'accumulated post-1986

9 deferred foreign income' means the post-1986 earn-

10 ings and profits except to the extent such earnings—

11   "(A) are attributable to income of the

12   specified foreign corporation which is effectively

13   connected with the conduct of a trade or busi-

14   ness within the United States and subject to

15   tax under this chapter, or

16   "(B) if distributed, would be excluded from

17   the gross income of a United States shareholder

18   under section 959.

19 To the extent provided in regulations or other guid-

20 ance prescribed by the Secretary, in the case of any

21 controlled foreign corporation which has share-

22 holders which are not United States shareholders,

23 accumulated post-1986 deferred foreign income shall

24 be appropriately reduced by amounts which would be

1 described in subparagraph (B) if such shareholders
2 were United States shareholders.

3 "(3) POST-1986 EARNINGS AND PROFITS.—The
4 term 'post-1986 earnings and profits' means the
5 earnings and profits of the foreign corporation (com-
6 puted in accordance with sections 964(a) and 986)
7 accumulated in taxable years beginning after Decem-
8 ber 31, 1986, and determined—

9   "(A) as of the date referred to in para-
10   graph (1) or (2) of subsection (a), whichever is
11   applicable with respect to such foreign corpora-
12   tion,

13   "(B) without diminution by reason of divi-
14   dends distributed during the taxable year end-
15   ing with or including such date, and

16   "(C) increased by the amount of any quali-
17   fied deficit (within the meaning of section
18   952(c)(1)(B)(ii)) arising before January 1,
19   2018, which is treated as a qualified deficit
20   (within the meaning of such section as amended
21   by the Tax Cuts and Jobs Act) for purposes of
22   such foreign corporation's first taxable year be-
23   ginning after December 31, 2017.

24 "(e) SPECIFIED FOREIGN CORPORATION.—

1   "(1) IN GENERAL.—For purposes of this sec-

2 tion, the term 'specified foreign corporation'

3 means—

4   "(A) any controlled foreign corporation,

5 and

6   "(B) any foreign corporation with respect

7 to which one or more domestic corporations is

8 a United States shareholder (determined with-

9 out regard to section 958(b)(4)).

10   "(2) APPLICATION TO CERTAIN FOREIGN COR-

11 PORATIONS.—For purposes of sections 951 and 961,

12 a foreign corporation described in paragraph (1)(B)

13 shall be treated as a controlled foreign corporation

14 solely for purposes of taking into account the sub-

15 part F income of such corporation under subsection

16 (a) (and for purposes of applying subsection (f)).

17   "(3) EXCEPTION FOR PASSIVE FOREIGN IN-

18 VESTMENT COMPANIES.—The term 'specified foreign

19 corporation' shall not include any passive foreign in-

20 vestment company (within the meaning of subpart D

21 of part VI of subchapter P) that is not a controlled

22 foreign corporation.

23   "(f) DETERMINATIONS OF PRO RATA SHARE.—For

24 purposes of this section, the determination of any United

25 States shareholder's pro rata share of any amount with

1 respect to any specified foreign corporation shall be deter-

2 mined under rules similar to the rules of section 951(a)(2)

3 by treating such amount in the same manner as subpart

4 F income (and by treating such specified foreign corpora-

5 tion as a controlled foreign corporation).

6 "(g) DISALLOWANCE OF FOREIGN TAX CREDIT,

7 ETC.—

8 "(1) IN GENERAL.—No credit shall be allowed

9 under section 901 for the applicable percentage of

10 any taxes paid or accrued (or treated as paid or ac-

11 crued) with respect to any amount for which a de-

12 duction is allowed under this section.

13 "(2) APPLICABLE PERCENTAGE.—For purposes

14 of this subsection, the term 'applicable percentage'

15 means the amount (expressed as a percentage) equal

16 to the sum of—

17 "(A) 85.7 percent of the ratio of—

18 "(i) the excess to which subsection

19 (c)(1)(A) applies, divided by

20 "(ii) the sum of such excess plus the

21 amount to which subsection (c)(1)(B) ap-

22 plies, plus

23 "(B) 65.7 percent of the ratio of—

24 "(i) the amount to which subsection

25 (c)(1)(B) applies, divided by

346

1   "(ii) the sum described in subpara-

2   graph (A)(ii).

3   "(3) DENIAL OF DEDUCTION.—No deduction

4 shall be allowed under this chapter for any tax for

5 which credit is not allowable under section 901 by

6 reason of paragraph (1) (determined by treating the

7 taxpayer as having elected the benefits of subpart A

8 of part III of subchapter N).

9   "(4) COORDINATION WITH SECTION 78.—Sec-

10 tion 78 shall not apply to any tax for which credit

11 is not allowable under section 901 by reason of para-

12 graph (1).

13   "(5) EXTENSION OF FOREIGN TAX CREDIT CAR-

14 RYOVER PERIOD.—With respect to any taxes paid or

15 accrued (or treated as paid or accrued) with respect

16 to any amount for which a deduction is allowed

17 under this section, section 904(c) shall be applied by

18 substituting 'first 20 succeeding taxable years' for

19 'first 10 succeeding taxable years'.

20 "(h) ELECTION TO PAY LIABILITY IN INSTALL-

21 MENTS.—

22   "(1) IN GENERAL.—In the case of a United

23 States shareholder of a deferred foreign income cor-

24 poration, such United States shareholder may elect

1   to pay the net tax liability under this section in 8

2   equal installments.

3   "(2) DATE FOR PAYMENT OF INSTALLMENTS.—

4   If an election is made under paragraph (1), the first

5   installment shall be paid on the due date (deter-

6   mined without regard to any extension of time for

7   filing the return) for the return of tax for the tax-

8   able year described in subsection (a) and each suc-

9   ceeding installment shall be paid on the due date (as

10   so determined) for the return of tax for the taxable

11   year following the taxable year with respect to which

12   the preceding installment was made.

13   "(3) ACCELERATION OF PAYMENT.—If there is

14   an addition to tax for failure to timely pay any in-

15   stallment required under this subsection, a liquida-

16   tion or sale of substantially all the assets of the tax-

17   payer (including in a title 11 or similar case), a ces-

18   sation of business by the taxpayer, or any similar

19   circumstance, then the unpaid portion of all remain-

20   ing installments shall be due on the date of such

21   event (or in the case of a title 11 or similar case,

22   the day before the petition is filed). The preceding

23   sentence shall not apply to the sale of substantially

24   all the assets of a taxpayer to a buyer if such buyer

25   enters into an agreement with the Secretary under

348

1   which such buyer is liable for the remaining install-

2   ments due under this subsection in the same manner

3   as if such buyer were the taxpayer.

4   "(4) PRORATION OF DEFICIENCY TO INSTALL-

5   MENTS.—If an election is made under paragraph (1)

6   to pay the net tax liability under this section in in-

7   stallments and a deficiency has been assessed with

8   respect to such net tax liability, the deficiency shall

9   be prorated to the installments payable under para-

10   graph (1). The part of the deficiency so prorated to

11   any installment the date for payment of which has

12   not arrived shall be collected at the same time as,

13   and as a part of, such installment. The part of the

14   deficiency so prorated to any installment the date

15   for payment of which has arrived shall be paid upon

16   notice and demand from the Secretary. This sub-

17   section shall not apply if the deficiency is due to

18   negligence, to intentional disregard of rules and reg-

19   ulations, or to fraud with intent to evade tax.

20   "(5) ELECTION.—Any election under paragraph

21   (1) shall be made not later than the due date for the

22   return of tax for the taxable year described in sub-

23   section (a) and shall be made in such manner as the

24   Secretary may provide.

349

1   "(6) NET TAX LIABILITY UNDER THIS SEC-

2   TION.—For purposes of this subsection—

3   "(A) IN GENERAL.—The net tax liability

4   under this section with respect to any United

5   States shareholder is the excess (if any) of—

6   "(i) such taxpayer's net income tax

7   for the taxable year in which an amount is

8   included in the gross income of such

9   United States shareholder under section

10   951(a)(1) by reason of this section, over

11   "(ii) such taxpayer's net income tax

12   for such taxable year determined—

13   "(I) without regard to this sec-

14   tion, and

15   "(II) without regard to any in-

16   come, deduction, or credit, properly

17   attributable to a dividend received by

18   such United States shareholder from

19   any deferred foreign income corpora-

20   tion.

21   "(B) NET INCOME TAX.—The term 'net

22   income tax' means the regular tax liability re-

23   duced by the credits allowed under subparts A,

24   B, and D of part IV of subchapter A.

350

1   "(i) SPECIAL RULES FOR S CORPORATION SHARE-

2 HOLDERS.—

3   "(1) IN GENERAL.—In the case of any S cor-

4   poration which is a United States shareholder of a

5   deferred foreign income corporation, each share-

6   holder of such S corporation may elect to defer pay-

7   ment of such shareholder's net tax liability under

8   this section with respect to such S corporation until

9   the shareholder's taxable year which includes the

10   triggering event with respect to such liability. Any

11   net tax liability payment of which is deferred under

12   the preceding sentence shall be assessed on the re-

13   turn as an addition to tax in the shareholder's tax-

14   able year which includes such triggering event.

15   "(2) TRIGGERING EVENT.—

16   "(A) IN GENERAL.—In the case of any

17   shareholder's net tax liability under this section

18   with respect to any S corporation, the trig-

19   gering event with respect to such liability is

20   whichever of the following occurs first:

21   "(i) Such corporation ceases to be an

22   S corporation (determined as of the first

23   day of the first taxable year that such cor-

24   poration is not an S corporation).

1   "(ii) A liquidation or sale of substan-

2   tially all the assets of such S corporation

3   (including in a title 11 or similar case), a

4   cessation of business by such S corpora-

5   tion, such S corporation ceases to exist, or

6   any similar circumstance.

7   "(iii) A transfer of any share of stock

8   in such S corporation by the taxpayer (in-

9   cluding by reason of death, or otherwise).

10   "(B) PARTIAL TRANSFERS OF STOCK.—In

11   the case of a transfer of less than all of the tax-

12   payer's shares of stock in the S corporation,

13   such transfer shall only be a triggering event

14   with respect to so much of the taxpayer's net

15   tax liability under this section with respect to

16   such S corporation as is properly allocable to

17   such stock.

18   "(C) TRANSFER OF LIABILITY.—A trans-

19   fer described in clause (iii) shall not be treated

20   as a triggering event if the transferee enters

21   into an agreement with the Secretary under

22   which such transferee is liable for net tax liabil-

23   ity with respect to such stock in the same man-

24   ner as if such transferee were the taxpayer.

1   "(3) NET TAX LIABILITY.—A shareholder's net

2   tax liability under this section with respect to any S

3   corporation is the net tax liability under this section

4   which would be determined under subsection (h)(6)

5   if the only subpart F income taken into account by

6   such shareholder by reason of this section were allo-

7   cations from such S corporation.

8   "(4) ELECTION TO PAY DEFERRED LIABILITY

9   IN INSTALLMENTS.—In the case of a taxpayer which

10   elects to defer payment under paragraph (1)—

11   "(A) subsection (h) shall be applied sepa-

12   rately with respect to the liability to which such

13   election applies,

14   "(B) an election under subsection (h) with

15   respect to such liability shall be treated as time-

16   ly made if made not later than the due date for

17   the return of tax for the taxable year in which

18   the triggering event with respect to such liabil-

19   ity occurs,

20   "(C) the first installment under subsection

21   (h) with respect to such liability shall be paid

22   not later than such due date (but determined

23   without regard to any extension of time for fil-

24   ing the return), and

1   "(D) if the triggering event with respect to

2   any net tax liability is described in paragraph

3   (2)(A)(ii), an election under subsection (h) with

4   respect to such liability may be made only with

5   the consent of the Secretary.

6   "(5) JOINT AND SEVERAL LIABILITY OF S COR-

7 PORATION.—If any shareholder of an S corporation

8 elects to defer payment under paragraph (1), such

9 S corporation shall be jointly and severally liable for

10 such payment and any penalty, addition to tax, or

11 additional amount attributable thereto.

12   "(6) EXTENSION OF LIMITATION ON COLLEC-

13 TION.—Notwithstanding any other provision of law,

14 any limitation on the time period for the collection

15 of a liability deferred under this subsection shall not

16 be treated as beginning before the date of the trig-

17 gering event with respect to such liability.

18   "(7) ANNUAL REPORTING OF NET TAX LIABIL-

19 ITY.—

20   "(A) IN GENERAL.—Any shareholder of an

21   S corporation which makes an election under

22   paragraph (1) shall report the amount of such

23   shareholder's deferred net tax liability on such

24   shareholder's return of tax for the taxable year

25   for which such election is made and on the re-

1   turn of tax for each taxable year thereafter

2   until such amount has been fully assessed on

3   such returns.

4   "(B) DEFERRED NET TAX LIABILITY.—

5   For purposes of this paragraph, the term 'de-

6   ferred net tax liability' means, with respect to

7   any taxable year, the amount of net tax liability

8   payment of which has been deferred under

9   paragraph (1) and which has not been assessed

10   on a return of tax for any prior taxable year.

11   "(C) FAILURE TO REPORT.—In the case of

12   any failure to report any amount required to be

13   reported under subparagraph (A) with respect

14   to any taxable year before the due date for the

15   return of tax for such taxable year, there shall

16   be assessed on such return as an addition to

17   tax 5 percent of such amount.

18   "(8) ELECTION.—Any election under paragraph

19   (1)—

20   "(A) shall be made by the shareholder of

21   the S corporation not later than the due date

22   for such shareholder's return of tax for the tax-

23   able year which includes the close of the taxable

24   year of such S corporation in which the amount

1 described in subsection (a) is taken into ac-

2 count, and

3   "(B) shall be made in such manner as the

4 Secretary may provide.

5 "(j) REPORTING BY S CORPORATION.—Each S cor-

6 poration which is a United States shareholder of a de-

7 ferred foreign income corporation shall report in its return

8 of tax under section 6037(a) the amount includible in its

9 gross income for such taxable year by reason of this sec-

10 tion and the amount of the deduction allowable by sub-

11 section (c). Any copy provided to a shareholder under sec-

12 tion 6037(b) shall include a statement of such share-

13 holder's pro rata share of such amounts.

14 "(k) INCLUSION OF DEFERRED FOREIGN INCOME

15 UNDER THIS SECTION NOT TO TRIGGER RECAPTURE OF

16 OVERALL FOREIGN LOSS, ETC.—For purposes of sections

17 904(f)(1) and 907(c)(4), in the case of a United States

18 shareholder of a deferred foreign income corporation, such

19 United States shareholder's taxable income from sources

20 without the United States and combined foreign oil and

21 gas income shall be determined without regard to this sec-

22 tion.

23 "(l) REGULATIONS.—The Secretary may prescribe

24 such regulations or other guidance as may be necessary

25 or appropriate to carry out the provisions of this section.".

356

1   (b) CLERICAL AMENDMENT.—The table of section

2 for subpart F of part III of subchapter N of chapter 1

3 is amended by striking the item relating to section 965

4 and inserting the following:

> "Sec. 965. Treatment of deferred foreign income upon transition to participa-
> tion exemption system of taxation.".

5 # Subtitle B—Modifications Related

6 # to Foreign Tax Credit System

7 **SEC. 4101. REPEAL OF SECTION 902 INDIRECT FOREIGN**

8   **TAX CREDITS; DETERMINATION OF SECTION**

9   **960 CREDIT ON CURRENT YEAR BASIS.**

10   (a) REPEAL OF SECTION 902 INDIRECT FOREIGN

11 TAX CREDITS.—Subpart A of part III of subchapter N

12 of chapter 1 is amended by striking section 902.

13   (b) DETERMINATION OF SECTION 960 CREDIT ON

14 CURRENT YEAR BASIS.—Section 960 is amended—

15   (1) by striking subsection (c), by redesignating

16   subsection (b) as subsection (c), by striking all that

17   precedes subsection (c) (as so redesignated) and in-

18   serting the following:

19 **"SEC. 960. DEEMED PAID CREDIT FOR SUBPART F INCLU-**

20   **SIONS.**

21   "(a) IN GENERAL.—For purposes of this subpart, if

22 there is included in the gross income of a domestic cor-

23 poration any item of income under section 951(a)(1) with

24 respect to any controlled foreign corporation with respect

1 to which such domestic corporation is a United States
2 shareholder, such domestic corporation shall be deemed to
3 have paid so much of such foreign corporation's foreign
4 income taxes as are properly attributable to such item of
5 income.

6   "(b) SPECIAL RULES FOR DISTRIBUTIONS FROM
7 PREVIOUSLY TAXED EARNINGS AND PROFITS.—For pur-
8 poses of this subpart—

9   "(1) IN GENERAL.—If any portion of a dis-
10   tribution from a controlled foreign corporation to a
11   domestic corporation which is a United States share-
12   holder with respect to such controlled foreign cor-
13   poration is excluded from gross income under section
14   959(a), such domestic corporation shall be deemed
15   to have paid so much of such foreign corporation's
16   foreign income taxes as—

17   "(A) are properly attributable to such por-
18   tion, and

19   "(B) have not been deemed to have to been
20   paid by such domestic corporation under this
21   section for the taxable year or any prior taxable
22   year.

23   "(2) TIERED CONTROLLED FOREIGN CORPORA-
24   TIONS.—If section 959(b) applies to any portion of
25   a distribution from a controlled foreign corporation

358

1   to another controlled foreign corporation, such con-

2   trolled foreign corporation shall be deemed to have

3   paid so much of such other controlled foreign cor-

4   poration's foreign income taxes as—

5   "(A) are properly attributable to such por-

6   tion, and

7   "(B) have not been deemed to have been

8   paid by a domestic corporation under this sec-

9   tion for the taxable year or any prior taxable

10   year.",

11   (2) and by adding after subsection (c) (as so re-

12   designated) the following new subsections:

13   "(d) FOREIGN INCOME TAXES.—The term 'foreign

14 income taxes' means any income, war profits, or excess

15 profits taxes paid or accrued to any foreign country or

16 possession of the United States.

17   "(e) REGULATIONS.—The Secretary may prescribe

18 such regulations or other guidance as may be necessary

19 or appropriate to carry out the provisions of this section.".

20   (c) CONFORMING AMENDMENTS.—

21   (1) Section 78 is amended to read as follows:

22 **"SEC. 78. GROSS UP FOR DEEMED PAID FOREIGN TAX**

23   **CREDIT.**

24   "If a domestic corporation chooses to have the bene-

25 fits of subpart A of part III of subchapter N (relating

1 to foreign tax credit) for any taxable year, an amount
2 equal to the taxes deemed to be paid by such corporation
3 under subsections (a) and (b) of section 960 for such tax-
4 able year shall be treated for purposes of this title (other
5 than sections 959, 960, and 961) as an item of income
6 required to be included in the gross income of such domes-
7 tic corporation under section 951(a) for such taxable
8 year.".

9   (2) Section 245(a)(10)(C) is amended by strik-
10   ing "sections 902, 907, and 960" and inserting
11   "sections 907 and 960".

12   (3) Sections 535(b)(1) and 545(b)(1) are each
13   amended by striking "section 902(a) or 960(a)(1)"
14   and inserting "section 960".

15   (4) Section 814(f)(1) is amended—

16   (A) by striking subparagraph (B), and

17   (B) by striking all that precedes "No in-
18   come" and inserting the following:

19   "(1) TREATMENT OF FOREIGN TAXES.—".

20   (5) Section 865(h)(1)(B) is amended by strik-
21   ing "sections 902, 907, and 960" and inserting
22   "sections 907 and 960".

23   (6) Section 901(a) is amended by striking "sec-
24   tions 902 and 960" and inserting "section 960".

1 (7) Section 901(e)(2) is amended by striking

2 "but is not limited to—" and all that follows

3 through "that portion" and inserting "but is not

4 limited to, that portion".

5 (8) Section 901(f) is amended by striking "sec-

6 tions 902 and 960" and inserting "section 960".

7 (9) Section 901(j)(1)(A) is amended by striking

8 "902 or".

9 (10) Section 901(j)(1)(B) is amended by strik-

10 ing "sections 902 and 960" and inserting "section

11 960".

12 (11) Section 901(k)(2) is amended by striking

13 "section 853, 902, or 960" and inserting "section

14 853 or 960".

15 (12) Section 901(k)(6) is amended by striking

16 "902 or".

17 (13) Section 901(m)(1) is amended by striking

18 "relevant foreign assets—" and all that follows and

19 inserting "relevant foreign assets shall not be taken

20 into account in determining the credit allowed under

21 subsection (a).".

22 (14) Section 904(d)(1) is amended by striking

23 "sections 902, 907, and 960" and inserting "sec-

24 tions 907 and 960".

361

1   (15) Section 904(d)(6)(A) is amended by strik-

2 ing "sections 902, 907, and 960" and inserting

3 "sections 907 and 960".

4   (16) Section 904(h)(10)(A) is amended by

5 striking "sections 902, 907, and 960" and inserting

6 "sections 907 and 960".

7   (17) Section 904 is amended by striking sub-

8 section (k).

9   (18) Section 905(c)(1) is amended by striking

10 the last sentence.

11   (19) Section 905(c)(2)(B)(i) is amended to read

12 as follows:

13   "(i) shall be taken into account for

14   the taxable year to which such taxes relate,

15   and".

16   (20) Section 906(a) is amended by striking "(or

17 deemed, under section 902, paid or accrued during

18 the taxable year)".

19   (21) Section 906(b) is amended by striking

20 paragraphs (4) and (5).

21   (22) Section 907(b)(2)(B) is amended by strik-

22 ing "902 or".

23   (23) Section 907(c)(3) is amended—

362

1   (A) by striking subparagraph (A) and re-
2 designating subparagraphs (B) and (C) as sub-
3 paragraphs (A) and (B), respectively, and

4   (B) by striking "section 960(a)" in sub-
5 paragraph (A) (as so redesignated) and insert-
6 ing "section 960".

7 (24) Section 907(c)(5) is amended by striking
8 "902 or".

9 (25) Section 907(f)(2)(B)(i) is amended by
10 striking "902 or".

11 (26) Section 908(a) is amended by striking
12 "902 or".

13 (27) Section 909(b) is amended—

14   (A) by striking "section 902 corporation"
15 in the matter preceding paragraph (1) and in-
16 serting "10/50 corporation",

17   (B) by striking "902 or" in paragraph (1),

18   (C) by striking "by such section 902 cor-
19 poration" and all that follows in the matter fol-
20 lowing paragraph (2) and inserting "by such
21 10/50 corporation or a domestic corporation
22 which is a United States shareholder with re-
23 spect to such 10/50 corporation.", and

363

1   (D) by striking "SECTION 902 CORPORA-

2   TIONS" in the heading thereof and inserting

3   "10/50 CORPORATIONS".

4   (28) Section 909(d)(5) is amended to read as

5 follows:

6   "(5) 10/50 CORPORATION.—The term '10/50

7 corporation' means any foreign corporation with re-

8 spect to which one or more domestic corporations is

9 a United States shareholder.".

10   (29) Section 958(a)(1) is amended by striking

11 "960(a)(1)" and inserting "960".

12   (30) Section 959(d) is amended by striking

13 "Except as provided in section 960(a)(3), any" and

14 inserting "Any".

15   (31) Section 959(e) is amended by striking

16 "section 960(b)" and inserting "section 960(c)".

17   (32) Section 1291(g)(2)(A) is amended by

18 striking "any distribution—" and all that follows

19 through "but only if" and inserting "any distribu-

20 tion, any withholding tax imposed with respect to

21 such distribution, but only if".

22   (33) Section 6038(c)(1)(B) is amended by

23 striking "sections 902 (relating to foreign tax credit

24 for corporate stockholder in foreign corporation) and

364

1 960 (relating to special rules for foreign tax credit)''

2 and inserting ''section 960''.

3 (34) Section 6038(c)(4) is amended by striking

4 subparagraph (C).

5 (35) The table of sections for subpart A of part

6 III of subchapter N of chapter 1 is amended by

7 striking the item relating to section 902.

8 (36) The table of sections for subpart F of part

9 III of subchapter N of chapter 1 is amended by

10 striking the item relating to section 960 and insert-

11 ing the following:

''Sec. 960. Deemed paid credit for subpart F inclusions.''.

12 (d) EFFECTIVE DATE.—The amendments made by

13 this section shall apply to taxable years beginning after

14 December 31, 2017.

15 **SEC. 4102. SOURCE OF INCOME FROM SALES OF INVEN-**

16 **TORY DETERMINED SOLELY ON BASIS OF**

17 **PRODUCTION ACTIVITIES.**

18 (a) IN GENERAL.—Section 863(b) is amended by

19 adding at the end the following: ''Gains, profits, and in-

20 come from the sale or exchange of inventory property de-

21 scribed in paragraph (2) shall be allocated and appor-

22 tioned between sources within and without the United

23 States solely on the basis of the production activities with

24 respect to the property.''.

365

1   (b) EFFECTIVE DATE.—The amendment made by
2 this section shall apply to taxable years beginning after
3 December 31, 2017.

Subtitle C—Modification of Subpart F Provisions

6 **SEC. 4201. REPEAL OF INCLUSION BASED ON WITHDRAWAL**
7 **OF PREVIOUSLY EXCLUDED SUBPART F IN-**
8 **COME FROM QUALIFIED INVESTMENT.**

9   (a) IN GENERAL.—Subpart F of part III of sub-
10 chapter N of chapter 1 is amended by striking section 955.

11   (b) CONFORMING AMENDMENTS.—

12   (1)(A) Section 951(a)(1)(A) is amended to read
13   as follows:

14   "(A) his pro rata share (determined under
15   paragraph (2)) of the corporation's subpart F
16   income for such year, and".

17   (B) Section 851(b)(3) is amended by striking
18   "section 951(a)(1)(A)(i)" in the flush language at
19   the end and inserting "section 951(a)(1)(A)".

20   (C) Section 952(c)(1)(B)(i) is amended by
21   striking "section 951(a)(1)(A)(i)" and inserting
22   "section 951(a)(1)(A)".

23   (D) Section 953(c)(1)(C) is amended by strik-
24   ing "section 951(a)(1)(A)(i)" and inserting "section
25   951(a)(1)(A)".

1   (2) Section 951(a) is amended by striking para-

2   graph (3).

3   (3) Section 953(d)(4)(B)(iv)(II) is amended by

4   striking "or amounts referred to in clause (ii) or (iii)

5   of section 951(a)(1)(A)".

6   (4) Section 964(b) is amended by striking ",

7   955,".

8   (5) Section 970 is amended by striking sub-

9   section (b).

10   (6) The table of sections for subpart F of part

11   III of subchapter N of chapter 1 is amended by

12   striking the item relating to section 955.

13   (c) EFFECTIVE DATE.—The amendments made by

14 this section shall apply to taxable years of foreign corpora-

15 tions beginning after December 31, 2017, and to taxable

16 years of United States shareholders in which or with which

17 such taxable years of foreign corporations end.

18 **SEC. 4202. REPEAL OF TREATMENT OF FOREIGN BASE COM-**

19   **PANY OIL RELATED INCOME AS SUBPART F**

20   **INCOME.**

21   (a) IN GENERAL.—Section 954(a) is amended by

22 striking paragraph (5), by striking the comma at the end

23 of paragraph (3) and inserting a period, and by inserting

24 "and" at the end of paragraph (2).

25   (b) CONFORMING AMENDMENTS.—

1   (1) Section 952(c)(1)(B)(iii) is amended by

2 striking subclause (I) and by redesignating sub-

3 clauses (II) through (V) as subclauses (I) through

4 (IV), respectively.

5   (2) Section 954(b)(4) is amended by striking

6 the last sentence.

7   (3) Section 954(b)(5) is amended by striking

8 "the foreign base company services income, and the

9 foreign base company oil related income" and insert-

10 ing "and the foreign base company services income".

11   (4) Section 954(b) is amended by striking para-

12 graph (6).

13   (5) Section 954 is amended by striking sub-

14 section (g).

15   (c) EFFECTIVE DATE.—The amendments made by

16 this section shall apply to taxable years of foreign corpora-

17 tions beginning after December 31, 2017, and to taxable

18 years of United States shareholders in which or with which

19 such taxable years of foreign corporations end.

20 **SEC. 4203. INFLATION ADJUSTMENT OF DE MINIMIS EXCEP-**

21   **TION FOR FOREIGN BASE COMPANY INCOME.**

22   (a) IN GENERAL.—Section 954(b)(3) is amended by

23 adding at the end the following new subparagraph:

24   "(D) INFLATION ADJUSTMENT.—In the

25   case of any taxable year beginning after 2017,

1   the dollar amount in subparagraph (A)(ii) shall

2   be increased by an amount equal to—

3   "(i) such dollar amount, multiplied by

4   "(ii) the cost-of-living adjustment de-

5   termined under section 1(c)(2)(A) for the

6   calendar year in which the taxable year be-

7   gins.

8   Any increase determined under the preceding

9   sentence shall be rounded to the nearest mul-

10   tiple of $50,000.".

11   (b) EFFECTIVE DATE.—The amendments made by

12 this section shall apply to taxable years of foreign corpora-

13 tions beginning after December 31, 2017, and to taxable

14 years of United States shareholders in which or with which

15 such taxable years of foreign corporations end.

16 **SEC. 4204. LOOK-THRU RULE FOR RELATED CONTROLLED**

17   **FOREIGN CORPORATIONS MADE PERMA-**

18   **NENT.**

19   (a) IN GENERAL.—Paragraph (6) of section 954(c)

20 is amended by striking subparagraph (C).

21   (b) EFFECTIVE DATE.—The amendments made by

22 this section shall apply to taxable years of foreign corpora-

23 tions beginning after December 31, 2019, and to taxable

24 years of United States shareholders in which or with which

25 such taxable years of foreign corporations end.

1 **SEC. 4205. MODIFICATION OF STOCK ATTRIBUTION RULES**

2   **FOR DETERMINING STATUS AS A CON-**

3   **TROLLED FOREIGN CORPORATION.**

4 (a) IN GENERAL.—Section 958(b) is amended—

5   (1) by striking paragraph (4), and

6   (2) by striking "Paragraphs (1) and (4)" in the

7 last sentence and inserting "Paragraph (1)".

8 (b) APPLICATION OF CERTAIN REPORTING REQUIRE-

9 MENTS.—Section 6038(e)(2) is amended by striking "ex-

10 cept that—" and all that follows through "in applying

11 subparagraph (C)" and inserting "except that in applying

12 subparagraph (C)".

13 (c) EFFECTIVE DATE.—The amendments made by

14 this section shall apply to taxable years of foreign corpora-

15 tions beginning after December 31, 2017, and to taxable

16 years of United States shareholders in which or with which

17 such taxable years of foreign corporations end.

18 **SEC. 4206. ELIMINATION OF REQUIREMENT THAT COR-**

19   **PORATION MUST BE CONTROLLED FOR 30**

20   **DAYS BEFORE SUBPART F INCLUSIONS**

21   **APPLY.**

22 (a) IN GENERAL.—Section 951(a)(1) is amended by

23 striking "for an uninterrupted period of 30 days or more"

24 and inserting "at any time".

25 (b) EFFECTIVE DATE.—The amendment made by

26 this section shall apply to taxable years of foreign corpora-

370

1 tions beginning after December 31, 2017, and to taxable

2 years of United States shareholders with or within which

3 such taxable years of foreign corporations end.

Subtitle D—Prevention of Base Erosion

SEC. 4301. CURRENT YEAR INCLUSION BY UNITED STATES SHAREHOLDERS WITH FOREIGN HIGH RETURNS.

9 (a) IN GENERAL.—Subpart F of part III of sub-

10 chapter N of chapter 1 is amended by inserting after sec-

11 tion 951 the following new section:

"SEC. 951A. FOREIGN HIGH RETURN AMOUNT INCLUDED IN GROSS INCOME OF UNITED STATES SHAREHOLDERS.

15 "(a) IN GENERAL.—Each person who is a United

16 States shareholder of any controlled foreign corporation

17 for any taxable year of such United States shareholder

18 shall include in gross income for such taxable year 50 per-

19 cent of such shareholder's foreign high return amount for

20 such taxable year.

21 "(b) FOREIGN HIGH RETURN AMOUNT.—For pur-

22 poses of this section—

23 "(1) IN GENERAL.—The term 'foreign high re-

24 turn amount' means, with respect to any United

1 States shareholder for any taxable year of such

2 United States shareholder, the excess (if any) of—

3   "(A) such shareholder's net CFC tested in-

4 come for such taxable year, over

5   "(B) the excess (if any) of—

6   "(i) the applicable percentage of the

7 aggregate of such shareholder's pro rata

8 share of the qualified business asset invest-

9 ment of each controlled foreign corporation

10 with respect to which such shareholder is

11 a United States shareholder for such tax-

12 able year (determined for each taxable year

13 of each such controlled foreign corporation

14 which ends in or with such taxable year of

15 such United States shareholder), over

16   "(ii) the amount of interest expense

17 taken into account under subsection

18 (c)(2)(A)(ii) in determining the share-

19 holder's net CFC tested income for the

20 taxable year.

21   "(2) APPLICABLE PERCENTAGE.—The term

22 'applicable percentage' means, with respect to any

23 taxable year, the Federal short-term rate (deter-

24 mined under section 1274(d) for the month in which

372

1   or with which such taxable year ends) plus 7 per-

2   centage points.

3   "(c) NET CFC TESTED INCOME.—For purposes of

4   this section—

5   "(1) IN GENERAL.—The term 'net CFC tested

6   income' means, with respect to any United States

7   shareholder for any taxable year of such United

8   States shareholder, the excess (if any) of—

9   "(A) the aggregate of such shareholder's

10   pro rata share of the tested income of each con-

11   trolled foreign corporation with respect to which

12   such shareholder is a United States shareholder

13   for such taxable year of such United States

14   shareholder (determined for each taxable year

15   of such controlled foreign corporation which

16   ends in or with such taxable year of such

17   United States shareholder), over

18   "(B) the aggregate of such shareholder's

19   pro rata share of the tested loss of each con-

20   trolled foreign corporation with respect to which

21   such shareholder is a United States shareholder

22   for such taxable year of such United States

23   shareholder (determined for each taxable year

24   of such controlled foreign corporation which

1 ends in or with such taxable year of such

2 United States shareholder).

3 "(2) TESTED INCOME; TESTED LOSS.—For pur-

4 poses of this section—

5 "(A) TESTED INCOME.—The term 'tested

6 income' means, with respect to any controlled

7 foreign corporation for any taxable year of such

8 controlled foreign corporation, the excess (if

9 any) of—

10   "(i) the gross income of such corpora-

11   tion determined without regard to—

12   "(I) any item of income which is

13   effectively connected with the conduct

14   by such corporation of a trade or

15   business within the United States if

16   subject to tax under this chapter,

17   "(II) any gross income taken into

18   account in determining the subpart F

19   income of such corporation,

20   "(III) except as otherwise pro-

21   vided by the Secretary, any amount

22   excluded from the foreign personal

23   holding company income (as defined

24   in section 954) of such corporation by

25   reason of section 954(c)(6) but only

374

1   to the extent that any deduction al-

2   lowable for the payment or accrual of

3   such amount does not result in a re-

4   duction in the foreign high return

5   amount of any United States share-

6   holder (determined without regard to

7   this subclause),

8   "(IV) any gross income excluded

9   from the foreign personal holding

10 company income (as defined in section

11 954) of such corporation by reason of

12 subsection (h) or (i) of section 954,

13   "(V) any gross income excluded

14 from the insurance income (as defined

15 in section 953) of such corporation by

16 reason of section 953(a)(2),

17   "(VI) any gross income excluded

18 from foreign base company income (as

19 defined in section 954) or insurance

20 income (as defined in section 953) of

21 such corporation by reason of section

22 954(b)(4),

23   "(VII) any dividend received

24 from a related person (as defined in

25 section 954(d)(3)), and

1   "(VIII) any commodities gross

2   income of such corporation, over

3   "(ii) the deductions (including taxes)

4   properly allocable to such gross income

5   under rules similar to the rules of section

6   954(b)(5) (or which would be so properly

7   allocable if such corporation had such

8   gross income).

9   "(B) TESTED LOSS.—The term 'tested

10   loss' means, with respect to any controlled for-

11   eign corporation for any taxable year of such

12   controlled foreign corporation, the excess (if

13   any) of the amount described in subparagraph

14   (A)(ii) over the amount described in subpara-

15   graph (A)(i).

16   "(d) QUALIFIED BUSINESS ASSET INVESTMENT.—

17 For purposes of this section—

18   "(1) IN GENERAL.—The term 'qualified busi-

19   ness asset investment' means, with respect to any

20   controlled foreign corporation for any taxable year of

21   such controlled foreign corporation, the aggregate of

22   the corporation's adjusted bases (determined as of

23   the close of such taxable year and after any adjust-

24   ments with respect to such taxable year) in specified

25   tangible property—

1   "(A) used in a trade or business of the

2   corporation, and

3   "(B) of a type with respect to which a de-

4   duction is allowable under section 168.

5   "(2) SPECIFIED TANGIBLE PROPERTY.—The

6 term 'specified tangible property' means any tangible

7 property to the extent such property is used in the

8 production of tested income or tested loss.

9   "(3) PARTNERSHIP PROPERTY.—For purposes

10 of this subsection, if a controlled foreign corporation

11 holds an interest in a partnership at the close of

12 such taxable year of the controlled foreign corpora-

13 tion, such controlled foreign corporation shall take

14 into account under paragraph (1) the controlled for-

15 eign corporation's distributive share of the aggregate

16 of the partnership's adjusted bases (determined as

17 of such date in the hands of the partnership) in tan-

18 gible property held by such partnership to the extent

19 such property—

20   "(A) is used in the trade or business of the

21   partnership, and

22   "(B) is used in the production of tested in-

23   come or tested loss (determined with respect to

24   such controlled foreign corporation's distribu-

1   tive share of income or loss with respect to such

2   property).

3 For purposes of this paragraph, the controlled for-

4 eign corporation's distributive share of the adjusted

5 basis of any property shall be the controlled foreign

6 corporation's distributive share of income and loss

7 with respect to such property.

8   "(4) DETERMINATION OF ADJUSTED BASIS.—

9   For purposes of this subsection, the adjusted basis

10   in any property shall be determined without regard

11   to any provision of this title (or any other provision

12   of law) which is enacted after the date of the enact-

13   ment of this section.

14   "(5) REGULATIONS.—The Secretary shall issue

15   such regulations or other guidance as the Secretary

16   determines appropriate to prevent the avoidance of

17   the purposes of this subsection, including regulations

18   or other guidance which provide for the treatment of

19   property if—

20   "(A) such property is transferred, or held,

21   temporarily, or

22   "(B) the avoidance of the purposes of this

23   paragraph is a factor in the transfer or holding

24   of such property.

378

1   "(e) COMMODITIES GROSS INCOME.—For purposes

2 of this section—

3   "(1) COMMODITIES GROSS INCOME.—The term

4   'commodities gross income' means, with respect to

5   any corporation, the gross income of such corpora-

6   tion from the disposition of commodities which are

7   produced or extracted by such corporation.

8   "(2) COMMODITY.—The term 'commodity'

9   means any commodity described in section

10   475(e)(2)(A) or section 475(e)(2)(D) (determined

11   without regard to clause (i) thereof and by sub-

12   stituting 'a commodity described in subparagraph

13   (A)' for 'such a commodity' in clause (ii) thereof).

14   "(f) TAXABLE YEARS FOR WHICH PERSONS ARE

15 TREATED AS UNITED STATES SHAREHOLDERS OF CON-

16 TROLLED FOREIGN CORPORATIONS.—For purposes of

17 this section—

18   "(1) IN GENERAL.—A United States share-

19   holder of a controlled foreign corporation shall be

20   treated as a United States shareholder of such con-

21   trolled foreign corporation for any taxable year of

22   such United States shareholder if—

23   "(A) a taxable year of such controlled for-

24   eign corporation ends in or with such taxable

25   year of such person, and

1   "(B) such person owns (within the mean-

2   ing of section 958(a)) stock in such controlled

3   foreign corporation on the last day, in such tax-

4   able year of such foreign corporation, on which

5   the foreign corporation is a controlled foreign

6   corporation.

7   "(2) TREATMENT AS A CONTROLLED FOREIGN

8   CORPORATION.—Except for purposes of paragraph

9   (1)(B) and the application of section 951(a)(2) to

10   this section pursuant to subsection (g), a foreign

11   corporation shall be treated as a controlled foreign

12   corporation for any taxable year of such foreign cor-

13   poration if such foreign corporation is a controlled

14   foreign corporation at any time during such taxable

15   year.

16   "(g) DETERMINATION OF PRO RATA SHARE.—For

17   purposes of this section, the pro rata shares referred to

18   in subsections (b)(2), (c)(1)(A), (c)(1)(B), and

19   (c)(2)(B)(ii), respectively, shall be determined under the

20   rules of section 951(a)(2) in the same manner as such sec-

21   tion applies to subpart F income.

22   "(h) COORDINATION WITH SUBPART F.—

23   "(1) TREATMENT AS SUBPART F INCOME FOR

24   CERTAIN PURPOSES.—Except as otherwise provided

25   by the Secretary any foreign high return amount in-

1   cluded in gross income under subsection (a) shall be

2   treated in the same manner as an amount included

3   under section 951(a)(1)(A) for purposes of applying

4   sections   168(h)(2)(B),   535(b)(10),   851(b),

5   904(h)(1), 959, 961, 962(c), 962(d), 993(a)(1)(E),

6   996(f)(1), 1248(b)(1), 1248(d)(1), 6501(e)(1)(C),

7   6654(d)(2)(D), and 6655(e)(4).

8   "(2) ENTIRE FOREIGN HIGH RETURN AMOUNT

9   TAKEN INTO ACCOUNT FOR PURPOSES OF CERTAIN

10   SECTIONS.—For purposes of applying paragraph (1)

11   with respect to sections 168(h)(2)(B), 851(b), 959,

12   961, 962(c), 962(d), 1248(b)(1), and 1248(d)(1),

13   the foreign high return amount included in gross in-

14   come under subsection (a) shall be determined by

15   substituting '100 percent' for '50 percent' in such

16   subsection.

17   "(3) ALLOCATION OF FOREIGN HIGH RETURN

18   AMOUNT   TO   CONTROLLED   FOREIGN   CORPORA-

19   TIONS.—For purposes of the sections referred to in

20   paragraph (1), with respect to any controlled foreign

21   corporation any pro rata amount from which is

22   taken into account in determining the foreign high

23   return amount included in gross income of a United

24   States shareholder under subsection (a), the portion

25   of such foreign high return amount which is treated

381

1   as being with respect to such controlled foreign cor-

2   poration is—

3   "(A) in the case of a controlled foreign

4   corporation with tested loss, zero, and

5   "(B) in the case of a controlled foreign

6   corporation with tested income, the portion of

7   such foreign high return amount which bears

8   the same ratio to such foreign high return

9   amount as—

10   "(i) such United States shareholder's

11   pro rata amount of the tested income of

12   such controlled foreign corporation, bears

13   to

14   "(ii) the aggregate amount deter-

15   mined under subsection (c)(1)(A) with re-

16   spect to such United States shareholder.

17   "(4) COORDINATION WITH SUBPART F TO DENY

18   DOUBLE BENEFIT OF LOSSES.—In the case of any

19   United States shareholder of any controlled foreign

20   corporation, the amount included in gross income

21   under section 951(a)(1)(A) shall be determined by

22   increasing the earnings and profits of such con-

23   trolled foreign corporation (solely for purposes of de-

24   termining such amount) by an amount that bears

25   the same ratio (not greater than 1) to such share-

1 holder's pro rata share of the tested loss of such

2 controlled foreign corporation as—

3   "(A) the aggregate amount determined

4   under subsection (c)(1)(A) with respect to such

5   shareholder, bears to

6   "(B) the aggregate amount determined

7   under subsection (c)(1)(B) with respect to such

8   shareholder.".

9 (b) FOREIGN TAX CREDIT.—

10   (1) APPLICATION OF DEEMED PAID FOREIGN

11 TAX CREDIT.—Section 960, as amended by the pre-

12 ceding provisions of this Act, is amended by redesig-

13 nating subsections (d) and (e) as subsections (e) and

14 (f), respectively, and by inserting after subsection (c)

15 the following new subsection:

16 "(d) DEEMED PAID CREDIT FOR TAXES PROPERLY

17 ATTRIBUTABLE TO TESTED INCOME.—

18   "(1) IN GENERAL.—For purposes of this sub-

19 part, if any amount is includible in the gross income

20 of a domestic corporation under section 951A, such

21 domestic corporation shall be deemed to have paid

22 foreign income taxes equal to 80 percent of—

23   "(A) such domestic corporation's foreign

24   high return percentage, multiplied by

1   "(B) the aggregate tested foreign income

2   taxes paid or accrued by controlled foreign cor-

3   porations with respect to which such domestic

4   corporation is a United States shareholder.

5   "(2) FOREIGN HIGH RETURN PERCENTAGE.—

6 For purposes of paragraph (1), the term 'foreign

7 high return percentage' means, with respect to any

8 domestic corporation, the ratio (expressed as a per-

9 centage) of—

10   "(A) such corporation's foreign high return

11   amount (as defined in section 951A(b)), divided

12   by

13   "(B) the aggregate amount determined

14   under section 951A(c)(1)(A) with respect to

15   such corporation.

16   "(3) TESTED FOREIGN INCOME TAXES.—For

17 purposes of paragraph (1), the term 'tested foreign

18 income taxes' means, with respect to any domestic

19 corporation which is a United States shareholder of

20 a controlled foreign corporation, the foreign income

21 taxes paid or accrued by such foreign corporation

22 which are properly attributable to gross income de-

23 scribed in section 951A(c)(2)(A)(i).".

24   (2) APPLICATION OF FOREIGN TAX CREDIT

25 LIMITATION.—

384

1   (A) SEPARATE BASKET FOR FOREIGN

2   HIGH RETURN AMOUNT.—Section 904(d)(1) is

3   amended by redesignating subparagraphs (A)

4   and (B) as subparagraphs (B) and (C), respec-

5   tively, and by inserting before subparagraph

6   (B) (as so redesignated) the following new sub-

7   paragraph:

8   "(A) any amount includible in gross in-

9   come under section 951A,".

10   (B) NO CARRYOVER OF EXCESS TAXES.—

11   Section 904(c) is amended by adding at the end

12   the following: "This subsection shall not apply

13   to taxes paid or accrued with respect to

14   amounts described in subsection (d)(1)(A)."

15   (3) GROSS UP FOR DEEMED PAID FOREIGN TAX

16   CREDIT.—Section 78, as amended by the preceding

17   provisions of this Act, is amended—

18   (A) by striking "any taxable year, an

19   amount" and inserting "any taxable year—

20   "(1) an amount", and

21   (B) by striking the period at the end and

22   inserting ", and

23   "(2) an amount equal to the taxes deemed to

24   be paid by such corporation under section 960(d) for

25   such taxable year (determined by substituting '100

1   percent' for '80 percent' in such section) shall be

2   treated for purposes of this title (other than sections

3   959, 960, and 961) as an increase in the foreign

4   high return amount of such domestic corporation

5   under section 951A for such taxable year.''.

6   (c) CONFORMING AMENDMENTS.—

7   (1) Section 170(b)(2)(D) is amended by strik-

8   ing ''computed without regard to'' and all that fol-

9   lows and inserting ''computed—

10   ''(i) without regard to—

11   ''(I) this section,

12   ''(II) part VIII (except section

13   248),

14   ''(III) any net operating loss

15   carryback to the taxable year under

16   section 172,

17   ''(IV) any capital loss carryback

18   to the taxable year under section

19   1212(a)(1), and

20   ''(ii) by substituting '100 percent' for

21   '50 percent' in section 951A(a).''.

22   (2) Section 246(b)(1) is amended by—

23   (A) striking ''and without regard to'' and

24   inserting ''without regard to'', and

1   (B) by striking the period at the end and

2   inserting '', and by substituting '100 percent'

3   for '50 percent' in section 951A(a).''.

4   (3) Section 469(i)(3)(F) is amended by striking

5 ''determined without regard to'' and all that follows

6 and inserting ''determined—

7   ''(i) without regard to—

8   ''(I) any amount includible in

9   gross income under section 86,

10   ''(II) the amounts allowable as a

11   deduction under section 219, and

12   ''(III) any passive activity loss or

13   any loss allowable by reason of sub-

14   section (c)(7), and

15   ''(ii) by substituting '100 percent' for

16   '50 percent' in section 951A(a).''.

17   (4) Section 856(c)(2) is amended by striking

18 ''and'' at the end of subparagraph (H), by adding

19 ''and'' at the end of subparagraph (I), and by insert-

20 ing after subparagraph (I) the following new sub-

21 paragraph:

22   ''(J) amounts includible in gross income

23   under section 951A(a);''.

24   (5) Section 856(c)(3)(D) is amended by strik-

25 ing ''dividends or other distributions on, and gain''

387

1 and inserting "dividends, other distributions on,

2 amounts includible in gross income under section

3 951A(a) with respect to, and gain".

4 (6) The table of sections for subpart F of part

5 III of subchapter N of chapter 1 is amended by in-

6 serting after the item relating to section 951 the fol-

7 lowing new item:

"Sec. 951A. Foreign high return amount included in gross income of United
States shareholders.".

8 (d) EFFECTIVE DATE.—The amendments made by

9 this section shall apply to taxable years of foreign corpora-

10 tions beginning after December 31, 2017, and to taxable

11 years of United States shareholders in which or with which

12 such taxable years of foreign corporations end.

13 **SEC. 4302. LIMITATION ON DEDUCTION OF INTEREST BY**

14 **DOMESTIC CORPORATIONS WHICH ARE MEM-**

15 **BERS OF AN INTERNATIONAL FINANCIAL RE-**

16 **PORTING GROUP.**

17 (a) IN GENERAL.—Section 163 is amended by redes-

18 ignating subsection (n) as subsection (p) and by inserting

19 after subsection (m) the following new subsection:

20 "(n) LIMITATION ON DEDUCTION OF INTEREST BY

21 DOMESTIC CORPORATIONS IN INTERNATIONAL FINAN-

22 CIAL REPORTING GROUPS.—

23 "(1) IN GENERAL.—In the case of any domestic

24 corporation which is a member of any international

1 financial reporting group, the deduction under this

2 chapter for interest paid or accrued during the tax-

3 able year shall not exceed the sum of—

4   "(A) the allowable percentage of 110 per-

5   cent of the excess (if any) of —

6   "(i) the amount of such interest so

7   paid or accrued, over

8   "(ii) the amount described in subpara-

9   graph (B), plus

10   "(B) the amount of interest includible in

11   gross income of such corporation for such tax-

12   able year.

13 "(2) INTERNATIONAL FINANCIAL REPORTING

14 GROUP.—

15   "(A) For purposes of this subsection, the

16   term 'international financial reporting group'

17   means, with respect to any reporting year, any

18   group of entities which—

19   "(i) includes—

20   "(I) at least one foreign corpora-

21   tion engaged in a trade or business

22   within the United States, or

23   "(II) at least one domestic cor-

24   poration and one foreign corporation,

1   "(ii) prepares consolidated financial

2   statements with respect to such year, and

3   "(iii) reports in such statements aver-

4   age annual gross receipts (determined in

5   the aggregate with respect to all entities

6   which are part of such group) for the 3-re-

7   porting-year period ending with such re-

8   porting year in excess of $100,000,000.

9   "(B) RULES RELATING TO DETERMINA-

10   TION OF AVERAGE GROSS RECEIPTS.—For pur-

11   poses of subparagraph (A)(iii), rules similar to

12   the rules of section 448(c)(3) shall apply.

13   "(3) ALLOWABLE PERCENTAGE.—For purposes

14   of this subsection—

15   "(A) IN GENERAL.—The term 'allowable

16   percentage' means, with respect to any domestic

17   corporation for any taxable year, the ratio (ex-

18   pressed as a percentage and not greater than

19   100 percent) of—

20   "(i) such corporation's allocable share

21   of the international financial reporting

22   group's reported net interest expense for

23   the reporting year of such group which

24   ends in or with such taxable year of such

25   corporation, over

390

1   ''(ii) such corporation's reported net

2   interest expense for such reporting year of

3   such group.

4   ''(B) REPORTED NET INTEREST EX-

5   PENSE.—The term 'reported net interest ex-

6   pense' means—

7   ''(i) with respect to any international

8   financial reporting group for any reporting

9   year, the excess of—

10   ''(I) the aggregate amount of in-

11   terest expense reported in such

12   group's consolidated financial state-

13   ments for such taxable year, over

14   ''(II) the aggregate amount of in-

15   terest income reported in such group's

16   consolidated financial statements for

17   such taxable year, and

18   ''(ii) with respect to any domestic cor-

19   poration for any reporting year, the excess

20   of—

21   ''(I) the amount of interest ex-

22   pense of such corporation reported in

23   the books and records of the inter-

24   national financial reporting group

25   which are used in preparing such

group's consolidated financial statements for such taxable year, over

"(II) the amount of interest income of such corporation reported in such books and records.

"(C) ALLOCABLE SHARE OF REPORTED NET INTEREST EXPENSE.—With respect to any domestic corporation which is a member of any international financial reporting group, such corporation's allocable share of such group's reported net interest expense for any reporting year is the portion of such expense which bears the same ratio to such expense as—

"(i) the EBITDA of such corporation for such reporting year, bears to

"(ii) the EBITDA of such group for such reporting year.

"(D) EBITDA.—

"(i) IN GENERAL.—The term 'EBITDA' means, with respect to any reporting year, earnings before interest, taxes, depreciation, and amortization—

"(I) as determined in the international financial reporting group's

1   consolidated financial statements for

2   such year, or

3   "(II) for purposes of subpara-

4   graph (A)(i), as determined in the

5   books and records of the international

6   financial reporting group which are

7   used in preparing such statements if

8   not determined in such statements.

9   "(ii) TREATMENT OF DISREGARDED

10   ENTITIES.—The EBITDA of any domestic

11   corporation shall not fail to include the

12   EBITDA of any entity which is dis-

13   regarded for purposes of this chapter.

14   "(iii) TREATMENT OF INTRA-GROUP

15   DISTRIBUTIONS.—The EBITDA of any do-

16   mestic corporation shall be determined

17   without regard to any distribution received

18   by such corporation from any other mem-

19   ber of the international financial reporting

20   group.

21   "(E) SPECIAL RULES FOR NON-POSITIVE

22   EBITDA.—

23   "(i) NON-POSITIVE GROUP EBITDA.—

24   In the case of any international financial

25   reporting group the EBITDA of which is

1   zero or less, paragraph (1) shall not apply

2   to any member of such group the EBITDA

3   of which is above zero.

4   "(ii) NON-POSITIVE ENTITY

5   EBITDA.—In the case of any group mem-

6   ber the EBITDA of which is zero or less,

7   paragraph (1) shall be applied without re-

8   gard to subparagraph (A) thereof.

9   "(4) CONSOLIDATED FINANCIAL STATEMENT.—

10   For purposes of this subsection, the term 'consoli-

11   dated financial statement' means any consolidated

12   financial statement described in paragraph (2)(A)(ii)

13   if such statement is—

14   "(A) a financial statement which is cer-

15   tified as being prepared in accordance with gen-

16   erally accepted accounting principles, inter-

17   national financial reporting standards, or any

18   other comparable method of accounting identi-

19   fied by the Secretary, and which is—

20   "(i) a 10-K (or successor form), or

21   annual statement to shareholders, required

22   to be filed with the United States Securi-

23   ties and Exchange Commission,

24   "(ii) an audited financial statement

25   which is used for—

394

1   "(I) credit purposes,

2   "(II) reporting to shareholders,

3   partners, or other proprietors, or to

4   beneficiaries, or

5   "(III) any other substantial

6   nontax purpose,

7   but only if there is no statement described

8   in clause (i), or

9   "(iii) filed with any other Federal or

10   State agency for nontax purposes, but only

11   if there is no statement described in clause

12   (i) or (ii), or

13   "(B) a financial statement which—

14   "(i) is used for a purpose described in

15   subclause (I), (II), or (III) of subpara-

16   graph (A)(ii), or

17   "(ii) filed with any regulatory or gov-

18   ernmental body (whether domestic or for-

19   eign) specified by the Secretary,

20   but only if there is no statement described in

21   subparagraph (A).

22   "(5) REPORTING YEAR.—For purposes of this

23 subsection, the term 'reporting year' means, with re-

24 spect to any international financial reporting group,

1   the year with respect to which the consolidated fi-

2   nancial statements are prepared.

3   "(6) APPLICATION TO CERTAIN ENTITIES.—

4   "(A) PARTNERSHIPS.—Except as other-

5   wise provided by the Secretary in paragraph

6   (8), this subsection shall apply to any partner-

7   ship which is a member of any international fi-

8   nancial reporting group under rules similar to

9   the rules of section 163(j)(3).

10   "(B) FOREIGN CORPORATIONS ENGAGED

11   IN TRADE OR BUSINESS WITHIN THE UNITED

12   STATES.—Except as otherwise provided by the

13   Secretary in paragraph (8), any deduction for

14   interest paid or accrued by a foreign corpora-

15   tion engaged in a trade or business within the

16   United States shall be limited in a manner con-

17   sistent with the principles of this subsection.

18   "(C) CONSOLIDATED GROUPS.—For pur-

19   poses of this subsection, the members of any

20   group that file (or are required to file) a con-

21   solidated return with respect to the tax imposed

22   by chapter 1 for a taxable year shall be treated

23   as a single corporation.

24   "(7) REGULATIONS.—The Secretary may issue

25   such regulations or other guidance as are necessary

1   or appropriate to carry out the purposes of this sub-

2   section.".

3   (b) CARRYFORWARD OF DISALLOWED INTEREST.—

4   (1) IN GENERAL.—Section 163(o) is amended

5   to read as follows:

6   "(o) CARRYFORWARD OF CERTAIN DISALLOWED IN-

7   TEREST.—The amount of any interest not allowed as a

8   deduction for any taxable year by reason of subsection

9   (j)(1) or (n)(1) (whichever imposes the lower limitation

10   with respect to such taxable year) shall be treated as inter-

11   est (and as business interest for purposes of subsection

12   (j)(1)) paid or accrued in the succeeding taxable year. In-

13   terest paid or accrued in any taxable year (determined

14   without regard to the preceding sentence) shall not be car-

15   ried past the 5th taxable year following such taxable year,

16   determined by treating interest as allowed as a deduction

17   on a first-in, first-out basis.".

18   (2) TREATMENT OF CARRYFORWARD OF DIS-

19   ALLOWED INTEREST IN CERTAIN CORPORATE ACQUI-

20   SITIONS.—For rules related to the carryforward of

21   disallowed interest in certain corporate acquisitions,

22   see the amendments made by section 3301(c).

23   (c) EFFECTIVE DATE.—The amendments made by

24   this section shall apply to taxable years beginning after

25   December 31, 2017.

1 **SEC. 4303. EXCISE TAX ON CERTAIN PAYMENTS FROM DO-**
2   **MESTIC CORPORATIONS TO RELATED FOR-**
3   **EIGN CORPORATIONS; ELECTION TO TREAT**
4   **SUCH PAYMENTS AS EFFECTIVELY CON-**
5   **NECTED INCOME.**

6   (a) EXCISE TAX ON CERTAIN AMOUNTS FROM DO-
7 MESTIC CORPORATIONS TO FOREIGN AFFILIATES.—

8   (1) IN GENERAL.—Chapter 36 is amended by

9   adding at the end the following new subchapter:

10 **"Subchapter E—Tax on Certain Amounts to**

11   **Foreign Affiliates**

"Sec. 4491. Imposition of tax on certain amounts from domestic corporations
to foreign affiliates.

12 **"SEC. 4491. IMPOSITION OF TAX ON CERTAIN AMOUNTS**

13   **FROM DOMESTIC CORPORATIONS TO FOR-**

14   **EIGN AFFILIATES.**

15   "(a) IN GENERAL.—There is hereby imposed on each

16 specified amount paid or incurred by a domestic corpora-

17 tion to a foreign corporation which is a member of the

18 same international financial reporting group as such do-

19 mestic corporation a tax equal to the highest rate of tax

20 in effect under section 11 multiplied by such amount.

21   "(b) BY WHOM PAID.—The tax imposed by sub-

22 section (a) shall be paid by the domestic corporation de-

23 scribed in such subsection.

398

1 "(c) EXCEPTION FOR EFFECTIVELY CONNECTED IN-

2 COME.—Subsection (a) shall not apply to so much of any

3 specified amount as is effectively connected with the con-

4 duct of a trade or business within the United States if

5 such amount is subject to tax under chapter 1. In the case

6 of any amount which is treated as effectively connected

7 with the conduct of a trade or business within the United

8 States by reason of section 882(g), the preceding sentence

9 shall apply to such amount only if the domestic corpora-

10 tion provides to the Secretary (at such time and in such

11 form and manner as the Secretary may provide) a copy

12 of the election made under section 882(g) by the foreign

13 corporation referred to in subsection (a).

14 "(d) DEFINITIONS AND SPECIAL RULES.—Terms

15 used in this section that are also used in section 882(g)

16 shall have the same meaning as when used in such section

17 and rules similar to the rules of paragraphs (5) and (6)

18 of such section shall apply for purposes of this section.".

19   (2) DENIAL OF DEDUCTION FOR TAX IM-

20   POSED.—Section 275(a) is amended by inserting

21   after paragraph (6) the following new paragraph:

22   "(7) Taxes imposed by section 4491.".

23   (3) CLERICAL AMENDMENT.—The table of sub-

24   chapters for chapter 36 is amended by adding at the

25   end the following new item:

"SUBCHAPTER E. TAX ON CERTAIN AMOUNTS TO FOREIGN AFFILIATES.".

1   (b) ELECTION TO TREAT CERTAIN PAYMENTS FROM

2 DOMESTIC CORPORATIONS TO RELATED FOREIGN COR-

3 PORATIONS AS EFFECTIVELY CONNECTED INCOME.—Sec-

4 tion 882 is amended by adding at the end the following

5 new subsection:

6   "(g) ELECTION TO TREAT CERTAIN PAYMENTS

7 FROM DOMESTIC CORPORATIONS TO RELATED FOREIGN

8 CORPORATIONS AS EFFECTIVELY CONNECTED INCOME.—

9   "(1) IN GENERAL.—In the case of any specified

10   amount paid or incurred by a domestic corporation

11   to a foreign corporation which is a member of the

12   same international financial reporting group as such

13   domestic corporation and which has elected to be

14   subject to the provisions of this subsection—

15   "(A) such amount shall be taken into ac-

16   count (other than for purposes of sections 245,

17   245A, and 881) as if such foreign corporation

18   were engaged in a trade or business within the

19   United States and had a permanent establish-

20   ment in the United States during the taxable

21   year and as if such payment were effectively

22   connected with the conduct of a trade or busi-

23   ness within the United States and were attrib-

24   utable to such permanent establishment,

1   "(B) for purposes of subsection (c)(1)(A),

2   no deduction shall be allowed with respect to

3   such amount and such subsection shall be ap-

4   plied without regard to such amount, and

5   "(C) there shall be allowed as a deduction

6   the deemed expenses with respect such amount.

7   "(2) SPECIFIED AMOUNT.—For purposes of

8   this subsection—

9   "(A) IN GENERAL.—The term 'specified

10   amount' means any amount which is, with re-

11   spect to the payor, allowable as a deduction or

12   includible in costs of goods sold, inventory, or

13   the basis of a depreciable or amortizable asset.

14   "(B) EXCEPTIONS.—The term 'specified

15   amount' shall not include—

16   "(i) interest,

17   "(ii) any amount paid or incurred for

18   the acquisition of any commodity described

19   in section 475(e)(2)(A) or section

20   475(e)(2)(D) (determined without regard

21   to subclause (i) thereof),

22   "(iii) except as provided in subpara-

23   graph (C), any amount with respect to

24   which tax is imposed under section 881(a),

25   and

1   "(iv) in the case of a payor which has

2   elected to use a services cost method for

3   purposes of section 482, any amount paid

4   or incurred for services if such amount is

5   the total services cost with no markup.

6   "(C) AMOUNTS TREATED AS EFFECTIVELY

7 CONNECTED TO EXTENT OF GROSS-BASIS

8 TAX.—Subparagraph (B)(iii) shall not apply to

9 any specified amount to the extent of the same

10 proportion of such amount as—

11   "(i) the rate of tax imposed under

12   section 881(a) with respect to such

13   amount, bears to

14   "(ii) 30 percent.

15   "(3) DEEMED EXPENSES.—

16   "(A) IN GENERAL.—The deemed expenses

17 with respect to any specified amount received

18 by a foreign corporation during any reporting

19 year is the amount of expenses such that the

20 net income ratio of such foreign corporation

21 with respect to such amount (taking into ac-

22 count only such deemed expenses) is equal to

23 the net income ratio of the international finan-

24 cial reporting group determined for such report-

1   ing year with respect to the product line to

2   which the specified amount relates.

3   "(B) NET INCOME RATIO.—For purposes

4   of this paragraph, the term 'net income ratio'

5   means the ratio of—

6   "(i) net income determined without

7   regard to interest income, interest expense,

8   and income taxes, divided by

9   "(ii) revenues.

10   "(C) METHOD OF DETERMINATION.—

11   Amounts described in subparagraph (B) shall

12   be determined on the basis of the consolidated

13   financial statements referred to in paragraph

14   (5)(A)(i) and the book and records of the mem-

15   bers of the internal financial reporting group

16   which are used in preparing such statements.

17   "(4) INTERNATIONAL FINANCIAL REPORTING

18   GROUP.—For purposes of this subsection—

19   "(A) IN GENERAL.—The term 'inter-

20   national financial reporting group' means any

21   group of entities, with respect to any specified

22   amount, if such amount is paid or incurred dur-

23   ing a reporting year of such group with respect

24   to which—

1   "(i) such group prepares consolidated

2   financial statements (within the meaning

3   of section 163(n)(4)) with respect to such

4   year, and

5   "(ii) the average annual aggregate

6   payment amount of such group for the 3-

7   reporting-year period ending with such re-

8   porting year exceeds \$100,000,000.

9   "(B) ANNUAL AGGREGATE PAYMENT

10   AMOUNT.—The term 'annual aggregate pay-

11   ment amount' means, with respect to any re-

12   porting year of the group referred to in sub-

13   paragraph (A)(i), the aggregate specified

14   amounts to which paragraph (1) applies (or

15   would apply if such group were an international

16   financial reporting group).

17   "(C) APPLICATION OF CERTAIN RULES.—

18   Rules similar to the rules of subparagraphs (A),

19   (B), and (D) of section 448(c)(3) shall apply

20   for purposes of this paragraph.

21   "(5) TREATMENT OF PARTNERSHIPS.—Any

22   specified amount paid, incurred, or received by a

23   partnership which is a member of any international

24   financial reporting group (and any amount treated

25   as paid, incurred, or received by a partnership under

1   this paragraph) shall be treated for purposes of this

2   subsection as amounts paid, incurred, or received,

3   respectively, by each partner of such partnership in

4   an amount equal to such partner's distributive share

5   of the items of income, gain, deduction, or loss to

6   which such amounts relate.

7   "(6) TREATMENT OF AMOUNTS IN CONNECTION

8   WITH UNITED STATES TRADE OR BUSINESS.—Any

9   specified amount paid, incurred, or received by a for-

10 eign corporation in connection with the conduct of a

11 trade or business within the United States (other

12 than a trade or business it is deemed to conduct

13 pursuant to this subsection) shall be treated for pur-

14 poses of this subsection as an amount paid, in-

15 curred, or received, respectively, by a domestic cor-

16 poration. For purposes of the preceding sentence, a

17 foreign corporation shall be deemed to pay, incur,

18 and receive amounts with respect to a trade or busi-

19 ness it conducts within the United States (other

20 than a trade or business it is deemed to conduct

21 pursuant to this subsection) to the extent such for-

22 eign corporation would be treated as paying, incur-

23 ring, or receiving such amounts from such trade or

24 business if such trade or business were a domestic

25 corporation.

1   "(7) JOINT AND SEVERAL LIABILITY OF MEM-

2   BERS OF INTERNAL FINANCIAL REPORTING

3   GROUP.—In the case of any underpayment with re-

4   spect to any taxable year of a foreign corporation

5   which is a member of an international financial ac-

6   counting group, each domestic corporation which is

7   a member of such group at any time during such

8   taxable year shall be jointly and severally liable

9   for—

10   "(A) so much of such underpayment as

11   does not exceed the excess (if any) of such un-

12   derpayment over the amount of such under-

13   payment determined without regard to this sub-

14   section, and

15   "(B) any penalty, addition to tax, or addi-

16   tional amount attributable to the amount de-

17   scribed in subparagraph (A).

18   "(8) DISALLOWANCE OF FOREIGN TAX CREDIT,

19   ETC.—

20   "(A) IN GENERAL.—No credit shall be al-

21   lowed under section 901 for any taxes paid or

22   accrued (or treated as paid or accrued) with re-

23   spect to any specified amount to which para-

24   graph (1) applies.

1   "(B) DENIAL OF DEDUCTION.—No deduc-

2   tion shall be allowed under this chapter for any

3   tax for which credit is not allowable under sec-

4   tion 901 by reason of paragraph (1) (deter-

5   mined by treating the taxpayer as having elect-

6   ed the benefits of subpart A of part III of sub-

7   chapter N).

8   "(9) RULES RELATED TO ELECTION.—Any

9 election under paragraph (1) shall—

10   "(A) be made at such time and in such

11   form and manner as the Secretary may provide,

12   and

13   "(B) apply for the taxable year for which

14   made and all subsequent taxable years unless

15   revoked with the consent of the Secretary.

16   "(10) REGULATIONS.—The Secretary may issue

17 such regulations or other guidance as are necessary

18 or appropriate to carry out the purposes of this sub-

19 section, including regulations or other guidance—

20   "(A) to provide for the proper determina-

21   tion of product lines, and

22   "(B) to prevent the avoidance of the pur-

23   poses of this subsection through the use of con-

24   duit transactions or by other means.".

25 (c) REPORTING REQUIREMENTS.—

1   (1) REPORTING BY FOREIGN CORPORATION.—

2   Section 6038C(b) is amended to read as follows:

3   "(b) REQUIRED INFORMATION.—

4   "(1) IN GENERAL.—The information described

5   in this subsection is—

6   "(A) the information described in section

7   6038A(b), and

8   "(B) such other information as the Sec-

9   retary may prescribe by regulations relating to

10   any item not directly connected with a trans-

11   action for which information is required under

12   subparagraph (A).

13   "(2) CERTAIN PAYMENTS FROM RELATED DO-

14   MESTIC CORPORATIONS.—

15   "(A) IN GENERAL.—In the case of any re-

16   porting corporation that receives during the

17   taxable year any amount to which section

18   882(g)(1) applies, the information described in

19   this subsection shall include, with respect to

20   each member of the international financial re-

21   porting group from which any such amount is

22   received—

23   "(i) the name and taxpayer identifica-

24   tion number of such member,

408

1   "(ii) the aggregate amounts received

2   from such member,

3   "(iii) the product lines to which such

4   amounts relate, the aggregate amounts re-

5   lating to each such product line, and the

6   net income ratio for each such product line

7   (determined under section 882(g)(3)(B)

8   with respect to the international financial

9   reporting group), and

10   "(iv) a summary of any changes in fi-

11   nancial accounting methods that affect the

12   computation of any net income ratio de-

13   scribed in clause (iii).

14   "(B) DEFINITIONS AND SPECIAL RULES.—

15   Terms used in this paragraph that are also

16   used in section 882(g) shall have the same

17   meaning as when used in such section and rules

18   similar to the rules of paragraphs (5) and (6)

19   of such section shall apply for purposes of this

20   paragraph.".

21   (2) REPORTING BY DOMESTIC GROUP MEM-

22   BERS.—

23   (A) IN GENERAL .—Subpart A of part III

24   of subchapter A of chapter 61 is amended by

1   inserting after section 6038D the following new

2   section:

3 **"SEC. 6038E. INFORMATION WITH RESPECT TO CERTAIN**

4   **PAYMENTS FROM DOMESTIC CORPORATIONS**

5   **TO RELATED FOREIGN CORPORATIONS.**

6   "(a) IN GENERAL.—In the case of any domestic cor-

7 poration which pays or accrues any amount to which sec-

8 tion 882(g)(1) applies, such person shall—

9   "(1) make a return according to the forms and

10   regulations prescribed the Secretary, setting forth

11   the information described in subsection (b), and

12   "(2) maintain (at the location, in the manner,

13   and to the extent prescribed in regulations) such

14   records as may be appropriate to determine liability

15   for tax pursuant to paragraphs (1) and (7) of sec-

16   tion 882(g).

17   "(b) REQUIRED INFORMATION.—The information de-

18 scribed in this subsection is—

19   "(1) the name and taxpayer identification num-

20   ber of the common parent of the international finan-

21   cial reporting group in which such domestic corpora-

22   tion is a member, and

23   "(2) with respect to any person who receives an

24   amount described in subsection (a) from such do-

25   mestic corporation—

410

1   "(A) the name and taxpayer identification

2   number of such person,

3   "(B) the aggregate amounts received by

4   such person,

5   "(C) the product lines to which such

6   amounts relate, the aggregate amounts relating

7   to each such product line, and the net income

8   ratio for each such product line (determined

9   under section $882(g)(3)(B)$ with respect to the

10   international financial reporting group), and

11   "(D) a summary of any changes in finan-

12   cial accounting methods that affect the com-

13   putation of any net income ratios described in

14   subparagraph (C).

15   "(c) DEFINITIONS AND SPECIAL RULES.—Terms

16 used in this paragraph that are also used in section $882(g)$

17 shall have the same meaning as when used in such section

18 and rules similar to the rules of paragraphs (5) and (6)

19 of such section shall apply for purposes of this para-

20 graph.".

21   (B) CLERICAL AMENDMENT.—The table of

22   sections for subpart A of part III of subchapter

23   A of chapter 61 is amended by inserting after

24   the item relating to section 6038D the following

25   new item:

"Sec. 6038E. Information with respect to certain payments from domestic corporations to related foreign corporations.".

1   (d) EFFECTIVE DATE.—The amendments made by
2 this section shall apply to amounts paid or accrued after
3 December 31, 2018.

Subtitle E—Provisions Related to Possessions of the United States

6 **SEC. 4401. EXTENSION OF DEDUCTION ALLOWABLE WITH**
7   **RESPECT TO INCOME ATTRIBUTABLE TO DO-**
8   **MESTIC PRODUCTION ACTIVITIES IN PUERTO**
9   **RICO.**

10   (a) IN GENERAL.—Section 199(d)(8)(C), prior to its
11 repeal by this Act, is amended—

12   (1) by striking "first 11 taxable years" and in-
13   serting "first 12 taxable years", and

14   (2) by striking "January 1, 2017" and insert-
15   ing "January 1, 2018".

16   (b) EFFECTIVE DATE.—The amendments made by
17 this section shall apply to taxable years beginning after
18 December 31, 2016.

19 **SEC. 4402. EXTENSION OF TEMPORARY INCREASE IN LIMIT**
20   **ON COVER OVER OF RUM EXCISE TAXES TO**
21   **PUERTO RICO AND THE VIRGIN ISLANDS.**

22   (a) IN GENERAL.—Section 7652(f)(1) is amended by
23 striking "January 1, 2017" and inserting "January 1,
24 2023".

1   (b) EFFECTIVE DATE.—The amendment made by
2 this section shall apply to distilled spirits brought into the
3 United States after December 31, 2016.

4 **SEC. 4403. EXTENSION OF AMERICAN SAMOA ECONOMIC**
5   **DEVELOPMENT CREDIT.**

6   (a) IN GENERAL.—Section 119(d) of division A of
7 the Tax Relief and Health Care Act of 2006 is amended—

8   (1) by striking "January 1, 2017" each place
9   it appears and inserting "January 1, 2023",

10   (2) by striking "first 11 taxable years" in para-
11   graph (1) and inserting "first 17 taxable years",
12   and

13   (3) by striking "first 5 taxable years" in para-
14   graph (2) and inserting "first 11 taxable years".

15   (b) EFFECTIVE DATE.—The amendments made by
16 this section shall apply to taxable years beginning after
17 December 31, 2016.

Subtitle F—Other International Reforms

20 **SEC. 4501. RESTRICTION ON INSURANCE BUSINESS EXCEP-**
21   **TION TO PASSIVE FOREIGN INVESTMENT**
22   **COMPANY RULES.**

23   (a) IN GENERAL.—Section 1297(b)(2)(B) is amend-
24 ed to read as follows:

1   "(B) derived in the active conduct of an in-

2   surance business by a qualifying insurance cor-

3   poration (as defined in subsection (f)),".

4   (b) QUALIFYING INSURANCE CORPORATION DE-

5 FINED.—Section 1297 is amended by adding at the end

6 the following new subsection:

7   "(f) QUALIFYING INSURANCE CORPORATION.—For

8 purposes of subsection (b)(2)(B)—

9   "(1) IN GENERAL.—The term 'qualifying insur-

10   ance corporation' means, with respect to any taxable

11   year, a foreign corporation—

12   "(A) which would be subject to tax under

13   subchapter L if such corporation were a domes-

14   tic corporation, and

15   "(B) the applicable insurance liabilities of

16   which constitute more than 25 percent of its

17   total assets, determined on the basis of such li-

18   abilities and assets as reported on the corpora-

19   tion's applicable financial statement for the last

20   year ending with or within the taxable year.

21   "(2) ALTERNATIVE FACTS AND CIR-

22   CUMSTANCES TEST FOR CERTAIN CORPORATIONS.—

23   If a corporation fails to qualify as a qualified insur-

24   ance corporation under paragraph (1) solely because

25   the percentage determined under paragraph (1)(B)

414

1   is 25 percent or less, a United States person that

2   owns stock in such corporation may elect to treat

3   such stock as stock of a qualifying insurance cor-

4   poration if—

5   "(A) the percentage so determined for the

6   corporation is at least 10 percent, and

7   "(B) under regulations provided by the

8   Secretary, based on the applicable facts and cir-

9   cumstances—

10   "(i) the corporation is predominantly

11   engaged in an insurance business, and

12   "(ii) such failure is due solely to run-

13   off-related or rating-related circumstances

14   involving such insurance business.

15   "(3) APPLICABLE INSURANCE LIABILITIES.—

16   For purposes of this subsection—

17   "(A) IN GENERAL.—The term 'applicable

18   insurance liabilities' means, with respect to any

19   life or property and casualty insurance busi-

20   ness—

21   "(i) loss and loss adjustment ex-

22   penses, and

23   "(ii) reserves (other than deficiency,

24   contingency, or unearned premium re-

25   serves) for life and health insurance risks

1   and life and health insurance claims with

2   respect to contracts providing coverage for

3   mortality or morbidity risks.

4   "(B) LIMITATIONS ON AMOUNT OF LIABIL-

5   ITIES.—Any amount determined under clause

6   (i) or (ii) of subparagraph (A) shall not exceed

7   the lesser of such amount—

8   "(i) as reported to the applicable in-

9   surance regulatory body in the applicable

10   financial statement described in paragraph

11   (4)(A) (or, if less, the amount required by

12   applicable law or regulation), or

13   "(ii) as determined under regulations

14   prescribed by the Secretary.

15   "(4) OTHER DEFINITIONS AND RULES.—For

16   purposes of this subsection—

17   "(A) APPLICABLE FINANCIAL STATE-

18   MENT.—The term 'applicable financial state-

19   ment' means a statement for financial reporting

20   purposes which—

21   "(i) is made on the basis of generally

22   accepted accounting principles,

23   "(ii) is made on the basis of inter-

24   national financial reporting standards, but

1   only if there is no statement that meets

2   the requirement of clause (i), or

3   "(iii) except as otherwise provided by

4   the Secretary in regulations, is the annual

5   statement which is required to be filed

6   with the applicable insurance regulatory

7   body, but only if there is no statement

8   which meets the requirements of clause (i)

9   or (ii).

10   "(B) APPLICABLE INSURANCE REGU-

11   LATORY BODY.—The term 'applicable insurance

12   regulatory body' means, with respect to any in-

13   surance business, the entity established by law

14   to license, authorize, or regulate such business

15   and to which the statement described in sub-

16   paragraph (A) is provided.".

17   (c) EFFECTIVE DATE.—The amendments made by

18 this section shall apply to taxable years beginning after

19 December 31, 2017.

20 **SEC. 4502. LIMITATION ON TREATY BENEFITS FOR CERTAIN**

21   **DEDUCTIBLE PAYMENTS.**

22   (a) IN GENERAL.—Section 894 is amended by adding

23 at the end the following new subsection:

24   "(d) LIMITATION ON TREATY BENEFITS FOR CER-

25 TAIN DEDUCTIBLE PAYMENTS.—

1 "(1) IN GENERAL.—In the case of any deduct-

2 ible related-party payment, any withholding tax im-

3 posed under chapter 3 (and any tax imposed under

4 subpart A or B of this part) with respect to such

5 payment may not be reduced under any treaty of the

6 United States unless any such withholding tax would

7 be reduced under a treaty of the United States if

8 such payment were made directly to the foreign par-

9 ent corporation.

10 "(2) DEDUCTIBLE RELATED-PARTY PAY-

11 MENT.—For purposes of this subsection, the term

12 'deductible related-party payment' means any pay-

13 ment made, directly or indirectly, by any person to

14 any other person if the payment is allowable as a de-

15 duction under this chapter and both persons are

16 members of the same foreign controlled group of en-

17 tities.

18 "(3) FOREIGN CONTROLLED GROUP OF ENTI-

19 TIES.—For purposes of this subsection—

20   "(A) IN GENERAL.—The term 'foreign

21 controlled group of entities' means a controlled

22 group of entities the common parent of which

23 is a foreign corporation.

24   "(B) CONTROLLED GROUP OF ENTITIES.—

25 The term 'controlled group of entities' means a

1   controlled group of corporations as defined in

2   section 1563(a)(1), except that—

3   "(i) 'more than 50 percent' shall be

4   substituted for 'at least 80 percent' each

5   place it appears therein, and

6   "(ii) the determination shall be made

7   without regard to subsections (a)(4) and

8   (b)(2) of section 1563.

9   A partnership or any other entity (other than a

10   corporation) shall be treated as a member of a

11   controlled group of entities if such entity is con-

12   trolled (within the meaning of section

13   954(d)(3)) by members of such group (includ-

14   ing any entity treated as a member of such

15   group by reason of this sentence).

16   "(4) FOREIGN PARENT CORPORATION.—For

17   purposes of this subsection, the term 'foreign parent

18   corporation' means, with respect to any deductible

19   related-party payment, the common parent of the

20   foreign controlled group of entities referred to in

21   paragraph (3)(A).

22   "(5) REGULATIONS.—The Secretary may pre-

23   scribe such regulations or other guidance as are nec-

24   essary or appropriate to carry out the purposes of

1   this subsection, including regulations or other guid-

2   ance which provide for—

3   "(A) the treatment of two or more persons

4   as members of a foreign controlled group of en-

5   tities if such persons would be the common par-

6   ent of such group if treated as one corporation,

7   and

8   "(B) the treatment of any member of a

9   foreign controlled group of entities as the com-

10   mon parent of such group if such treatment is

11   appropriate taking into account the economic

12   relationships among such entities.".

13   (b) EFFECTIVE DATE.—The amendment made by

14   this section shall apply to payments made after the date

15   of the enactment of this Act.

TITLE V—EXEMPT
ORGANIZATIONS
Subtitle A—Unrelated Business
Income Tax

20   SEC. 5001. CLARIFICATION OF UNRELATED BUSINESS IN-

21   COME TAX TREATMENT OF ENTITIES TREAT-

22   ED AS EXEMPT FROM TAXATION UNDER SEC-

23   TION 501(a).

24   (a) IN GENERAL.—Section 511 is amended by adding

25   at the end the following new subsection:

1 "(d) ORGANIZATIONS AND TRUSTS EXEMPT FROM

2 TAXATION NOT SOLELY BY REASON OF SECTION

3 501(a).—For purposes of subsections (a)(2) and (b)(2),

4 an organization or trust shall not fail to be treated as ex-

5 empt from taxation under this subtitle by reason of section

6 501(a) solely because such organization is also so exempt,

7 or excludes amounts from gross income, by reason of any

8 other provision of this title.".

9 (b) EFFECTIVE DATE.—The amendments made by

10 this section shall apply to taxable years beginning after

11 December 31, 2017.

SEC. 5002. EXCLUSION OF RESEARCH INCOME LIMITED TO PUBLICLY AVAILABLE RESEARCH.

14 (a) IN GENERAL.—Section 512(b)(9) is amended by

15 striking "from research" and inserting "from such re-

16 search".

17 (b) EFFECTIVE DATE.—The amendments made by

18 this section shall apply to taxable years beginning after

19 December 31, 2017.

Subtitle B—Excise Taxes

SEC. 5101. SIMPLIFICATION OF EXCISE TAX ON PRIVATE FOUNDATION INVESTMENT INCOME.

23 (a) RATE REDUCTION.—Section 4940(a) is amended

24 by striking "2 percent" and inserting "1.4 percent".

421

1   (b) REPEAL OF SPECIAL RULES FOR CERTAIN PRI-
2 VATE FOUNDATIONS.—Section 4940 is amended by strik-
3 ing subsection (e).

4   (c) EFFECTIVE DATE.—The amendments made by
5 this section shall apply to taxable years beginning after
6 December 31, 2017.

7 **SEC. 5102. PRIVATE OPERATING FOUNDATION REQUIRE-**
8 **MENTS RELATING TO OPERATION OF ART**
9 **MUSEUM.**

10   (a) IN GENERAL.—Section 4942(j) is amended by
11 adding at the end the following new paragraph:

12   "(6) ORGANIZATION OPERATING ART MU-
13   SEUM.—For purposes of this section, the term 'oper-
14   ating foundation' shall not include an organization
15   which operates an art museum as a substantial ac-
16   tivity unless such museum is open during normal
17   business hours to the public for at least 1,000 hours
18   during the taxable year.".

19   (b) EFFECTIVE DATE.—The amendments made by
20 this section shall apply to taxable years beginning after
21 December 31, 2017.

22 **SEC. 5103. EXCISE TAX BASED ON INVESTMENT INCOME OF**
23   **PRIVATE COLLEGES AND UNIVERSITIES.**

24   (a) IN GENERAL.—Chapter 42 is amended by adding
25 at the end the following new subchapter:

1 **"Subchapter H—Excise Tax Based on Invest-**

2 **ment Income of Private Colleges and Uni-**

3 **versities**

"Sec. 4969. Excise tax based on investment income of private colleges and universities.

4 **"SEC. 4969. EXCISE TAX BASED ON INVESTMENT INCOME**

5 **OF PRIVATE COLLEGES AND UNIVERSITIES.**

6 "(a) TAX IMPOSED.—There is hereby imposed on

7 each applicable educational institution for the taxable year

8 a tax equal to 1.4 percent of the net investment income

9 of such institution for the taxable year.

10 "(b) APPLICABLE EDUCATIONAL INSTITUTION.—For

11 purposes of this subchapter—

12 "(1) IN GENERAL.—The term 'applicable edu-

13 cational institution' means an eligible educational in-

14 stitution (as defined in section 25A(e)(3))—

15 "(A) which has at least 500 students dur-

16 ing the preceding taxable year,

17 "(B) which is not described in the first

18 sentence of section 511(a)(2)(B), and

19 "(C) the aggregate fair market value of

20 the assets of which at the end of the preceding

21 taxable year (other than those assets which are

22 used directly in carrying out the institution's

23 exempt purpose) is at least $100,000 per stu-

24 dent of the institution.

1   "(2) STUDENTS.—For purposes of paragraph

2 (1), the number of students of an institution shall

3 be based on the daily average number of full-time

4 students attending such institution (with part-time

5 students taken into account on a full-time student

6 equivalent basis).

7   "(c) NET INVESTMENT INCOME.—For purposes of

8 this section, net investment income shall be determined

9 under rules similar to the rules of section 4940(c).".

10   (b) CLERICAL AMENDMENT.—The table of sub-

11 chapters for chapter 42 is amended by adding at the end

12 the following new item:

> "SUBCHAPTER H—EXCISE TAX BASED ON INVESTMENT INCOME OF PRIVATE COLLEGES AND UNIVERSITIES".

13   (c) EFFECTIVE DATE.—The amendments made by

14 this section shall apply to taxable years beginning after

15 December 31, 2017.

16 **SEC. 5104. EXCEPTION FROM PRIVATE FOUNDATION EX-**

17   **CESS BUSINESS HOLDING TAX FOR INDE-**

18   **PENDENTLY-OPERATED PHILANTHROPIC**

19   **BUSINESS HOLDINGS.**

20   (a) IN GENERAL.—Section 4943 is amended by add-

21 ing at the end the following new subsection:

22   "(g) EXCEPTION FOR CERTAIN HOLDINGS LIMITED

23 TO INDEPENDENTLY-OPERATED PHILANTHROPIC BUSI-

24 NESS.—

424

1   "(1) IN GENERAL.—Subsection (a) shall not

2 apply with respect to the holdings of a private foun-

3 dation in any business enterprise which for the tax-

4 able year meets—

5   "(A) the ownership requirements of para-

6 graph (2),

7   "(B) the all profits to charity distribution

8 requirement of paragraph (3), and

9   "(C) the independent operation require-

10 ments of paragraph (4).

11   "(2) OWNERSHIP.—The ownership require-

12 ments of this paragraph are met if—

13   "(A) 100 percent of the voting stock in the

14 business enterprise is held by the private foun-

15 dation at all times during the taxable year, and

16   "(B) all the private foundation's ownership

17 interests in the business enterprise were ac-

18 quired not by purchase.

19   "(3) ALL PROFITS TO CHARITY.—

20   "(A) IN GENERAL.—The all profits to

21 charity distribution requirement of this para-

22 graph is met if the business enterprise, not

23 later than 120 days after the close of the tax-

24 able year, distributes an amount equal to its net

1   operating income for such taxable year to the

2   private foundation.

3   "(B) NET OPERATING INCOME.—For pur-

4   poses of this paragraph, the net operating in-

5   come of any business enterprise for any taxable

6   year is an amount equal to the gross income of

7   the business enterprise for the taxable year, re-

8   duced by the sum of—

9   "(i) the deductions allowed by chapter

10   1 for the taxable year which are directly

11   connected with the production of such in-

12   come,

13   "(ii) the tax imposed by chapter 1 on

14   the business enterprise for the taxable

15   year, and

16   "(iii) an amount for a reasonable re-

17   serve for working capital and other busi-

18   ness needs of the business enterprise.

19   "(4) INDEPENDENT OPERATION.—The inde-

20   pendent operation requirements of this paragraph

21   are met if, at all times during the taxable year—

22   "(A) no substantial contributor (as defined

23   in section 4958(c)(3)(C)) to the private founda-

24   tion, or family member of such a contributor

25   (determined under section 4958(f)(4)) is a di-

1   rector, officer, trustee, manager, employee, or

2   contractor of the business enterprise (or an in-

3   dividual having powers or responsibilities simi-

4   lar to any of the foregoing),

5   "(B) at least a majority of the board of di-

6   rectors of the private foundation are not—

7   "(i) also directors or officers of the

8   business enterprise, or

9   "(ii) members of the family (deter-

10   mined under section 4958(f)(4)) of a sub-

11   stantial contributor (as defined in section

12   4958(c)(3)(C)) to the private foundation,

13   and

14   "(C) there is no loan outstanding from the

15   business enterprise to a substantial contributor

16   (as so defined) to the private foundation or a

17   family member of such contributor (as so deter-

18   mined).

19   "(5) CERTAIN DEEMED PRIVATE FOUNDATIONS

20   EXCLUDED.—This subsection shall not apply to—

21   "(A) any fund or organization treated as a

22   private foundation for purposes of this section

23   by reason of subsection (e) or (f),

24   "(B) any trust described in section

25   4947(a)(1) (relating to charitable trusts), and

1   "(C) any trust described in section

2   4947(a)(2) (relating to split-interest trusts).".

3   (b) EFFECTIVE DATE.—The amendments made by

4 this section shall apply to taxable years beginning after

5 December 31, 2017.

Subtitle C—Requirements for Organizations Exempt From Tax

SEC. 5201. CHURCHES PERMITTED TO MAKE STATEMENTS RELATING TO POLITICAL CAMPAIGN IN ORDINARY COURSE OF RELIGIOUS SERVICES AND ACTIVITIES.

12   (a) IN GENERAL.—Section 501 is amended by adding

13 at the end the following new subsection:

14   "(s) SPECIAL RULE RELATING TO POLITICAL CAM-

15 PAIGN STATEMENTS OF CHURCHES, INTEGRATED AUXIL-

16 IARIES, ETC.—

17   "(1) IN GENERAL.—For purposes of subsection

18   (c)(3) and sections 170(c)(2), 2055, 2106, 2522,

19   and 4955, an organization described in section

20   508(c)(1)(A) shall not fail to be treated as organized

21   and operated exclusively for a religious purpose, nor

22   shall it be deemed to have participated in, or inter-

23   vened in any political campaign on behalf of (or in

24   opposition to) any candidate for public office, solely

25   because of the content of any homily, sermon, teach-

428

1   ing, dialectic, or other presentation made during re-

2   ligious services or gatherings, but only if the prepa-

3   ration and presentation of such content—

4   "(A) is in the ordinary course of the orga-

5   nization's regular and customary activities in

6   carrying out its exempt purpose, and

7   "(B) results in the organization incurring

8   not more than de minimis incremental ex-

9   penses.".

10   (b) EFFECTIVE DATE.—The amendments made by

11   this section shall apply to taxable years ending after the

12   date of the enactment of this Act.

13   **SEC. 5202. ADDITIONAL REPORTING REQUIREMENTS FOR**

14   **DONOR ADVISED FUND SPONSORING ORGA-**

15   **NIZATIONS.**

16   (a) IN GENERAL.—Section 6033(k) is amended by

17   striking "and" at the end of paragraph (2), by striking

18   the period at the end of paragraph (3), and by adding

19   at the end the following new paragraphs:

20   "(4) indicate the average amount of grants

21   made from such funds during such taxable year (ex-

22   pressed as a percentage of the value of assets held

23   in such funds at the beginning of such taxable year),'

24   and

429

1   "(5) indicate whether the organization has a

2 policy with respect to donor advised funds (as so de-

3 fined) for frequency and minimum level of distribu-

4 tions.

5 Such organization shall include with such return a copy

6 of any policy described in paragraph (5).".

7   (b) EFFECTIVE DATE.—The amendment made by

8 this section shall apply for returns filed for taxable years

9 beginning after December 31, 2017.

www.ingramcontent.com/pod-product-compliance
Lightning Source LLC
Chambersburg PA
CBHW080603270326
41928CB00016B/2908